HB
99.7
K395
1986

KEYNES' ECONOMIC LEGACY

KEYNES' ECONOMIC LEGACY

Contemporary Economic Theories

Edited by

James L. Butkiewicz
Kenneth J. Koford
Jeffrey B. Miller

PRAEGER SPECIAL STUDIES • PRAEGER SCIENTIFIC

New York • Philadelphia • Eastbourne, UK
Toronto • Hong Kong • Tokyo • Sydney

Library of Congress Cataloging-in-Publication Data
Main entry under title:

Keynes' economic legacy.

Bibliography: p.
Includes index.
1. Keynesian economics—Addresses, essays, lectures. I. Butkiewicz, James L. II. Koford, Kenneth J. III. Miller, Jeffrey B.
HB99.7.K395   1985   330.15′6   85-9508
ISBN 0-03-004202-X (alk. paper)

Published in 1986 by Praeger Publishers
CBS Educational and Professional Publishing, a Division of CBS Inc.
521 Fifth Avenue, New York, NY 10175 USA

© 1986 by Praeger Publishers

All rights reserved

6789 052 987654321

Printed in the United States of America on acid-free paper

INTERNATIONAL OFFICES

Orders from outside the United States should be sent to the appropriate address listed below. Orders from areas not listed below should be placed through CBS International Publishing, 383 Madison Ave., New York, NY 10175 USA

Australia, New Zealand
Holt Saunders, Pty, Ltd., 9 Waltham St., Artarmon, N.S.W. 2064, Sydney, Australia

Canada
Holt, Rinehart & Winston of Canada, 55 Horner Ave., Toronto, Ontario, Canada M8Z 4X6

Europe, the Middle East, & Africa
Holt Saunders, Ltd., 1 St. Anne's Road, Eastbourne, East Sussex, England BN21 3UN

Japan
Holt Saunders, Ltd., Ichibancho Central Building, 22-1 Ichibancho, 3rd Floor, Chiyodaku, Tokyo, Japan

Hong Kong, Southeast Asia
Holt Saunders Asia, Ltd., 10 Fl, Intercontinental Plaza, 94 Granville Road, Tsim Sha Tsui East, Kowloon, Hong Kong

Manuscript submissions should be sent to the Editorial Director, Praeger Publishers, 521 Fifth Avenue, New York, NY 10175 USA

Acknowledgments

A conference volume is the result of the efforts of many people, and this is no exception. The conference itself would not have occurred without the financial support provided by the Office of Special Sessions at the University of Delaware. Janet Gross, coordinator of special sessions, was most supportive of the idea of a conference honoring the centenary of Keynes' birth. Clair Garrison and Nancy Lynam were responsible for the actual organization of the conference.

The editors were assisted in the preparation of the manuscript by Lorraine Holton, Jimmie Gail Madison, Sandra DeVore, David Carey, and Emma Lou Elston-Gray. Barbara Leffel, our editor at Praeger Publishers, provided valuable assistance in bringing the project to completion.

Cambridge University Press generously granted permission to use Professor Leijonhufvud's chapter, which previously appeared in *Keynes and the Modern World* by Worswick and Trevithek.

Contents

ACKNOWLEDGMENTS	v
Introduction Kenneth J. Koford, James L. Butkiewicz, and Jeffrey B. Miller	1

1
What Would Keynes Have Thought of Rational Expectations?
Axel Leijonhufvud — 25

Comment by Barry Bosworth	52
Comment by Christopher Pissarides	55
Comment by Paul Davidson	58
Comment by Karl Brunner	59
Reply by Axel Leijonhufvud	61

2
Financial Markets and Macroeconomic Fluctuations
Robert J. Shiller — 65

Comment by Karl Brunner	88
Comment by Paul Davidson	94
Comment by Joseph Stiglitz	102
Reply by Robert Shiller	105
Rejoinder by Karl Brunner	108

3
Policies for Reducing the Natural Rate of Unemployment
Richard A. Jackman, Richard Layard, and Christopher Pissarides — 111

Comment by Barry Bosworth	133
Comment by Paul Davidson	135
Comment by Laurence Seidman	143
Comment by Joseph Stiglitz	144
Comment by David Colander	145
Reply by Richard Layard	149

4
Theories of Wage Rigidity
Joseph E. Stiglitz — 153

    Comment by Christopher Pissarides — 206
    Comment by Karl Brunner — 209
    Comment by Richard Layard — 215
    Comment by Costas Azariadis — 216
    Reply by Joseph Stiglitz — 219

INDEX — 223

ABOUT THE CONTRIBUTORS — 227

Introduction

Kenneth J. Koford, James L. Butkiewicz, and Jeffrey B. Miller

This volume collects the papers presented at the conference "Keynes' Economic Legacy: Contemporary Macroeconomic Theories" held at the University of Delaware on January 11-13, 1984. The presentations attracted lively comments and discussion which we have included as well.

The conference used the occasion of the centenary of Keynes' birth to examine how his economic views are faring. In contrast to conferences that took a retrospective and somewhat depressive view, finding Keynesian ideas in retreat and even in eclipse, we looked at new work in the Keynesian tradition. Ten years ago that endeavor might have been futile, but not now. A variety of lines of research, imbued with a combination of Keynesian perspective and new, rigorous microeconomic foundations, are gaining attention.

This "new Keynesian" research is still very much in progress. It has yet to produce a complete, consistent model of the macroeconomy, although numerous results have been obtained.[1] Many of its major results are derived from, or in response to, the new classical economics of Lucas, Sargent, Prescott, and Barro. The four major papers at the conference, by Axel Leijonhufvud, Robert Shiller, Richard Layard, and Joseph Stiglitz, bring out different facets of this new Keynesian research.

The first part of this introduction is a summary, with some critical discussion, of the four papers and the comments that followed each. The second part provides our analysis of how this research contributes to a "new Keynesian" approach to macroeconomics.

SUMMARY OF THE PROCEEDINGS

In the introductory chapter, summarized below, Axel Leijonhufvud provides a historical overview, bringing out the issues that led to the decline of traditional Keynesianism and the defects of the new classical approach that have been exploited by the new Keynesians. The author emphasizes the difference in approach between finding adjustment failures in real and in nominal magnitudes.

The conference papers indicate different lines of research for the financial (or nominal) and the real sectors. The financial sector of the economy is examined by Robert Shiller and also in some of Leijonhufvud's comments. Shiller questions whether financial markets are consistent with rational expectations theory and finds that prices on capital markets vary too much to represent the underlying streams of real returns that new classical theory says should determine prices. Leijonhufvud reminds us that Keynes was very concerned prior to the General Theory with financial instability. His solution, which Leijonhufvud agrees with, was "monetary reform." Inflation was not to be tolerated or even reduced, but to be eradicated. Leijonhufvud calls such an all-out policy a "change of regimes" and argues that only such a permanent, unyielding commitment to a stable price level can restore nominal-value stability. We summarize these arguments in the section on the nominal sector.

Two chapters examine real-sector adjustment failures. Joseph Stiglitz discusses recent theories of wage rigidity and, finding them unsatisfactory, proposes an alternative theory of wage rigidity that appears able to account for the stylized facts of labor market adjustment failures. Richard Layard's chapter, written jointly with Robert Jackman and Christopher Pissarides, examines models in which workers search for jobs. Each model has a different market-clearing mechanism, from union control to firms' price setting, to a rent-sharing solution. In all of the models, the equilibrium level of unemployment is higher than optimal due to externalities in the search and wage bargaining process. Layard finds that tax incentives applied to wage rates and rates of wage increase could reduce the equilibrium level of unemployment. These analyses are developed in the section on the real sector.

Keynesian Economics in Perspective

Leijonhufvud first examines the recent history of macroeconomic thought, to see how the ideas of Keynes and the Keynesians have fared in their competition with the monetarist tradition.

During the Great Depression of the 1930s, a new way of thinking about the aggregate economy developed. Previous approaches that emphasized microeconomic factors and were cautious about intervening in business cycles passed out of vogue. By 1960 Keynesian economics dominated macroeconomic thought and was considered to have succeeded both theoretically and empirically. Yet within a decade it suffered fatal blows, both empirically and theoretically.

Leijonhufvud argues that the crucial error of the Keynesians of the time was adopting the Phillips curve. Some relationship between inflation and unemployment was necessary, and none had existed in the models of the 1950s. But by wholeheartedly supporting the Phillips curve, and putting it to policy use soon after its discovery, the Keynesians extended their model in a uniquely falsifiable way. The Keynesians of the 1950s also flirted with a strongly antimonetarist stand; that money does not matter at all. There again, they proved to be poor forecasters, even if they were roughly correct for some earlier periods. (Some recent empirical work noted in the conclusion to this Introduction shows that the Keynesian model worked well prior to 1960.)

The inflation of the 1960s and 1970s devastated the Keynesian position. However, its worst problems were with the inflation-unemployment tradeoff (the Phillips curve), which Leijonhufvud points out was not an essential part of the Keynesian model and might even be considered inconsistent with Keynes' views. The basic source of the inflation was clearly monetary, although the evidence for an extreme monetarist position that *only* money matters was rather weak.

Leijonhufvud believes that the new classical economics that developed in the 1970s, in large part in response to the deficiencies of the Keynesian position, has brought several crucial lessons from which Keynesians (new Keynesians, perhaps) must learn. He emphasizes that the new classical school does not support just a single principle, but rather three: monetarism, rational expectations, and market clearing. Monetarism holds that the main source of macroeconomic disturbances is the money supply and that the appropriate policy solution is steady growth in the quantity of money. Leijonhufvud notes that Lucas developed his new classical models to provide a micro foundation for Friedman's monetarist and natural rate of unemployment beliefs.

Of the three principles, Leijonhufvud believes that rational expectations is the one most compatible with Keynesian analysis. He focuses on the concept of "monetary regimes," that people in one monetary policy regime will correctly expect quite different inflationary and cyclical behavior than they will in another. Prior to the 1960s, many countries followed a "convertibility" monetary principle, that is, keeping their currency convertible into some outside goods, such as gold or silver or another currency. In that regime monetary policy cannot create inflation; the convertibility constraint forces monetary policy to be consistent with a single price level. Then it is unlikely for rational expectations to lead to inflationary expectations. If the money goal were to keep employment high, however, as has occurred in recent years, there is no constraint upon inflation. And when people realize that they are in such a policy regime, they will expect inflation to accompany any increase in the money supply.

Leijonhufvud finds the third new classical principle, continuous market clearing, to be the least plausible. In fact, most of the new Keynesian research has been on non-market-clearing models with rational expectations. However, Leijonhufvud does not find the current disequilibrium models unsatisfactory.

Leijonhufvud develops a typology of macroeconomic models that is novel, and, as the discussion shows, controversial. He identifies in each macroeconomic theory a source of shocks to the system and a source of adjustment failures. Each source can be either real or nominal. He characterizes Keynes' theory as a real-real model, in which the shock is a shift of the marginal efficiency of investment, and the real interest rate fails to adjust. In contrast, Friedman proposed a nominal-nominal model in which erroneous monetary policy caused shocks, and nominal wages failed to adjust. The Keynesians proposed a less elegant hybrid: a real-nominal model, in which real shocks (these days, perhaps oil shocks) are the source of the disturbance, but it is nominal magnitudes, mostly wages, that fail to adjust. The new classicals have moved to the nominal-real category, although some of their models may now be in the real-real category. Monetary shocks are the source of problems, but real values—intertemporal substitution or information costs—cause adjustment "failures."

We find it worth noting that none of the other conference papers develops a model that clearly illustrates Leijonhufvud's major points. Shiller, for example, finds disequilibrium in the financial markets that may be self-generating or the result of disturbances elsewhere in the economy, but whether it is a source of wider disturbance is not developed. While Leijonhufvud emphasizes disequilibrium, Layard's models are of low-level equilibrium states. Thus, contrary to Keynes' method of using short-run equilibrium models to examine disequilibrium, Layard's models are in long-run equilibrium with high unemployment. Their adjustment failure is real, but there is, properly speaking, no source of a shock. Stiglitz's models fit the scheme most clearly. The source of shocks is not specified, but he is concerned with adjustment failures in wage rates. Either nominal or real values could be rigid in Stiglitz's model. Leijonhufvud's typology seems worth examining further, but these authors have not asked his question of their own models.

Near the end of his analysis of the history of thought Leijonhufvud has a comment that makes a striking challenge. He notes that over the last two decades the "Keynesian" position has shifted regularly. Every time, that shift was in response to a challenge from the monetarist camp. Today, Leijonhufvud suggests, the "Keynesian" position is merely that held by the intellectually hindmost.

Such intellectual conservatism has been common among Keynesians for a long time, perhaps because they were followers and interpreters of a major thinker. But we think it is fairly clear that the current generation of macrotheorists we are calling the "new Keynesians" do not fit that mold. Their roots are not in the old Keynes or the Keynesians, but in the new microeconomics, just as the new classicals owe little to Ricardo. It is fair to say that the other chapter authors are among the elders of the new Keynesians, and it is significant that each has done most of his work in microeconomics.

Leijonhufvud's chapter is discussed by Barry Bosworth, Christopher Pissarides, Paul Davidson, and Karl Brunner. Bosworth questions whether it is fair to separate economists so strictly into Keynesians and monetarists; rather, he argues that there are many centrists who include the good ideas of each point of view. He doubts that markets always clear as the new classicals claim and concludes that, as Keynesians believe, they do not. He emphasizes the usefulness of the *IS-LM* framework, presenting the debates of the 1960s in its own terms, rather than in terms of Leijonhufvud's intertemporal disequilibrium story. (We note here the continuing tension in macroeconomics between equilibrium models and disequilibrium beliefs. Meir Kohn [forthcoming] has claimed that Keynes used short-run equilibrium as a simplifying device to tell a disequilibrium story. Disequilibrium models remain poorly specified, so that it is not clear what is meant for a model to be "out of equilibrium.")

Pissarides examines the rational expectations hypothesis that Leijonhufvud considers desirable. One rational expectaions approach without market clearing uses search models. Despite advances in these models, they do not yet explain unemployment behavior. Pissarides also doubts that Lucas' islands model fits into Leijonhufvud's typology; what drives Lucas' model is a combination of real and nominal shocks, such that agents cannot tell which is which. Finally, Pissarides emphasizes the importance of multiplier effects in creating employment. They could occur due to imperfect capital markets, or bankruptcy, or due to elastic expectations about quantities, as in the Malinvaud/Benassy models.

Davidson contrasts our views with Keynes'. Unemployment for Keynes is the normal state of affairs, while our current models say full employment is normal. Keynes combined real and monetary factors, with real problems causing monetary ills, which is the reverse of the monetarists' belief that monetary errors cause real problems.

Karl Brunner finds more agreement between monetarists and Keynesians than did Leijonhufvud. Monetarists and Keynesians agree that relative wage inflexibility is a problem, and they both lack a real micro foundation—as do the new classicals. And while monetarists once emphasized monetary shocks, recently they have added real shocks, creating a legitimate real business cycle theory.

Leijonhufvud's response clears up apparent disagreements with Davidson and Brunner. He also predicts increasing empirical trouble for the new classical school. It denies any micro-macro distinction, rather than creating a micro foundation for macroeconomics, which is something that still remains to be done properly.

The Nominal Sector: Problems and Policy

Robert Shiller questions whether the combined theories of efficient markets and rational expectations give us an adequate theory of speculative financial markets. Keynes had argued that stock markets act "irrationally," being determined by short-term psychology largely unrelated to long-run fundamentals. Shiller regards Keynes' veiw as a "nontheory" that is not testable but is a possible "residual" theory if others fail. And Shiller has strong evidence that the efficient market theory fails empirically. That theory assumes that the market value of stocks reflects the stream of underlying dividends, and movements in stock prices should reflect movements in expected future dividends.

The first evidence that Shiller considers is whether the stock market follows a random walk. He finds that it does not; rather it has a tendency to return to some underlying value. (Since the stock market is supposed to represent the value of the firms in the U.S. economy, this finding is perhaps not so surprising, but theory currently assumes a random walk.) In addition, while stock prices and dividends sometimes move together, there have been numerous stock market booms and crashes during which dividends stayed nearly constant.

The second major piece of evidence compares the variance of stock prices with what the variance should be if it is caused by variations in dividends. Shiller has found that stocks vary far too much to be explained by actual changes in dividends. He examines whether the variance could be explained by some potential disaster that would wipe out all future dividends, even though there is no evidence for it in the dividend series since the disaster has not yet occurred. And he looks for the possibility that some enormous windfall that has not yet occurred, but might, causes the variation in prices. Both of these models seem implausible.

Shiller also looks briefly at long-term interest rates and finds that they are also too volatile in comparison with short-term rates to accord with rational expectations.

Shiller then explains a model that he and Sanford Grossman developed, the consumption-based asset pricing theory. This theory claims that, when people all want to save, the discount rate underlying stocks falls; when they all want to consume out of savings, the discount rate rises. During recessions people are having a hard time and want to consume by selling stocks; they do not care that stocks then are a good investment—they need the money. Shiller finds that this theory could be a good explanation of stock price variation. However, the data on similar assets that people might sell in bad times—bonds, housing, and land—do not show similar fluctuations, as they should if the theory is correct. Shiller concludes that there is still no theory of financial markets that is consistent with the facts.

Shiller's first discussant, Paul Davidson, argues that Keynes believed that stock markets were nonergodic; they did not follow a fixed pattern that could be projected into the future. If stock marekts see a continual creation of new facts and situations, then their results will not follow a predictable path. Also Keynes claimed that there was insufficient intertemporal substitution for intertemporal markets to be stable. And Davidson asks whether nominal values of stocks, bonds, real estate really do not matter. Yet Shiller's work is all in terms of real values. People use stocks, bonds, and so on as a speculative "time machine" to carry value to the future, and they value liquidity, the ability to get their money back. That makes the "time machine" have unstable values, as Shiller-Grossman claim.

Karl Brunner's comment defends the efficient market hypothesis. He notes that the random walk is often violated in small samples, but that the autocorrelation found does not last into other samples. There are *some* violations of the rational expectations hypothesis, which are currently being investigated. In contrast, Keynes' irrationality hypothesis is untestable.

Joseph Stiglitz states that there is plenty of additional evidence that markets are not efficient.[2] He notes the paradoxes that firms pay dividends rather than buying up their shares and that they long used FIFO accounting when LIFO would have reduced taxes. He asks whether the stock market had received information in 1983 that was sufficient for it to go up 40 percent—what news was that good? Stiglitz's view is that the stock market is a gambling casino for the affluent. Its behavior is plainly inconsistent with rational risk-averse behavior.

But then Stiglitz asks if we should worry about the macroeconomic effects of the irrationality and volatility of the stock market. The answer is no because firms do not use it for capital; they use banks to get capital. And banks do not use market interest rates, but rather ration credit. (Greenwald, Stiglitz, and Weiss [1984] have developed this theory further; it is closely analogous to the rigid wages theory Stiglitz develops in this volume.)

Shiller's response makes several points. Contrary to Brunner, there is much evidence contradicting stock market efficiency. He agrees with Davidson that the stock market seems to have a lot of one-time-only events that do not fit into the Rational Expectations Hypothesis (REH) statistical framework. He notes that credit constraints have not been considered in work up to now but might solve the puzzle. He agrees with Stiglitz in that in 1929, for example, there was hardly enough bad news prior to the stock market crash to drive prices down so deeply. (We should make note that the random walk theory is about the relationships of closely related asset prices, such as pricing on consecutive days. The concern of macroeconomists is whether asset prices reflect the underlying values of the income streams. Asset prices could easily follow a random walk without accurately reflecting underlying values.

Leijonhufvud's policy discussion is relevant to Shiller's empirical results. The former basically agrees with Shiller's view that financial markets are not inherently stable. But he emphasizes that the degree of instability is in large part the result of the monetary regime, a point that he sees in Keynes' (1923) strong case for all-out "monetary reform" during an earlier unsatisfactory monetary regime. A regime that can credibly assure economic agents that the price level will remain constant reduces instability. Such a regime also guarantees that any policy errors—overshooting—will be corrected. While speculative markets may still be inherently unstable, one wants to avoid policies that make rational calculation impossible.

Leijonhufvud claims that optimally a stable regime is based not on the monetarist quantity rule, but on the convertibility rule—that the monetary authorities should promise to exchange money for some other bundle of equivalents. When that is the case, monetary policy becomes endogenous. Any exogenous changes in the money supply would be ineffective, since they must be reversed to be consistent with the convertibility rule. But real shocks are transmitted through the system, since the monetary authority automatically accomodates them.

Leijonhufvud has outlined a convincing case for a guaranteed monetary standard here and elsewhere.[3] We would suggest that like other rules, this one might as well be fixed in law. That could be done by a legal injunction to the Federal Reserve or by a policy like Lerner and Colander's MAP (discussed in more detail below), which requires that the price level remain constant.

The Real Sector: Theory and Policy

In contrast to the financial sector, where there are problems with the established model and where the policies proposed aim at making the world more consistent with theory (i.e., more rational), the real sector is wide open for micro-foundation theorists and policymakers with new approaches. Jackman, Layard, and Pissarides (referred to as Layard, who presented the paper) present labor search models that explain unemployment in long-run equilibrium—why an economy may be permanently stuck at high levels of unemployment. Stiglitz looks at theories of short-run wage rigidity that lead to high levels of unemployment when demand varies. Stiglitz's model also provides an explanation for long-term steady-state unemployment, as unemployed workers queue for good jobs rather than take the poor jobs that are available.

Layard accepts that there is a long-term "natural" rate of unemployment, one that depends upon the institutions of the labor market. He notes that unemployment benefits increase the natural rate (although he does not propose major cuts in those benefits). Layard considers the effects of two policies on the natural rate of unemployment: tax-based incomes policies (TIP) and targeted labor subsidies to low-wage workers. He sets up five models of equilibrium unemployment and finds that in each of these models TIP reduces equilibrium unemployment.

All five models are neoclassical in their assumptions and methodology. In each model, some party to the wage contract sets a wage rate, based upon what other wages are offered, upon the unemployment rate, and upon the TIP tax-subsidy rate. At equilibrium identical wage setters all choose the same wage rate. And with free entry and exit, all firms earn zero economic profits.

In Model 1 firms set the wages. Workers quit if wages are too low; quits cost the firm money; increased unemployment reduces the quit rate.

In Model 2, an efficiency-wage model comparable to those Stiglitz describes, output is determined by the relative wage rate chosen by the firm. Increased unemployment encourages workers to work harder, as do higher wages.

Model 3 includes quitting, hiring, and vacancies, providing a rather complex and comprehensive model of the labor market. Firms create vacancies—which they want to fill—at some cost, and workers quit as before. Relative wages and the unemployment rate determine both quit rates and hiring rates. If a firm reduces its wage rate, it reduces labor costs, but hires fall and quits rise. The long-run equilibrium wage balances these effects, so that the firm maintains a constant labor force.

In these three models, the TIP mechanism reduces equilibrium unemployment and reduces real wages, for the following reasons. First, firms are taxed when they raise wages and receive subsidies when they reduce wages. So for any set of external conditions (unemployment rate and other wages), each firm will choose lower wages. At the old equilibrium level of unemployment and these lower wages, quits will remain constant, since relative wages have not changed. But now firms have an increased incentive to create vacancies, as the profits from filling a vacancy are positive. Firms suck up unemployed workers until their probability of filling a vacancy, which is reduced due to the falling level of unemployment, becomes too low.

Firms' behavior in these models is explicitly modeled as an optimizing problem over the major factors that firms face in the labor market—wages, hires, and quits. However, while Layard's firms optimize, his workers do not. Thus, while these models have many positive properties, they do not represent a complete solution to the labor market search problem.

In Model 4 unions set the wages, with firms responding by choosing the level of employment. The TIP tax reduces unions' incentives to increase wages, since part of the increase in wages is taxed away.

In Model 5 there is a partly unionized economy, with the wages in the rest of the economy determined by supply and demand. Increased union wages drive workers into the supply-demand sector, but at lower wages fewer workers are willing to work and so become "unemployed"— perhaps on welfare, retired, or at home. The tax reduces wages in the unionized sector. At those lower wages fewer workers are driven into the supply-demand sector. Wages are then higher there, and fewer workers are driven into "unemployment."

While Layard emphasizes the usefulness of these models in showing the advantages of a wage TIP, they are of general theoretical interest as well. They provide a definite microeconomic search foundation for the macro economy. Labor search in a stochastic model is one way to describe how unemployed resources can occur in equilibrium. Still, these models are not fully developed. For instance, while firms and unions act optimally, so far workers act reasonably but parametrically. Workers' utility-maximizing strategies need to be determined and brought to the fore.[4] In addition, while these models emphasize long-run equilibrium, short-run dynamics are also important. Do these models cause Keynesian short-run behavior? What if in the short run expectations are rational, but foresight is not perfect—do business cycles and Clower-type disequilibria occur?

Layard next shows how targeted employment subsidies can reduce unemployment. With a minimum wage, or unemployment benefits, the subsidy increases the margin between that level of income and the worker's income on the job. When there is a difference in elasticities of labor supply across industries, subsidies to the high-elasticity industry can reduce discouraged worker unemployment. Training targeted at workers in low-wage occupations also can increase wages in that occupation, reducing the number of discouraged workers. Union reform that reduced wages in high-wage occupations down toward the competitive level would also reduce unemployment and increase output.

There are five comments on the Layard chapter. Barry Bosworth argues that Layard's model does not fully explain the unemployment behavior of workers. He asks why increased quits are associated with reduced unemployment. Bosworth wants a more complete model of the search process, including hiring and layoffs. (We would note that workers' search choices *have* been examined empirically by Hall [1982] and Akerlof and Main [1980]. That evidence provides stylized facts that could be used in building search models. Labor search behavior has been modeled in detail as an optimizing problem [Lippman and McCall 1976], and those models could be used to complete these macro search models.)

Paul Davidson notes that while Layard looks at long-term equilibrium, Keynes had a short-term disequilibrium theory that is inconsistent with a natural rate of unemployment. While Keynes believed in disequilibrium, his supposed followers today—even Clower, Leijonhufvud, and Malinvaud—believe only in coordination problems. In a coordination failure, which they view as a temporary disequilibrium, the short side of the market prevails and unemployment occurs. But Keynes did not say that. In fact, in Keynes, people can spend more than they earn by borrowing.

Laurence Seidman wonders if a TIP would improve the inflation-unemployment tradeoff when applied as a short-run policy to bring inflation down. And, in the long-run, does TIP get one closer to the optimal rate of unemployment? Layard's model does not show what rate is optimal. (For a model that *does* look at optimality, the reader should see Pissarides 1984.)

Stiglitz notes that wage subsidies can do harm as well as good—one must look at the general equilibrium solution, which is always complicated. He responded to Seidman's query: we know that the natural rate of unemployment is not optimal, but it is hard to be sure that the government can improve matters.

David Colander doubts that the "natural rate" is an appropriate term. It suggests that the amount of search is optimal. But is there are externalities in the search process, then NAIRU, the non-accelerating inflation rate of unemployment, is more accurate. Colander describes a model in which agents engaging in dynamic monopolization lead to a long-run increase in the NAIRU above the natural rate. Colander criticizes Layard's view that wage-only TIPs are superior to value-added TIPs, since the Layard models contain only labor and have no returns to inputs except for wages. But in reality firms have quasi rents, which a dynamic model should allow for. Then a value-added TIP can squeeze these quasi rents without necessarily reducing wages.[5]

Layard's reply responds to several of the discussants. His answer to Bosworth is that quitting workers need not be unemployed—usually they take another job immediately. So an inverse relationship between quits and unemployments is reasonable. Davidson had claimed that the search unemployment model is really just a supply and demand model. While Layard illustrates his models with a supply-demand picture, conventional supply-demand principles do not drive the models. Rather, search unemployment does, and it implies involuntary unemployment, as in Keynes. Layard agrees that he assumes there is a natural rate of unemployment—that the economy tends to some rate of unemployment. He disagrees with Colander about the merits of a value-added TIP. Such a TIP is too complex to explain politically—a crude, simple policy seems better.

Joseph Stiglitz's paper also examines real-sector adjustment failures. He first asks whether wage rigidity can explain unemployment. The original theories of rigid wages, the implicit contracts theories, fail to explain cyclical unemployment as it actually occurs. However, the new efficiency wage theories *are* consistent with a positive level of equilibrium unemployment, and with the major patterns of unemployment. Keynes assumed that wages were exogenous; to see why wage rigidities occur, we need an explanation. (We think it is interesting, and perhaps a critical stylized fact, that while stock prices vary a lot in Keynes, interest rates and wage rates are extremely stable—too stable, in fact. Perhaps interest and wage rate stability should both be explained in the same way, as Greenwald, Stiglitz, and Weiss [1984] have recently proposed.)

Stiglitz's stylized facts of unemployment are: workers are laid off, rather than having wages or hours reduced; layoffs and hires are common, so workers and firms are not permanently tied; some unemployed are as qualified as the employed and willing to work at the same wages. He asks, why are people laid off rather than being offered lower wages? Why are laid-off workers not immediately rehired by other firms, as should be true in supply and demand markets? Why is unemployment concentrated in certain parts of the labor market? Why do people generally dislike being unemployed?

The implicit contracts theories failed to explain these problems. According to these theories; risk-averse workers are insured by risk-neutral firms against income losses. But the theories provide no clear rationale for unemployment. If unemployment occurs to let workers receive unemployment compensation and leisure, workers should be happy to lose their jobs. Job rotation, giving every worker a chance to be laid off, would be the rule. But that does not happen.

Stiglitz brings out many other problems with the implicit contract approach. We note just two: First, explicit contracts are hard to write out and to enforce. But with an implicit, unwritten "contract," conditions are very difficult to specify and there is no enforcement mechanism. How is it upheld? Second, under reasonable assumptions, risk-neutral firms would provide full, or more than full employment, contrary to the conclusion of implicit contract theory. Instead, only under quite special conditions do firms find underemployment profitable.

Stiglitz then turns to the efficiency-wage approach. In these models productivity is a positive function of the wage rate. Reducing wages can reduce productivity even more. Since the wage-productivity relationship differs across industries, the equilibrium wage for similar workers varies too. So queues of unemployed workers form to obtain the high-wage jobs.

Stiglitz gives five separate explanations for efficiency wages, any or all of which may occur, and all of which give the same basic empirical regularities.

1. Minimum nutrition levels: a minimum level of subsistence is needed for effective work.
2. Turnover at low wages: workers quit at low wages, and the firm bears some of the costs of turnover, so the firm suffers reduced average labor productivity.
3. Imperfect information about worker quality: the quality mix of job applicants improves as the firm offers higher wages.
4. High costs of monitoring workers: if workers receive a margin above their alternative wages, the cost of being caught shirking is higher, so they shirk less. That increases productivity.
5. Sociological theories: workers expect "fair treatment" including a standard wage and work much less well when they receive less.

Unemployment patterns appear consistent with the efficiency wage models. Some groups of workers are fully employed, others are partially employed, and still other groups are largely rationed out of the market. Changes in aggregate demand affect different labor markets quite differently, depending on the specific relationships. For instance, if wages drop below a "fair" level, workers may quit or shirk. On the other hand, if wages drop, but not below that fair level, workers may go on as before. Similarly, the tradeoff between quits and wages (and costs of replacing workers) should be different for each industry, meaning different layoff and wage rate policies across industries. And laid-off workers' choices will depend on the labor practices of the neighboring industries.

Appropriate labor market policy varies with the specific model. For example, increasing unemployment compensation will make things worse in the shirking model. Workers do not mind being fired so much, so they shirk more and stay unemployed longer. But suppose that the quality mix story is correct. Then low-productivity workers will search less, and so it is easier for employers wanting high-productivity workers to get them at relatively modest wages. Efficiency increases and unemployment falls.

Cyclical fluctuations cause big disequilibria in these models. Wage rates are not all adjusted at once; they are administered. And relative wages among a group of firms are crucial. The first firm to adjust wages to eliminate the disequilibrium will lose, as its workers quit or shirk or become angry.

In addition, the gains to changing wages are small. They are the result of an optimizing process, so that the firm is at the top of a profit hill with respect to the wage rate. Adjusting wages gives only second-order increases in profits (corresponding to the curvature of the profit hill). In the traditional analysis, changing wages toward the optimum gives large immediate (first-order) gains.

Finally, Stiglitz tries to fit his analysis into Leijonhufvud's nominal-real framework. The analysis is in real terms, but adjustment failures could occur because contracts are in nominal terms.

The discussants have widely varied views of Stiglitz's model. Pissarides agrees with Stiglitz that the implicit contract theory is unsatisfactory. However, there are still many unanswered questions about the efficiency wage argument. He notes that Hicks developed an efficiency wage theory in his *Theory of Wages* (1932).

Karl Brunner points out that for Keynes, as opposed to the Keynesians, nominal wage rigidity was a minor element. Rather, Keynes has a "real" theory with a real business cycle. In Keynes wage rigidity "serves to anchor nominal values," like the money supply in classical theory. Brunner finds some of the efficiency wage theories quite reasonable, particularly the turnover and shirking theories. He finds the optimal contracts approach problematical in that it starts with an Arrow-Debreu world with complete markets and then removes particular markets. A more reasonable approach, Brunner believes, is to begin with widespread uncertainty—with agents trying to create more certainty. Stable prices help agents to do that. Brunner sees pitfalls in using the very simple functional form of the efficiency relationship that Stiglitz has chosen. For example, wage rates of other firms and the firm's hierarchical control system are not included. Finally, he emphasizes the importance of workers' perceptions and expectations and how they are formed via institutional arrangements (a point that Leijonhufvud also makes).

Layard is interested in how nominal wage rigidity is maintained in these models. Under a deflationary policy, there are many uncoordinated firms/workers with staggered contracts. How can they adjust? (Layard's models emphasize the importance of large numbers of markets, industries, or firms, all of which set prices. While Lucas' islands model has large numbers of firms, the simpler classical and Keynesian models have just a few huge aggregates. Only models with an Arrow-Debreu heritage, such as Benassy [1982], emphasize large numbers of closely related markets.) Finally, Layard queries, what is a plausible natural rate of unemployment in these models? Could it be 50 percent or more? It should be determined whether the models lead to plausible levels of unemployment.

Costas Azariadis asked for "equal time" to respond to the criticisms of the implicit contracts approach. He begins with criticisms of several efficiency wage models. The turnover or quitting models are deficient in that they erroneously predict that quits are highest in recessions, not in booms. The shirking model, on the other hand, contains an implicit contract—a given level of work effort to be performed. Azariadis notes that firms can shirk too, in which case vacancies are perhaps a way of disciplining firms.

Azariadis argues, contrary to Brunner, that implicit contracts are *not* in an Arrow-Debreu framework but have special information held by workers and their employers not available to outsiders—much as Brunner desires. Finally, Azariadis argued that the enforcement of implicit contracts may not be as difficult as some believe. Reputation and arbitration are available. And there may be certain sorts of contracts that are self-enforcing. That question is worth looking at.

Finally, Stiglitz responds to the critiques. When a firm's optimal wages depended on the wages of other firms, as in Layard's model, the dynamics are very interesting, particularly with staggered contracts. Stiglitz prefers Leijonhufvud's real-real model; the effort to turn efficiency-wage stories into nominal ones seems stretched. Why couldn't people write contracts to solve that problem?

SOME OBSERVATIONS AND CONCLUSIONS

We think that the essays contained in this volume are representative of an important new development in macroeconomics: the creation of a research agenda that is leading toward a macroeconomics based on microeconomic foundations.

The Microeconomic Foundations of Macroeconomics

For many years, while macroeconomics has appeared empirically correct, it has lacked clear microeconomic foundations. To be sure, there have been plausible stories, such as those Keynes told about markets, interest rates, and the stock market; or as Brunner tells here about the inability to contract freely; or as Friedman told about the natural rate of unemployment. Nevertheless, there was very little actual derivation of macroeconomic relationships from the assumed micro principles. And so there could be no testing of the combined micro-macro assumptions.

The new classical economics brought radical changes. It was rigorously based upon competitive supply and demand in individual markets, and then aggregation to the economy as a whole; and it allowed for empirical tests of the combined micro-macro hypothesis. Unfortunately, the assumptions of the new classical model, taken as a whole, have turned out to be inconsistent with the empirical evidence.

There are two, largely separable, fundamental assumptions about behavior in the new classical model: rational expectations and market-clearing. In principle, rational expectations is a theory for modeling individual behavior, while market clearing is a theory of aggregate behavior. In practice, however, both assumptions are applied to aggregates. A conservative research strategy is to give up one of the assumptions while maintaining the other.

Rational Expectations and Speculative Asset Markets

There are good reasons for doubting the rational expectations assumption. It assumes in the formal models that implement it that all agents have the same model of economy, and they only differ in their beliefs about some specific parameters. Yet it appears probable that people have extremely varied ideas of how the economy works. As essays in Frydman and Phelps (1983) show, Bayesian learners are very unlikely to come to the consensus assumed in the new classical models. That is to say, in order to get aggregate rational expectations, extremely strong assumptions about individual knowledge of others' knowledge must be assumed. A tempting, but very difficult, alternative is to assume that individuals are rational Bayesians and then see how likely it is that aggregate expectations are rational. Or we might find an alternative expectations hypothesis more consistent with individual behavior and aggregate empirical results.

Another reason for doubting the rational expectations hypothesis is the large and growing literature in psychology showing it to be false. Even when people do their best to be rational, when they make decisions under uncertainty, they fail. The essays collected in Kahneman, Slovic, and Tversky (1982) describe some of the major errors that people consistently make.

People are, it is fairly clear, unaware of the laws of Bayesian decision theory, which economists have accepted on the standard for optimal decision making. People jump to conclusions on small numbers of observations. People use easily available rules of thumb. And people hate to admit that they have lost and will take very risky gambles to try to gain enough to make up for such a loss. But rational expectations requires the correct, or optimal, use of available information. If people individually cannot do that, we may need to give up on rational expectations or find evidence of social structures that develop forecasts superior to what any individual can develop and that pass them on to most other agents. Thus markets with many professionals interacting could provide a way for many different expectations to be correct and improved. We also might find that agents in different sectors of the economy have quite different models of the economy. Agents in the financial sector and very large firms may have complex and sophisticated views of the overall economy, akin to the new classical approach. Other agents, such as small firms, workers, and consumers, may have much simpler views that are not consistent with each other or with more sophisticated models. Such an economy could easily have forecast differences that could lead to disequilibrium via Clower's (1967) dual-decision hypothesis, as worked out in Barro and Grossman's (1976) and Benassy's (1982) dynamic disequilibrium models.

It must also be noted that the new classical model's informational requirements are very substantial. They run counter to what is often perceived to be a major advantage of the market system. Hayek (1945) has argued persuasively that the market system is very efficient because prices provide so much information. If a market economy actually needs the detailed information about the structure of the economy that rational expectations models assume that all agents have, it would be much harder to distinguish the workings of a market economy from the planned economics that Hayek was criticizing.

The failure of people to be perfectly rational could well be the source of the instability Shiller finds in the stock market. (Certainly the stock market has competitive market clearing). These Tversky-Kahneman psychological principles appear to explain our gambling and risk-taking instincts (which are emphasized by Adam Smith [1776], Frank Knight [1921], and Stiglitz, in his 1982 essay and his comments on Shiller in this volume), so they could explain excessive instability in speculative markets. And better theories of those instincts should help us explain human behavior on speculative markets.

People often conflate two rather different questions about speculative markets: do the prices follow a random walk, so that no one can make money off the pattern of past prices, and do prices represent present values of the underlying assets? Keynes was, and macroeconomists are, concerned with the second question. If prices do not properly represent underlying values—for example, if the bond market overstates the appropriate discount rate—macroeconomic harm will result, even if the price follows a random walk.

Some recent work has examined whether price changes are comparable to the change in underlying values (Madeo and Pincus 1985). But we really do not know if stock or other asset prices are good representations of underlying values. When stock market speculators claim that the stock of huge corporations is billions of dollars undervalued, it certainly suggests a remarkable divergence between stock prices and underlying values. Often the stock prices do adjust as the speculators want, so they are not just making idle claims. And we have trouble identifying the "new information" that led to the 1929 stock market crash or the 1983 boom. So maybe, as Ackley (1983) claims, these markets do largely track changes in our ignorance: prices shift in the direction implied by new information, but since we are so ignorant about the future, the size of the shifts and the levels attained are only remotely related to underlying "values."

For speculative asset markets, and the investment decisions based partly on them, we think questioning the REH makes sense as a research strategy.

Market Disequilibrium and Rigid Wages

For many other markets, particularly labor markets, we think that market clearing is the assumption to drop, while rational expectations should be kept as a maintained hypothesis. (We are not adverse to replacing the REH with an alternative, when one becomes available. However, most recent work on disequilibrium has assumed rational expectations.) How can the assumption of market clearing be replaced?

The efforts of the early 1970s give us some guidance. First, there was the disequilibrium approach proposed by Clower (1965, 1967) and carried out most fully by Barro and Grossman (1976). Clower appears to give good insight into the nature of macroeconomic market failure, and Barro and Grossman's approach seems to give qualitatively plausible comparative-dynamics results. However, in their work a rationale for rigidity (largely of wages) was not provided; rather, rigidity was assumed.

The second effort was the implicit contracts approach of Azariadis (1975) and Baily (1974). It began with the reasonable viewpoint that labor markets are long-term agreements, presumably contractual in nature. Certainly labor markets do not look much like auction markets, as the new classical theorists assume them to be. But why and how labor markets have long-term agreements is not so clear. And how such agreements cause wage rigidity or unemployment is not clear either.

Three strands of more recent work help to show why labor market disequilibrium could occur and persist. (They do not explain *equilibrium* unemployment.) Two were emphasized at this conference; all three have their effect by making the chosen wage rate (or price) the result of an optimization process. First, as Stiglitz points out, any error in the choice of wage has small, only second-order, effects on profits. That is, an optimal decision is at the top of a profit hill. So small changes in the chosen level of the decision variable (wage, price) cause only very small effects on profits. If for some reason the firm makes a small mistake, or if underlying parameters change slightly, the loss of profits is very small. If optimizing is costly, or there are adjustment costs, then it may be sensible for a firm to let a disequilibrium persist.

Second, Benassy (1982) develops a model in which firms choose fairly rigid prices in the short run because they do not know the extent of excess demand or supply. Firms will adjust toward the equilibrium price, but since they do not know how far away from it they are, the adjustment is slow. Price-setting firms suffer asymmetrical losses from errors that lead to excess supply (Benassy 1982, chap. 9). Firms with excess demand could just raise price at the same quantity, while firms with excess supply may prefer to cut quantity rather than reduce price on all units sold. Simon and Rice (1983–84) have a similar analysis.

Third, in Stiglitz's efficiency-wage model and Layard's search models, the optimal wage balances several hard-to-observe factors: quits, hires, average quality of new hires, and worker discontent. It is easy for a firm to err in such an estimate and to take a long time to recognize a change in underlying conditions. The costs of that error are very small, following Stiglitz's analysis.

These reasons for gradual or imperfect adjustment mean that considerable unemployment (of capital as well as labor) can easily occur. All that is needed is a sudden shock, or an error in optimizing.

All of these models, and particularly Benassy's, emphasize interaction among multiple markets. Lucas' islands model (1972) includes something similar. But in these models, the forces pushing toward equilibrium are weak, so that disequilibrium in one market causes disequilibrium in other markets; the disequilibria feed on each other in a chain-reaction or multiplier manner. So far, this part of Benassy's model has not been fully developed. But other disequilibrium models, such as Barro and Grossman's and Malinvaud's, show that this interaction among sectors gives fascinating and important results. The Malinvaud (1977) typology of disequilibrium—Keynesian, classical, repressed inflation—is a good beginning of that analysis.

In even more recent work, Drazan (1985) combines search unemployment and multiple unemployment equilibria, in a model that at least notionally has many markets. Diamond (1984) also finds multiple equilibria in a search model. In these models the economy could become "stuck" at some high-unemployment equilibrium or could be pushed by random stocks from one equilibrium to another.

Equilibrium levels of unemployment are modeled by Layard's search unemployment model, by his unionization model, and by Stiglitz's efficiency wage models.[6] These models can explain a single economy-wide level of unemployment, but not differences in unemployment across sectors. It is important to see if they have implications consistent with the actual flow of hires and quits, and with actual unemployment rates under varying conditions.

But the most promising line of research seems to be the multisector efficiency wage model. Does it replicate actual patterns of unemployment? Does it explain why unemployment occurs—why many labor markets have institutions that cause continual high unemployment to the workers and firms in those industries? The model should also be able to show why some specific markets seem never to have significant unemployment while unemployment is continually high in other markets.

Some Policy Ideas

Policies can be put under two headings: stability and incentives. Stability seems most appropriate as a policy goal for monetary policy, while incentives apply to the real sector. (Some incentive proposals, such as MAP, have both monetary and real effects.) The aggregate economy seems to lack strong stability properties, according to both the disequilibrium theorists and Stiglitz's second-order condition argument. So our first policy objective is to keep macroeconomic policy as stable, and as stabilizing, as possible. A constant money growth rate or an aggregate nominal demand target is one route; tying the price level to some permanent constant value should also help. We think that work on a permanent price-level rule, as a quite different "regime" from the current one, would be fruitful. The economy should be different in fundamental ways when the price level is stable than when the price level, in Leijonhufvud's terms, follows a "random walk." Turnovsky and Wohar (1984) find a considerable change in the structure of the U.S. economy during the "great inflation" of the 1960s and 1970s, compared to the period before the 1960s, when the price level was viewed as stable. In the earlier period, they found that the economy was more "Keynesian," apparently because people assumed monetary policy would not be allowed to lead to inflation.

Turning to real policy, we accept Colander's (and Lerner's) view that the average, or NAIRU, rate of unemployment is higher than the optimal level. The reasons may be incomplete contracts, unemployment compensation, or something else. To change this situation, some new incentives are required.

First, the clearly perverse aspects of the unemployment compensation system could be changed. The unemployment compensation tax on firms can be experience rated, and part of the payments to the unemployed could be loans. Second, an incentive policy to reduce the equilibrium level of unemployment is highly desirable, if a workable policy can be found.[7] The incentives of TIPs, both wage TIPs as discussed by Layard, and value-added TIPs, are a step in the right direction for reducing unemployment.[8] So are the incentives of MAP, the market-based incentive on value-added, devised by Lerner and Colander (1980). MAP acts as a tax on monopoly throughout the economy, making it profitable for firms to reduce price and increase output. That also increases efficiency and reduces unemployment (Koford 1984). Whether these policies can be implemented in practice is another question that needs investigation.

New Keynesian theorists agree that the economy's markets are incomplete and that some form of externality exists due to that lack of markets. However, the precise nature of macroeconomic externality has not been determined, and appropriate policy depends on what sort of externality it is. The current candidates include a labor search externality in an equilibrium setting, a search externality that leads to multiple equilibria (Diamond 1984), or a short-run disequilibrium externality fed by multipliers across multiple markets. Colander's theory of a monopolization externality, driven by the continual creation and distribution of temporary monopolies, is an attractive new candidate. When the nature of the externality is identified, then a policy aimed directly at the externality can be developed. Since MAP imposes both a stable price level and an incentive to increase output, it is an attractive policy, and may be close to the optimal policy in theory. But there may be other policies, as yet not fully developed, such as Weitzman's (1984) share economy proposal that could be superior. And we do not want to exclude the possibility that correcting the government's macroeconomic instability and microeconomic perverse incentives would solve the bulk of the problem of excess unemployment.

In summary, we see room for new theoretical work on the instability of asset prices and the stability of wages. We see the first, essential government policy to be maintenance of a permanently stable price level and stable aggregate demand. And we regard the investigation of incentive policies to reduce unemployment as an important new item on the micro-macro agenda.

NOTES

1. All of the papers at this conference report research on parts of the story. Malinvaud (1977, 1980) might be the best early integration of the parts into a whole.
2. Stiglitz develops his skeptical views on stock market rationality in greater detail in his 1982 paper.
3. See Leijonhufvud's book, *Information and Coordination*, particularly Chapter 7.
4. For example, Christopher Pissarides, "Efficiency Aspects of the Financing of Unemployment Insurance and Other Government Expenditure," *Review of Economic Studies* (January 1983), develops a model of optimal labor search interacting with a tax/benefit system. However, the optimal behavior of firms is not fully modeled.
5. Pissarides (forthcoming) and Koford (1984) have developed such models.
6. Annable (1984) develops a theory of wage based on satisfaction much like the Akerlof theory.
7. Atkinson and Stiglitz (1980, Lecture 7; Part 5) indicate some of the incentive problems of taxes in a disequilibrium framework.
8. See Pissarides (forthcoming) and Koford and Miller (forthcoming) for two analyses of value-added incentive plans (TIP and MAP) that obtain this result.

REFERENCES

Ackley, Gardner. 1983. "Commodities and Capital: Prices and Quantities." *American Economic Review* (March).

Akerlof, George A., and Main, Brian G. M. 1980. "Unemployment Spells and Unemployment Experience." *American Economic Review*, 70, pp. 885-93.

Annable, James E., Jr. 1984. *The Price of Industrial Labor*. Lexington, Mass.: D. C. Health.

Atkinson, Anthony B., and Joseph E. Stiglitz. 1980. *Lectures on Public Economics*. New York: McGraw-Hill.

Azariadis, Costas. 1975. "Implicit Contracts and Underemployment Equilibria." *Journal of Political Economy* (December).

Baily, Martin N. 1974. "Wages and Employment Under Uncertain Demand." *Review of Economic Studies* (January).

Barro, Robert, and H. I. Grossman. 1976. *Money, Employment and Inflation*. New York: Cambridge University Press.

Benassy, J. P. 1982. *The Economics of Market Disequilibrium*. New York: Academic Press.

Clower, Robert. 1967. "A Reconsideration of the Foundation of Monetary Theory." *Western Economic Journal*. Vol. 6, pp. 1-9.

_____. 1965. "The Keynesian Counter-Revolution: A Theoretical Appraisal." In F. H. Hahn and F. P. R. Breckling, eds., *The Theory of Interest Rates*. London: Macmillan.

Diamond, Peter. 1984. "Money in Search Equilibrium." *Econometrica* (January).

Drazan, Allan. 1985. "Involuntary Unemployment and Aggregate Demand Spillovers in an Optimal Search Model." Foerder Institute Working Paper, March.

Frydman, Roman, and Edmund S. Phelps, eds. 1983. *Individual Forecasting and Aggregate Outcomes*. New York: Cambridge University Press.
Greenwald, Bruce, Joseph E. Stiglitz, and Andrew Weiss. 1984. "Information Imperfections in the Capital Market and Macroeconomic Fluctuations." *American Economic Review* (May).
Hall, Robert. 1982. "The Importance of Lifetime Work in the U.S. Economy." *American Economic Review* (September).
Hayek, F. A. 1945. "The Use of Knowledge in Society." *American Economic Review* 35 (September):4.
Hicks, John R. 1932. *The Theory of Wages*. New York: Macmillan.
Kahneman, Daniel, Paul Slovic, and Amos Tversky. 1982. *Judgement Under Uncertainty. Heuristic and Biases*. Cambridge: Cambridge University Press.
Keynes, J. M. 1923. *A Tract on Monetary Reform*. London: Harcourt, Brace.
Knight, Frank. 1921. *Risk, Uncertainty and Profit*. Chicago: University of Chicago Press.
Koford, Kenneth. 1984. "Do Incentive Anti-Inflation Plans Reduce the Natural Rate of Unemployment?" Unpublished paper.
Koford, Kenneth, and Jeffrey B. Miller. Forthcoming. "Incentive Anti-Inflation Policies in a Model of Market Disequilibrium." In David C. Colander, ed., *Incentive Anti-Inflation Plans*. New York: Ballinger.
Kohn, Meir. Forthcoming. "Monetary Analysis, the Equilibrium Method, and Keynes' *General Theory*." *American Economic Review*.
Leijonhufvud, Axel. 1981. *Information and Coordination*. Cambridge: Cambridge University Press.
Lerner, Abba, and David C. Colander. 1980. *MAP: A Market Anit-Inflation Plan*. New York: Harcourt Brace Jovanovich.
Lippman, Steven, and J. J. McCall. 1976. "The Economics of Job Search: A Survey." *Economic Inquiry* (June).
Lucas, Robert E., Jr. 1972. "Expectations and the Neutrality of Money." *Journal of Economic Theory*.
Madeo, Silvia, and Morton Pincus. 1985. "Stock Market Behavior and Tax Rule Changes: The Case of the Disallowance of Certain Interest Deductions Claimed by Banks." *Accounting Review* (July).
Malinvaud, Edmond. 1980. *Profitability and Unemployment*. London: Cambridge University Press.
_____. 1977. *The Theory of Unemployment Reconsidered*. London: Halsted.
Pissarides, Christopher. Forthcoming. "Equilibrium Effects of Tax-Based Incomes Policies." In David C. Colander, ed., *Incentive Anti-Inflation Plans*. New York: Ballinger.
_____. 1984. "Search Intensity, Job Advertising, and Efficiency." *Journal of Labor Economics* (January): 128–43.
Simon, Julian, and Ed Rice. 1983–84. "The Theory of Price Changing and Monopoly Power." *Journal of Post-Keynesian Economics* (Winter).
Smith, Adam. 1776. *The Wealth of Nations*, New York: Random House (1965 edition).
Stiglitz, Joseph E. 1982. "Information and Capital Markets." In William F. Sharpe

and Cathryn M. Cootner, eds., *Financial Economics: Essays in Honor of Paul Cootner.* Englewood Cliffs, N.J.: Prentice-Hall.

Turnovsky, Stephen, and Mark E. Wohar. 1984. "Monetarism and the Aggregate Economy: Some Longer-Run Evidence." *Review of Economics and Statistics* (November).

Weitzman, Martin. 1984. *The Share Economy.* Cambridge, Mass.: Harvard University Press.

1
What Would Keynes Have Thought of Rational Expectations?

Axel Leijonhufvud

INTRODUCTION

The Keynes Centenary celebrations would be more festive if the Keynesian tradition were in intellectual good health and vigor for the occasion. Unfortunately, it is not. Unsuccessful policies and confused debates have left Keynesian economics in disarray.

In recent years, the intellectual excitement in macroeconomic theory has centered around the development of the rational expectations approach. Many economists have concluded that rational expectations spells the end of Keynesian economics—and many more seem to fear that this is so, even while they dispute it. What has caused the most commotion, however, is not so much rational expectations *per se* but rather the so-called New Classical Economics. *Rational Expectations* is but one of the characteristic components of NCE. The other two are *Monetarism* and *Market Clearing*.

It does not seem particularly fruitful to speculate on how Keynes might have reacted to theoretical developments taking place thirty years or so after his death.[1] Economists who still regard themselves as 'Keynesians' (in some sense) will, however, have to define their positions *vis-à-vis* these new developments. What should we learn from this recent work? What criticisms of Keynesian economics have to be accepted? What lessons of Keynesian economics must not be abandoned? How can they most persuasively be reasserted?

This chapter has been reprinted with permission from David Worswick and James Trevithick, *Keynes and the Modern World* (Cambridge: Cambridge University Press, 1983).

The relevance of Keynes' contributions to current concerns is best reaffirmed by providing good, clear answers to these questions. Many retorts to the New Classical Economics have been impatient outbursts, tinged with moral indignation. They have gotten us precisely nowhere. Quite generally, Keynesian economics has adapted badly to opposition. As a consequence, it is losing the battles for the best young talent in economics. In the United States, this has been true for a decade or more. To the younger generation of economists, Keynesian economics—all of it, not just Keynes himself—belongs to the history of economic thought.[2]

MONETARISM IN THREE LESSONS

How did Keynesian economics end up in such a sorry state? Although some of us have not conceded defeat, it is obviously a widely held view that Keynesianism was vanquished by Monetarism. James Tobin has distinguished two Monetarist creeds: Mark I and Mark II.[3] It is useful, I think, to distinguish two stages in the development of his Mark I Monetarism and, correspondingly, to recognize three stages of the long controversy.

In the first stage, through the mid-1960s,[4] the discussion concerned the Monetarist causal interpretation of money–income correlations. The stability of the demand function for a well-specified stock of 'money' and the predominance of supply over money demand in the determination of that money stock were the core tenets of this Stage I Monetarism. In claiming that monetary policy would be an effective regulator of nominal income this Monetarism differed markedly from Keynesian views of that time. In almost every respect the policy doctrine advanced by Friedman and Brunner was diametrically opposed to that of the Radcliffe Report.

In the second stage of the controversy, many Keynesians embraced the Phillips-curve and the Monetarists challenged its stability. Arguments based on the anticipation of inflation became central to the debate for the first time. Although not logically entailed by labor-market anticipation of inflation, the Natural Rate of Unemployment hypothesis was made a Monetarist doctrine. This natural rate doctrine sharpened the crowding-out arguments against fiscal stabilization policies. The Monetarists found use for the anticipated inflation model (AIM) also in accounting for Gibson's paradox, i.e. the (pro-cyclical) pattern of nominal interest rates. Friedman's presidential address (1968) authoritatively summarized this Stage II Monetarism.

In the third stage, Lucas (1972) succeeded in providing a model, carefully built on rational expectations foundations, within which Friedman's (1968) conjectures about the short-run and long-run Phillips curves hold true. A breakthrough in the systematic modelling of informational assumptions, this immensely influential paper married the rational expectations approach to Stage II Monetarism from the outset. Sargent (1973) generalized the policy-ineffectiveness proposition which was then further developed by Sargent and Wallace (1976) and Barro (1976). The 'New Classical Economics' gained currency as the label for this Stage III Monetarism.

The reason for distinguishing between the Stages I and II is that the former is capable of a 'weak' and a 'strong' interpretation of the money-income correlation. In the strong version, exogenous changes in a purely supply-determined money stock interact with a stable money demand function to 'cause' the observed movements in money income. The 'weak' version allows a reciprocal influence from real income movements via real money demand to the money stock. The weak version nonetheless implies that control of the money stock will yield control of money income. Recall the oft-quoted summing up of Friedman and Schwartz's *Monetary History*:

> Mutual interaction, but with money rather clearly the senior partner in longer-run movements and in major cyclical movements, and more nearly an equal partner with money-income and prices in shorter-run and milder movements—this is the generalization suggested by our evidence.[5]

Sufficiently diluted, Stage I Monetarism can be made weak enough, obviously, to be stomached by almost all Keynesians, most of whom use a stable money demand function in any case. Stage II Monetarism, however, pretty much excludes this weaker interpretation. In the absence of monetary shocks, employment stays at the Natural Rate level. The permanent income corresponding to the Natural Rate of Unemployment determines the demand for real balances which is, therefore, a constant in the absence of monetary shocks. This leaves us with 'money causes income,' *without* the reciprocal influence. It is this strong version, consequently, that is carried over into Stage III New Classical Theory.

Where then did Keynesianism founder? At Stage II, obviously, on the Phillips curve or, more generally, on the failure to incorporate inflation rate expectations in the Keynesian model. When the American inflation picked up steam, the misbehavior of the Phillips curve and the inflation premium in nominal interest rates became obvious for all to see. Monetarists, who had predicted these things by reasoning from the neoclassical anticipated inflation model, made enormous headway within the economics profession and without. Keynesians, who had continued to argue the usefulness of the Phillips curve and to disparage the empirical relevance of the anticipated inflation model, lost face and lost influence.

It was a debacle. A bad enough debacle that the profession proclaimed the long controversy a Monetarist victory and, by and large, turned its interest elsewhere. This collective reaction left a number of things muddled.

First, the Phillips curve and Gibson's Paradox were both late-comers among the issues of the Monetarist controversy. When the verdict was rendered on the basis of the obvious significance of inflationary expectations, the *original* (Stage I) issues were not thereby settled. Rather they were forgotten or at least tabled for a number of years. I would agree with Tobin that 'the question whether money causes income or income money or both is still undecided.'[6]

Second, the stable Phillips curve had not been an integral part of earlier Keynesian theory. It was added on to that theory in the 1960s, not without opposition by some Keynesians.[7] It is not obvious, therefore, that the destruction of this excrescence by unfolding events should be reagrded as tantamount to the demolition of the central structure.

Third, although the Natural Rate hypothesis is pedagogically effective as the polar opposite to the stable Phillips trade-off hypothesis, it is not the case that empirical rejection of the latter establishes the former. Suppose that fully anticipated, purely nominal shocks have no employment effects. Other things (such as changes in the 'marginal efficiency of capital') might still have such effects. The ability to anticipate inflation (or 'absence of money illusion'), then, does not by itself imply some sort of strong stability of the economic system around full employment, be it 'Natural' or not.

THE OUT-OF-FOCUS KEYNES

What do the Three Stages of Monetarism have to do with Keynes? How do we bring Keynes into some sort of relation with developments decades after his death?

In all the debates over Keynesian economics in the last twenty years or so, there is one Keynes that has remained curiously out of focus. This is true also of my own writings. I mean Keynes, the monetary reformer. After more than fifteen muddled years of inflation, preoccupied as we are with intractable problems of monetary stabilization, it seems natural to give some thought to the Keynes who gave so many years of his life, from Versailles to Bretton Woods, to the cause of a stable and workable international financial order.

The Phillips curve debacle coincided in time with the elimination of the last vestiges of the Bretton Woods system. The heritage of Keynes, the theorist, came to grief when the legacy of Keynes, the monetary reformer, had been squandered. Is this just a curious coincidence? Or should we make more of it?

Keynesian theory failed to incorporate inflation expectations. Before the Great American inflation, the theory was widely accepted as an adequate guide to reality. Once the inflation picked up momentum and became both high and volatile, the Keynesian neglect of nominal expectations became fatal. But the international monetary order that Keynes had striven for should have had responsible international central bank policy by the reserve currency countries and everyone else disciplined by fixed exchange rates. In such a regime, rational agents should not have volatile nominal expectations, and a theory in which they do not is appropriate to the regime.

This is a rational expectations argument. The concept of 'monetary regime' figures prominently in the more recent rational expectations literature. It links expectations and institutions. It may be defined as follows: A monetary regime is a system of expectations that governs the behavior of the public and that is sustained by the consistent behavior of the policy-making authorities. Since the responses of an economy to shocks or to policy actions depend on the public's expectations, we need, in effect, a different short-run macrotheory for each different regime.

The regime approach is a highly useful one—certainly, one of the most useful developments to come out of the rational expectations movement so far. I suggest we use it on Keynes and ask what regimes (if any) his theory would fit and also what his opinions were of various regimes. First, we need to consider his treatment of expectations.

EXPECTATIONS

It used to be one of the proud boasts of Keynesian economics that it incorporated expectations in a significant way. Sir John Hicks in his first review of the *General Theory* gave pride of place among the book's contributions to its treatment of expectations:

> If we assume given, not only the tastes and resources ordinarily assumed given in static theory, but also people's anticipations of the future, it is possible to regard demands and supplies as determined by these tastes, resources and anticipations, and prices as determined by demands and supplies. Once the missing element—anticipations—is added, equilibrium analysis can be used, not only in the remote stationary conditions to which many economists have found them-

selves driven back, but even in the real world, even in the real world in 'disequilibrium'.

This is the general method of [the *General Theory*]; it may be reckoned the first of Mr Keynes's discoveries.[8]

The claim Hicks made for Keynes was that, by bringing in expectations in the right way, he had succeeded in significantly extending the scope of equilibrium analysis. This is precisely the claim now being made for Lucas, Sargent & Co. although for rather different reasons. Keynes extended the use of the Marshallian equilibrium method by treating long-term investment expectations as *exogenous* determinants of his short-run income equilibrium. Lucas extended the use of neo-Walrasian equilibrium analysis by making short-run nominal expectations strictly *endogenous* again while shifting to a stochastic equilibrium concept that allows realizations to diverge from expected values.

By the early thirties, business cycle theorists had come to realize that use of the equilibrium toolbox could be strictly justified only for stationary and perfect foresight processes.[9] This pretty much excluded business cycles—and there was no other toolbox. Keynes' new method successfully *evaded* this dilemma. Lucas's new method attempts to *solve* it.

That, however, is not the whole story. Keynes' innovation concerned the long-term expectations of real magnitudes, while NCE theory has dealt mainly with the short-term expectations of nominal magnitudes. Keynes, on the whole, ignored nominal expectations and the rational expectations pioneers have only recently begun to turn their attention to long-term investment expectations.

Keynes' own treatment of short-term expectations should give pause to anyone tempted to attack the NCE on the grounds that it assumes too much foresight on the part of agents:[10]

> it will often be safe to omit express reference to *short-term* expectations in view of the fact that in practice ... there is a large overlap between the effects on employment of the realized sale-proceeds of recent output and those of the sale-proceeds expected from current input ...

The omission of 'express reference' is achieved, of course, by simply equating expected and realized real income, a procedure subsequently imbedded in the Keynesian cross, in *IS=LM*, and thus in the entire Keynesian literature. This is 'perfect foresight' such as the rational expectations people have not allowed themselves to indulge in! Keynes, I would think, should have appreciated the considerable weakening of this assumption achieved through the use of a stochastic equilibrium concept.

Long-term expectations are another story. In the early stages of the rational expectations debate, *the* issue was the Phillips curve, and the focus, therefore, was entirely on expectations over the most immediate future only. The ability of agents to infer more or less correctly the immediate price-level consequences of current monetary policies was emphasized to the neglect of their inability to infer much of anything about the future nominal values that will emerge from longer sequences of discretionary policy actions.[11] As a consequence, this early rational expectations literature provides very little in the way of theoretical foundation for the opposition to inflationary policies (and discretionary policies in general) that also characterizes it.[12] This temporary neglect does not mean that the rational expectations approach implies negligible social costs of inflation. Nor does it mean that it somehow precludes sensible study of this problem on which Keynes held such strong views.[13] On the contrary, progress beyond the point reached in the *Tract* requires, I think, careful specification of the 'inflationary regime' in question—requires, in other words, a rational expectations approach.

Nonetheless, long-term expectations pose the question of how far the endogenization of expectations can be taken. Elsewhere, I have used a distinction between 'well-behaved' and 'ill-behaved' expectations.[14] Well-behaved expectations bear a stable relationship to the observable state variables of a macroeconomic model and can therefore be treated as fully endogenous. Expectations are 'ill-behaved' if not explainable by the model. If, in addition, they are unobservable (or unmeasurable), ill-behaved expectations will spell trouble for our ability to forecast.

In these terms, Keynes' short-term expectations were (excessively) well-behaved but his long-term expectations ill-behaved in that they shifted for reasons not incorporated in the model. The rational expectations approach to this problem will, of course, be to strive for a behavior-description in which long-term investment expectations are completely endogenized.[15] Keynes would presumably have raised philosophical objections to so foolhardy an attempt to harness the 'dark forces of time and ignorance' with the actuarial calculus.

From the standpoint of rational expectations methodology, a refusal to attempt to *endogenize* all expectations is perhaps nothing but obscurantism. The Keynesian trick of explaining income movements by invoking exogenous (and perhaps also unobservable) 'shifts in MEC' appears as nothing more than putting a verbal label on our quantitative ignorance. Clearly, we are better off the more success this ambitious rational expectations programme has. Meanwhile, a label for one's ignorance is a very useful thing—if it helps remind one that one *is* ignorant.

PRICES AND QUANTITIES

During the course of the Monetarist controversy it was often said that the two sides differed in their explanations of changes in nominal income but 'were in the same boat' when it came to explaining the breakdown of nominal income changes into their price and quantity components. But surely the two approaches do not belong in the same boat? Throughout the entire history of modern macroeconomics, I feel, there has been something profoundly unsatisfactory, something thoroughly befuddled, about our handling of the relationships between nominal and real magnitudes.

I have no precise diagnosis of what has been the problem. I do have a hunch about it, namely, that the trouble may stem from a failure to keep straight the differences between monetary (or nominal) and real business cycle hypotheses.

Any business cycle 'story' will have, as two of its elements, first, a shock or disturbance and, second, the failure of some endogenous variable or variables to adjust appropriately to the shock. The disturbances can be nominal or real (or, of course, mixed) and so can the adjustment failures. Thus, we obtain the 'Swedish flag' classification of Figure 1.1 where the mixed cases are slighted for the purposes of the present discussion.

A '(purely) nominal disturbance' is one that requires a scaling up or down of all nominal values for the re-equilibration of the system. Thus, nominal shocks are neutral by definition. A 'real shock' is one that

		Nominal	Mixed	Real
Shocks	Nominal	N/N $dM\|\bar{w}$		N/R $dM\|\bar{E}(r)$
	Mixed			
	Real	R/N $dMEC\|\bar{w}$		R/R $dMEC\|\bar{r}$

FIGURE 1.1 Adjustment 'Failures'

requires some reallocation of resources and, correspondingly, changes in real relative prices. Keynes' shifting 'marginal efficiency of capital' is the case we will deal with here (oil shocks and other newfangled inventions will be ignored). MEC shocks change perceived intertemporal oportunities and require, therefore, adjustments in intertemporal prices, i.e., in the structure of real rates of interest.

In a nominal/nominal (N/N) theory, the disturbance requires a rescaling of nominal values. A truly exogenous change in a purely supply-determined money stock might approximate such a case. If money wages (for instance) were to be inflexible—for whatever reason—the maladjustment would show up in changes in employment. Friedman's (1968) explanation of deviations from the natural rate of unemployment exemplifies this brand of theory.

In the diagonally opposed R/R case, the MEC shift requires a reallocation of resources between production for present and production for future consumption. (To the extent that intertemporal substitution elasticities in labor-supply vs. leisure choices are of significant magnitude, it may also call for a change in the present 'natural' level of employment.) If the intertemporal price structure proves inflexible, saving and investment cannot be appropriately coordinated and the maladjustment, again, shows up in changes in employment. Keynes' (1936) *General Theory* is, of course, of this variety.

If we could have had a Monetarist controversy of this clear-cut N/N versus R/R variety, modern macroeconomics would be more easily understandable than is now the case. That a failure of nominal values to adjust to a nominal disturbance will mean trouble is not a very complex idea. That a failure of relative prices to adjust to a real disturbance likewise spells trouble is not that much harder to grasp.

The actual discussion has seldom been that straightforward. First, the most widely accepted version of Keynesian economics combines shifts in MEC with rigidity of money wage rates. This R/N story is not at all as transparent as our first two examples. If we start with a real disturbance requiring changes in the allocation of resources and in relative prices, but not in the level of nominal values, why should rigid money wages give us trouble? At best a crucial link is missing from this story. At worst it is confused.

One of the consequences of 'Keynesian' economists shifting their ground in this way was a rather confused altercation with the Monetarists over unemployment theory. In this discussion, the Monetarists—who are obliged to invoke some nominal adjustment failure to explain how the real cycle results from nominal shocks—were steadfast in denying any rigidity of wages, while the Keynesians—who should have no particular use for the assumption—eventually made it the touchstone of Keynesian doctrine.[16] Probably, nothing could have done more to make wage rigidity seem an essential Keynesian tenet than the objections to it from Karl Brunner and Milton Friedman.

At the same time, of course, Friedman assumed temporary 'stickiness' of wages to explain how nominal shocks would cause temporary deviations of unemployment from its 'natural rate.' In constructing an equilibrium model with the properties conjectured by Friedman, Lucas transformed the temporary maladjustment into an intertemporal one. The canonical version of NCE, therefore, has nominal disturbances causing misperceptions of the real rate of return which give rise, in turn, to intertemporal substitution adjustments in employment.[17]

Thus, the New Classicists have, in effect, shifted the Monetarist position from a N/N one to a N/R one. This moves the muddled conflict over unemployment theory onto the R/N to N/R off-diagonal, which frankly does not help much. It leaves us with Keynesians blaming sticky money wages confronting Monetarists blaming real return misperceptions.

The slow quadrille continues. It may be that most American Keynesians see little difference between the R/N and N/N positions. From $IS=LM$, one learns that both monetary and real shocks can produce changes in nominal income; it appears, then, that the point one must insist on is that changes in nominal income produce changes in real output and employment only if money wages or prices are sticky. Quite a few former Keynesians, moreover, have come to agree that it takes monetary impulses to produce aggregative movements. These people actually occupy the original Monetarist position (at N/N) but still regard themselves as quite non-Monetarist in their insistence on the inflexibility of wages; they do so with some reason since the leading younger Monetarists have vacated these premises in favor of a position (at N/R) allowing a principled insistence on market-clearing wages.

Meanwhile—are you following me?—doubts have arisen in the Rational Expectations camp concerning the Monetarist causation hypothesis. Indeed, Sims has moved already from a reconsideration (1980) to rejection (1983) of the monetary business cycle explanation. Here I must ask you to stand by for further developments. It is, as yet, too early to tell whether Sims will lead the New Classical Economists to occupy the original Keynes position (at R/R), while the Old Keynesians make themselves at home in Friedman's quarters (at N/N).

This will remind you, I am sure, of that great Cambridge contemporary of Keynes, Sir Dennis Robertson (1954):

> highbrow opinion is like a hunted hare; if you stand in the same place, or nearly the same place, it can relied upon to come round to you in a circle.

Whether Robertson was here expressing a Rational Expectation or merely voicing the autoregressive prejudice of his five lagged decades in the profession, I will not presume to judge. If, in this clockwise dance, highbrow opinion were to come back to 'nearly the same place' as Keynes, it may still not be perceived as a vindication, for by now the term 'Keynesian' is little more than a label for the hindmost.

The long controversy between Keynesians and Monetarists is thus a very complicated story. That acknowledged, I will proceed 'as if' the basic conflict, all along, had been between a Keynesian real disturbance/real maladjustment theory and a Monetarist nominal disturbance/nominal maladjustment theory.

MONETARY REGIMES

There are two basic but contrasting conceptions of how control of nominal values can be achieved which we may call the *quantity principle* and the convertibility principle, respectively. Monetary regimes may be distinguished inter alia according to how closely they approximate a system of pure quantity control or one of pure convertibility control.[18]

The quantity principle seeks control of the price level through control of some monetary aggregate usually referred to loosely as the 'quantity of money'. The logically tidiest version of such a system will be on a pure fiat standard. It requires central banking. The private sector must be prevented from creating perfect substitutes for the government controlled 'money' since otherwise control of the latter might not achieve control of the general price level. Hence the system usually has government monopoly of the note issue and more or less far-reaching governmental control of the banking system. Basically, the government decides on the quantity of money, and the private sector sets the price level.

An extreme version of this regime would arise if the government, in changing the quantity of money, did so only be means of currency reforms that change the nominal value of outstanding contracts and of the real balances held by the public. (The 1958 French replacement of old by new francs is an example.) In this unrealistic case, the 'nominal scalar' case, the government could directly manipulate the nominal scale of all real magnitudes.

The convertibility principle, in contrast, requires the government to set the legal price of some commodity (such as gold), allows banks to produce 'money' redeemable into the commodity, and lets the private non-bank sector decide the quantity of paper money and bank deposits it desires to hold. Suppose, just for a moment, that the government could set the legal nominal price of a basket of commodities, and that redeemability of money into baskets could be made operable. Such a 'basket case' monetary regime would be the diametric opposite to the 'nominal scalar': the government sets the price level and the private sector determines the quantity of money.

We may thus consider a spectrum of institutional possibilities with the commodity standard regimes toward the convertibility control extreme at one end and the fiat regimes toward the quantity control end. Early banking history shows us systems relying altogether on convertibility for monetary control. The present system retains no shred of convertibility, but relies altogether on governmental quantity control. In between, we could array, in rough historical sequence, the managed gold standard, the gold exchange standard, and the Bretton Woods system in its various stages of ascendancy and decline. The historical process has not been a smooth and gradual transition from commodity to fiat standards, of course. War-time lapses into inconvertible paper were repeatedly followed by the reestablishment of regimes in which convertibility had a more or less significant role to play. With some backing and filling, the secular process has nonetheless been one away from convertibility and toward quantity control of fiat money.

Most of the historical experience relevant to the present discussion is not well represented by either of my two extreme cases. Nonetheless it is instructive to note what kind of monetary theories and monetary policy doctrines would fit these extremes. We should also ask what relationship might be established between the previous classification of business cycle theories and the present one of monetary regimes.

Obviously, the quantity control fiat standard is made for Monetarist theory. In Friedman's theory (particularly, Stage II), the central bank sets the quantity of money and the private sector adjusts first nominal income but ultimately only the price level. The monetary authorities can control nominal magnitudes but, in equilibrium, real ones are beyond their grasp. Attempts to control what cannot be controlled produce undesirable results. Pursuit of a low interest target, for instance, would eventually produce an explosive inflation. Monetary policy should be directed at monetary targets, and the latter should not be adjusted with an eye to variables, such as employment, that are ultimately beyond nominal control. And so on.

The (unrealistic) case of 'basket convertibility' would be a convenient one for Radcliffe monetary policy doctrine. The price level is set and the public rationally expects its future to be regulated by convertibility. The non-bank public's trading of real IOU's for real deposits with the banking system determines the monetary aggregates. To the extent that the central bank can affect the terms of this exchange, i.e., mainly the real rate of interest, it will have some small degree of influence on real investment, output, and the real money stock, but control of the nominal scale of real magnitudes in the economy is essentially beyond its powers. Monetary policy operates within narrow limits to affect real credit conditions and liquidity. The use of interest targets does not carry any imminent danger of liquidity. The use of interest targets does not carry any imminent danger of nominal instability in this setting where both the price level and price expectations are kept in check by convertibility.

Now, of course, not even the late 19th century gold standard resembled this 'basket convertibility' regime at all closely. It had an anchor for nominal values in the sense that price level fluctuations were constrained to those of the relative value of gold in terms of other commodities. Mean-reverting price level expectations helped stabilize prices. Even so, a variable supply of new gold, a small and price-inelastic non-monetary demand and a vanishing non-bank monetary demand meant that the bounds which gold convertibility put on the price level could be uncomfortably wide. The wider these bounds, the more room the system gave for the 'Credit Cycle', as Keynes called it.[19] Management of the standard, for reasons beyond merely protecting the solvency of the banking system against 'drains,' became increasingly desirable.

The last attempt, in the 1920s, to control nominal values through gold convertibility ended in total disaster. Convertibility for the public disappeared and was never seen again. One by one, the features of the commodity standard were removed, making central bank control increasingly important. With redeemability gone, the public could no longer protect itself against inflationary policies. Until 1971, small open economies were still disciplined to some degree by fixed exchange rates but retained a significant ability to sterilize reserve flows, particularly in periods when capital flows were restricted.[20]

The international system of multiple fiat regimes, snakes, tunnels, dirty floats, and flexible exchange rates is far removed from the old gold standard world. But although the peoples of the Western world have had to become accustomed to the instability of nominal values and even though the correct anticipation of nominal changes is of the utmost importance in such a setting, the present system of multilateral monetary mismanagement does not closely approximate my 'nominal scalar' extreme.

So, our historical experience lies well inside these extremes. But the never-ceasing theoretical debate juxtaposes two traditions of monetary analysis each of which interprets that experience as if it 'essentially' belonged close to one of the extremes. Very often, moreover, the battle between Monetarism and the 'New View' over the interpretation of some regime midway between the extremes is carried out in terms that suggest that the two theories are regarded as mutually exclusive so that one must be True and the other False.[21] My own unprincipled belief is that both theories are about half true and that we can be dangerously misled if we base policy wholly on one to the total exclusion of the other.

REGIMES AND CYCLES

Turning now to business cycle theories, it is clear that those postulating purely nominal shocks are relevant only at the fiat extreme, whereas at the convertibility extreme only real shock hypotheses are admissible. The (strong) Monetarist causal chain from exogenous money shock via nominal inflexibility to real output and employment is familiar. The Keynesian chain from changes in real intertemporal prospects via real interest rate maladjustments to real income and endogenous movements in inside money, even if familiar, is out of fashion. We may sketch both an equilibrium and a 'disequilibrium' version of it.

In the equilibrium version, we start with a rise (exogenous in relation to the model specified) in the future real income perceived as derivable from present factor employment in some sizeable sector of the economy. All agents are equally informed about this change in the situation, and all evaluate it in the same way. The entire system responds as would Robinson Crusoe therefore. Suppose, for the sake of argument, a high degree of intertemporal elasticity of labor/leisure substitution, so that we obtain a significant supply response to this change in the future return to present labor. This will allow a temporary equilibrium employment expansion in one sector without equal contraction elsewhere. Hence, the natural rate of unemployment is not a constant but depends on the marginal efficiency of capital. The expansion of output is financed by an expansion of bank and non-bank trade credit. As income increases more real money balances are demanded so that the additional saving matching the increased investment ends up being partly intermediated by the banking system. Investment, real interest rates, and employment all rise, and the expansion of the banking system (and of non-bank credit) allows this to happen without downward pressure on money prices.

Note that this sketch follows the rational expectations equilibrium ground rules, although it is non-Monetarist. The money stock varies with income for purely endogenous reasons. Employment covaries with money income for reasons that have nothing to do with nominal misperceptions or other maladjustments of wages or prices.

The disequilibrium version is the Wicksell–Keynes story. Here it is *not* the case that all agents get the same information. Individual firms see improvements in the future return to present activity, but no one has an overview of what is happening to the economy-wide marginal efficiency of investment. Since, historically, the average real rate of return has not been a volatile variable, speculation stabilizes the real rate of interest, and firms adjust their rates of investment to it. When the real interest rate fails to find its 'natural' level, household saving and business investment are not properly coordinated. In the upswing, (over)expansion of credit allows investment to exceed planned saving, putting upward pressure on money prices and wages. In recession, the contraction of credit will similarly put downward pressure on prices. The cycle, therefore, would leave a Phillips curve pattern of observations even in this system where nominal values are anchored by convertibility.

Suppose this is a serviceable description of the kind of cycle that occurs toward the end of our spectrum where convertibility more or less guarantees against the occurrence of purely nominal shocks. What then happens to the cyclical behavior of the economy as the historical trend away from convertibility control takes it toward pure quantity control? What does *not* happen is that the Keynesian R/R cycle fades out to be replaced by a Monetarist N/N cycle. Two things might happen. *Either* the quantity control is handled in such a way that shocks requiring adjustments in the nominal scale of real magnitudes do not occur; *or* it is mismanaged in which case a N/N cycle is superimposed on the R/R one.

Recent history presents us with about two decades of one and two of the other. What seems most interesting about the Bretton Woods regime in retrospect is that a system of expectations basically appropriate to an economy with convertible money was sustained by quantity control and with the central convertibility mechanism removed. A system of price level expectations consistent with the convertibility principle means that people expect prices to revert to the longer term trend if and when they go above or below trend. For such expectations to be maintained when the economy is not in fact on a standard where non-discretionary, objective factors determine the trend, the central bank must, in effect, 'mimic' such a standard. It does so by imposing monetary restraint above trend and applying monetary stimulus below it. The government must also maintain the faith that this pattern of behavior will be continued indefinitely. An (at least implicit) monetary constitution will be of help in this regard. For small open economies, a habit of defending a fixed exchange rate may be the way to accomplish this task—if, that is, the reserve currency country behaves responsibly. This can be a big 'if.' In any case, public confidence in the indefinite maintenance of this pattern of monetary control will require budgetary policies consistent with this objective.[22]

In the United States, monetary stability was maintained in this way until the mid-sixties. With the private sector firmly expecting a quite low and not very variable rate of inflation, the Federal Reserve System could affect the availability and price of 'real' credit to some extent. Monetary policy could play a limited, but constructive role in attempts to stabilize employment. But the continuance of the regime required continued restraint on the part of the authorities.

The one-time Keynesian (or Radcliffe) doctrine of the 'ineffectiveness' of monetary policy would seem to have served, however inadvertently, as a myth protecting the Bretton Woods regime. Like the belief in the stickiness of nominal wages, it is a doctrine fitting a true convertible standard—where the monetary authorities cannot play around with the nominal scalar, rational agents will not expect that adjustments in the nominal scale of contracts will be needed. When the Friedmanite doctrine that the quantity of money is an effective regulator of nominal income gradually gained acceptance, however, it was inevitable that advocates of discretionary policy would put it to use. To economists who explained unemployment by the stickiness of money wages, this Monetarist doctrine suggested that the stock of money might serve as an effective regulator of employment. If so, it was almost a moral imperative that it be used. But vigorous manipulation of the supply of outside nominal money will destroy the system of expectations that makes nominal values relatively inflexible. The Phillips curve will then start to misbehave.

INVOLUNTARY UNEMPLOYMENT

At the outset I noted that the New Classical Economics was made up of Rational Expectations, Monetarism, and Market Clearing. It remains to comment on the last of the three.[23]

The equilibrium approach has caused more uproar among Keynesians than any other aspect of the work of Lucas, Sargent & Co. The reason is that the market clearing assumption is taken to be inconsistent with 'involuntary unemployment,' a concept which most Keynesians feel obliged to defend to the bitter end of their creed. Much ink has been spilt and a considerable volume of hot air expended, therefore, in criticizing or satirizing the rational expectations approach on this score. From the rational expectations side, scorn is heaped on the arbitrary fix-price constraints of 'disequilibrium' theory while the concept of excess demand is declared inoperational and the notion of 'involuntary' behavior spurned as inexplicable in utility-maximizing terms.

In my opinion, however, the issue has hardly been joined, so that not much can be sensibly said about the debate as it relates to Keynes. One reason for this is that few, if any, people on either side care much about what Keynes might have meant by 'involuntary unemployment' and that most proceed to use the term as if whatever associations happen to come to mind are good enough at least for polemical purposes.[24] The term, without a doubt, is one of the most unfortunate new coinages in the history of economics. The problem to which the term refers is not therefore nonsensical. Keynes was concerned with a *systemic* problem that could be defined neither in terms of individual decision situations nor in terms of interactions between buyers and sellers in a single market. His 'involuntary' unemployment is the result of *effective demand failures*.[25]

Two distinct effective demand failures are involved in Keynes' persistent involuntary unemployment state. One is the intertemporal (R/R) one discussed above which arises because

> a decision not to have dinner to-day ... does not necessitate a decision to have dinner or to buy a pair of boots a week hence or a year hence or to consume any specified thing at any specified date.[26]

Hence, it does not pay to organize all the markets for specified things at all specified dates. In their absence, it is possible to have an effective excess supply of present goods to which there corresponds a notional excess demand for future goods which is nowhere registered in a market. The other one, predicated on the prior occurrence of the first, occurs between the spot markets for labor and for consumption goods because unemployed people without money cannot bid for consumption goods so that an effective excess supply of labor may have as its Walras' Law counterpart an ineffective excess demand for goods.

Now, this kind of situation does not have fix-price rationing as a prerequisite. Suppose atomistic markets where, every day, sellers of commodities and buyers of labor post prices and wages and buyers of commodities and sellers of labor have to decide on their demand-price and reservation-wage schedules.[27] These prices are set using the best information available. Suppose further that agents find a way to carry out all transactions compatible with these prior valuation decisions. 'Markets clear.' If, however, the system has been perturbed in some way such that not all agents are equally informed about the developing situation, these information asymmetrics will make realized transactions deviate from their 'equilibrium' volume (if by 'equilibrium' we mean the transactions that would be consistent with plans based on some universally shared view of what the true situation is). So the 'market clears' at a 'disequilibrium' volume.

In the first round of a Keynesian recession, demand price schedules for capital goods shift down because expectations about their future rental values have deteriorated and the rate of interest at which expected rentals are discounted has not declined commensurably. The derived demand for labor in those industries consequently declines but suppliers of labor, who have little reason to believe that realizable real wages have declined throughout the entire system, keep their reservation wages up. So the market clears at reduced employment with not much change in the observed wage level.

Now, this first round outcome may be described in various ways. To say, as I once did to my frequent regret, that 'In the Keynesian macrosystem the Marshallian ranking of price- and quantity-adjustment speeds is reversed'[28] is too mechanical to be helpful. It reads as an open invitation to fix-price rationing modelling of the sort that pays little attention to the determination of prices. In my 1968 story, prices were not 'rigid' but held up temporarily (in atomistic markets) because of speculation based on 'inelastic expectations.' This story does not give both sides of the labor market the same information sets. But it does not otherwise differ significantly from the way in which later rational expectations models deal with variations in employment.[29]

In the New Classical models, however, tomorrow's another day (drawn from the distribution of pretty nice days). Tomorrow you try it again, starting from scratch. Today's decline in employment has no persistent consequences. (A reason for persistence, in fact, has to be invented.)

In Clower's version of the Keynesian story, the temporary curtailment in employment means that tomorrow's consumption demand is constrained by today's realized income. The derived demand for labor in the consumption goods industries is now also affected. By a familiar route, multiplier repercussions bring the system into a state where the inability of the unemployed to back their notional consumption demands with cash is a major reason for the persistence of unemployment. The unemployment that persists in the system *for this reason* Keynes called 'involuntary.'[30, 31]

Now, I will agree that the theory of effective demand failures raises more questions than it answers and, also, that it has made no progress (as far as I know) for several years. But the nature of the problem that it poses should be clear. Individuals interact on the basis of incomplete information. The consequence is a price vector reflecting the incompleteness of information and a pattern of realized transactions which leaves some agents disappointed. Will this set in motion a learning process that leads to a coordinated solution? If price adjustments were governed by notional excess demands, then neo-Walrasian stability theorems will tell us under which conditions the answer is Yes. Effective demand theory argues, I think persuasively, that there is no reason to suppose that, whatever the trial-and-error process that capitalist economies rely on, the successive trials will in fact be governed by these notional errors. Consequently, *tâtonnement* stability theorems are suspect.

To my knowledge, the New Classical literature contains nothing of any relevance one way or another to these issues. When 'excess demand' is simply dismissed as an inoperational concept, inquiries into its 'notional' or 'effective' nature are somewhat discouraged. The oft-paraphrased point that 'rational agents will act to exhaust perceived gains from trade' may serve very well as a pedagogical note of caution vis-à-vis certain fix-price constructions, but as a contribution to our understanding of the stability of general equilibrium it ranks somewhere below the Law of Jean-Baptiste Say.

This debate, to repeat, has not been joined.

THE 1920s AND THE 1980s

To many people, my assigned subject is worth discussing mostly in so far as it leads up to a stand for or against Mrs. Thatcher or President Reagan. It should be developed in adversary terms: Keynes vs. Rational Expectations. Aggregate demand management in a world of sticky wages versus policy ineffectiveness in a world of neutral money. Re-inflation versus continued disinflation.

My own belief, in contrast, is that this way of seeing the issues gets neither Keynes nor the Rational Expectations people right. I do not believe it gets the alternatives currently before us right either.

There was one period, the early twenties, when Keynes had to deal with a monetary regime resembling our own, which is to say, a system of flexible exchange rates, unbalanced budgets, and unanchored fiat currencies. His main reaction to it, evidently, was that it urgently demanded Monetary Reform. The *Tract* was not a book about how best to muddle along from year to year within the existing system. It argued for a change of regime.

The 1920s have recently drawn the renewed interest of balance-of-payments theorists and monetary economists. In a recent paper on the problem of 'Stopping Moderate Inflations,' Sargent (1981) compares the methods of Poincaré and Thatcher. He criticizes Mrs. Thatcher for carrying through with disinflation without reforming the policy regime and attributes the 1926 Poincaré 'miracle' to a systematic fiscal and monetary regime change.

The diagnosis of the French situation and the precise recipe for the miracle had been given by Keynes more than two years before Poincaré reluctantly acted on these lines. Keynes' diagnosis, item by item, was then exactly the one that Sargent has now rediscovered.[32] For example:

> What... will determine the value of the franc? First, the quantity, present and prospective, of the francs in circulation.... (T)he quantity of the currency, depends mainly on the loan and budgetary policies of the French Treasury.
>
> What course should the French Treasury now take in face of the dangers surrounding them? It is soon said. First, the government must so strengthen its fiscal position that its power to control the volume of the currency is beyond doubt.

Obviously, Keynes had an adequate working knowledge of that 'unpleasant monetarist arithmetic'![33] A more detailed reading of Keynes and Sargent only makes the agreement between the two even more remarkable.

The *Tract on Monetary Reform* is a very monetarist book. Many latter-day Keynesians like to think that Keynes successfully kicked this habit soon afterward and went on to write the *Treatise*, which he in turn discarded as the *General Theory* began to take shape in his mind. But it is also possible to see this progression less as a series of radical changes in Keynes' fundamental theoretical beliefs than as reorientations of his theoretical efforts to meet changing problems.

This characteristic of Keynes' work—that he adapted his theory to changing problems—has often been remarked upon. Practical political economists approve; pure theorists disapprove. Rational expectations economists might recognize in this adaptability of Keynes' something more than an engaging or irritating character quirk. Rational expectations theory tells us that the short-run effects of particular disturbances or policy actions will depend upon the expectations of the public and, therefore, on the regime that the public believes to be in effect. We need a different applied macrotheory for each monetary regime. The lesson is that we all must, like Keynes, adopt our theories to a changing world.

The *Tract* denounced 'instability of the standard of value' in strong, colorful terms. We do not find him retracting these opinions later. Instead, throughout the rest of his life, he strove for an international economic order that would anchor nominal values and provide 'fixed' exchange rates while leaving scope for discretionary domestic policies and, in particular, giving Britain time to adjust.[34] His work in theory, subsequent to the *Tract*, assumed a regime in which the nominal scale of real magnitudes was not being manipulated. The influence of nominal expectations on behavior was correspondingly neglected. His theory did assume, of course, that one would have to face a business cycle even in the absence of nominal shocks. Absence of obstacles to money wage adjustment does not suffice to guarantee rapid convergence on the natural rate of unemployment in this theory, since intertemporal coordination failures ('saving exceeding investment') are not corrected by changes in nominal values.[35] The strong version of Monetarism, therefore, cannot hold in this theory.

CONCLUSIONS

Keynesian economics used to be the mainstream. Now, the younger generation of macrotheorists and econometricians regard it just as a backwater, look to Monetarism for navigable channels, and find their real white water thrills in the technically demanding rapids of Rational Expectations. This ageing Keynesian thinks the main channel is still where it used to be. But it obviously has silted up, is full of accumulated debris, and must be thoroughly dredged and cleared, before one can hope that it will see much traffic again.

Mainly, I suggest, the Keynesian tradition has had trouble in keeping the analysis straight on nominal versus real shocks and adjustments. This happened to surface in the squabble over the Phillips curve. But the trouble goes deeper and begins earlier. When I was a student, over twenty years ago, two of the tenets (for example) that were taught to us as 'Keynesian' were (1) that unemployment was due to the rigidity of nominal wages, and (2) that monetary policy could not bring about sizeable changes in nominal income. Both propositions are basically true if we can take a framework of monetary stability as part of the (unstated) *ceteris paribus* conditions. Both are false as matters of 'general theory.' As it happens, you will be all right as long as you firmly believe both of them. Unlearning (2) while still holding on to (1) led to confusion and produced the Phillips curve debacle.

One does not revive Keynesian economics again by insisting that nominal wages are sticky or by denying that governmental money creation causes inflation. The doctrine that unemployment is produced by nominal income changes (without distinction as to their cause) interacting with sticky wages keeps pointing us in the wrong direction, namely, toward using nominal instruments to try to bring about real change.

Keynesians should learn from Monetarism (if need be) that manipulation of the nominal money stock has strong effects on nominal income in discretionary fiat money regimes. From Rational Expectations they should learn that nominal expectations (of price-setting agents, in particular) are endogenous in regimes where the nominal scale is subject to manipulation; also that stabilization policy is better thought of in terms of the design of policy regimes with desirable overall, long-run properties rather than in terms of one short-horizon policy choice at a time. But there are also fashionable things they should refuse to learn. We do not have sufficient reason to accept the strong version of Monetarism; we have reason to reject the Natural Rate of Unemployment doctrine;[36] and we have no reason to pay much attention to Rational Expectations denials of effective demand failures and the possibility of involuntary unemployment.

We should seek a return to a monetary order that should as far as possible minimize nominal shocks. They do us no good but cause us much harm.[37] A return to monetary stability—*if* we can find a way—requires us to forswear policies that are built on the hope of exploiting temporary money illusions, or the incomplete indexing of contracts, or other information imperfections. This includes forswearing fiscal deficits financed by borrowing today but by money creation tomorrow.

In a world where the nominal scale were firmly anchored, business fluctuations would presumably still take place (and they would probably leave behind a record of observations looking much like a stable Phillips curve.) It is conceivable that these would be socially optimal in some sense or other, but we have no substantive reasons to give much weight to this possibility. The amplitude of these real cycles and the incidence of their social cost can be modified by policy regimes designed to have real effects on real variables: unemployment insurance, functional finance, built-in stabilizers. The lessons of Hansenian Keynesianism would come back into their own.

As in the 1920s, so in the 1980s: the times call for Monetary Reform. That will be easier said than done. Simply money growth-rules, assuming their operational feasibility, are probably too tight as constraints on systems where not only does '(nominal) money cause (nominal) income' but '(real) income also causes (real) money.'[38] We should have no longings for the 'barbarous relic.' And there can be no returning to Bretton Woods. From Keynes, the monetary reformer, we get a useful suggestion on where to start:

> First, the government must so strengthen its position that its power to control the volume of the currency is beyond doubt.

But hardly any help beyond that point. As is proper for an economist, I am thus led to a dismal conclusion—namely, we have to start thinking for ourselves.

NOTES

1. In the past, I have sometimes been accused of claiming knowledge of "what Keynes really meant." The present title was assigned to me by Royal (Economic Society) Decree. In trying to write a paper to fit it, I have had occasional bouts of the unworthy suspicion that it was meant to goad me into some sort of spiritualist seance before witnesses. I would like to declare from the outset, therefore, that I have not been in touch with Maynard about this!

2. A recent Lucas and Sargent paper (1979) is entitled "After Keynesian Macroeconomics." (It deals, however, to a very large extent with econometric issues outside the scope of my discussion.)

3. Tobin (1981). For the material in this section, see also Laidler (1981, 1982).

4. Friedman's (1956) "Restatement" through the years in which Friedman and Schwartz's (1963) *Monetary History* and related to works by Cagan, Brunner, and Meltzer were absorbed by the profession.

5. Friedman and Schwartz (1963), p. 695.

6. Tobin (1981), p. 41.

7. See esp. Phelps (1968). I may also refer to my own comment, ibid.

8. Sir John Hicks (1936), reprinted as " 'The General Theory' a First Impression," in Hicks (1982), p. 86.

9. See, again, J. R. Hicks (1933), reprinted as "Equilibrium and the Cycle," in his (1982). Compare also Robert E. Lucas, Jr. (1980), reprinted in his (1981), esp. section 5.

10. See Keynes (1936), pp. 50-51. My colleague, Robert Clower, reads this passage simply as assuming static expectations. Even on that reading, however, the solution states of Keynes' model will be perfect foresight equilibria.

11. See Leijonhufvud (1981b, 1983a).

12. That the New Classical Economics does not provide sufficient reasons for its strong aversion to inflationary policies is a complaint often voiced by critics. See, e.g., Tobin, op. cit., or Hahn (1983), pp. 101ff.

13. Keynes' (1971b) "Preface." It is true, of course, that Keynes' thought changed and developed from the *Tract* on. It is also true, however, that the world of the *Tract* resembles our current regime of fiduciary standards and flexible exchange rates more than does the world of the *Treatise* or that of the *General Theory*. One must insist, moreover, that we do not have evidence from Keynes' later years that would indicate a change of mind on his part with regard to the consequences of inflation.

14. Leijonhufvud (1983a).

15. Early in his career, Lucas was best known for his work on investment. He returns to it, in context of a complete macromodel and from a rational expectations perspective in his (1975). For the growing interest of the rational expectations group in explaining the cyclical behavior of investment, see the "Introduction" to Lucas (1981) and for recent work, e.g., Kydland and Prescott (1982).

16. E.g., Okun (1981), Gordon (1981), or Solow (1980).

17. See Lucas (1975) and Barro (1980).

18. I have discussed the material in this and the following sections more extensively in my (1982a, 1982b).

19. Keynes (1971b).

20. For an assessment of the scope for independent monetary policies, cf., Darby, Lothian et al. (1983).

21. For the strong anti-Monetarist position, see Kaldor (1982).

22. See the "Unpleasant Arithmetic" of Sargent and Wallace (1981), and Keynes' advice to Poincaré quoted in Section IX below.

23. The following remarks will deal only with "involuntary unemployment" which is the aspect of the matter that has the most to do with Keynes. For a broader discussion of the equilibrium methodology of the New Classicists, see the last section of my (1983a) and also my (1983b).

24. Lucas (1978), for example, concludes his discussion of the concept as follows: "In summary, it does not appear possible, even in principle, to classify individual unemployed people as either voluntarily or involuntarily unemployed depending upon the characteristics of the decision problems they face." Lucas may have had in mind, perhaps, Barro and Grossman (1971), Benassy (1975), or Malinvaud (1977), etc., but his comment is simply irrelevant to Keynes' concept.

25. One should recall that the Keynesian categories of "frictional" and "voluntary" unemployment covered vast territories, and especially a number of possibilities that latter-day Keynesians often like to bring into their quarrel with the rational expectations equilibrium theorists. The *General Theory* (1936, p. 6) briskly lumps into the *voluntary* category, for instance,

> unemployment due to the refusal or inability of a unit to labour, as a result of legislation or social practices or of combination for collective bargaining or of slow response to change or of mere human obstinacy, to accept reward corresponding to the value of the product attributable to its marginal productivity.

Note especially that the "*inability...*" is "voluntary"!

26. See *General Theory*, p. 210.

27. This is basically the conception from which I began in my (1968b). It will not serve very far before a more structured picture of how trade is organized in the system becomes required. Cf. Robert Clower (1975).

28. Leijonhufvud (1968b), p. 52.

29. An important class of rational expectations models, exemplified by Barro (1976), has what amounts to Hicksian "inelastic expectations" as a central feature. Most of the "action" in realized transactions comes from a term in the supply and demand functions which measures the difference between current and expected future price. When the expected future price fails to reflect a disturbance appropriately, the result is speculative intertemporal substitution effects that affect the price and volume of transactions in the spot markets.

Asymmetries of information between the two sides of the market are against the rules of the game that apply to this class of models, however. They occur only in the market where the central bank conducts its open market operations.

30. See Clower (1965, 1967), Leijonhufvud (1968b, Chapter II:3), and for second thoughts on how prevalent such effective demand failures may be, Leijonhufvud (1973).

31. If you will permit one paragraph of self-indulgence, I have this to add. In my 1968 book my discussion of involuntary unemployment ended on this note:

> One must conclude, I believe, that Keynes' theory, although obscurely expressed and doubtlessly not all that clear even in his own mind, was still in substance that to which Clower has recently given precise statement.

Although this interpretation was the only one that made sense to me, I was nonetheless conscious of having done a good deal of reading between the lines. A number of colleagues who did not agree that "one must conclude" anything of the sort poked some fun at the claim. When Volumes XIII and XIV of the *Collected Writings* appeared, I skimmed them solely to see whether my interpolations had been too imaginative. Somewhat to my consternation, I could not find anything that seemed relevant to the problem one way or another! In the Fall of 1974, I visited Cambridge as an Overseas Fellow of Churchill College and took the opportunity of a dinner at King's to ask my host, Lord Kahn, and also Lord Kaldor and Professor Robinson whether the Circus had not discussed Chapter 2 of the *General Theory* and why no background material had come to light. They did not recall any such discussion—which left me somewhat mystified.

Some time ago, Mr. C. W. S. Torr brought to my attention that the "Tilton Laundry hamper" had contained the answer. Much of Vol. XXIX is devoted to some discarded introductions to the *General Theory* in which "the contrast between a Co-operative and an Entrepreneur Economy" is treated as fundamental.

Keynes' "Co-operative Economy," as it turned out, was one in which labor is bartered for goods, so that the supply of labor is always an effective demand for goods. In his "Entrepreneur Economy" the Clowerian rule applies: Labor buys money and money buys goods but labor does not buy goods. In the entrepreneur economy, therefore, effective demand failures are possible and so, consequently, is "involuntary unemployment."

That, I think, should settle the matter. See Keynes (1979), pp. 63–102.

32. See the March 1924 "Preface to the French Edition" of Keynes (1971a). Also the 1926 and 1928 commentaries reprinted as "The French Franc" in Keynes (1972).

33. See Sargent and Wallace (1981).

34. See Tumlir (1983). I am grateful to Tumlir for insisting in conversation that I should go back and read Keynes on the French franc.

35. See "The Wicksell Connection" in Leijonhufvud (1981a), esp. sections IX and X.

36. See my "Wicksell Connection," loc. cit.

37. See Leijonhufvud (1981b).

38. For a monetary rule allowing limited scope for discretion, see the discussion in Leijonhufvud (1982b).

REFERENCES

Barro, Robert J. 1980. "A Capital Market in an Equilibrium Business Cycle Model." *Econometrica* (September).

———. 1976. "Rational Expectations and the Role of Monetary Policy." *Journal of Monetary Economics* (January).

Barro, Robert J., and Hershel I. Grossman. 1971. "A General Disequilibrium Model of Income and Employment." *American Economic Review* (March).

Benassy, Jean-Paul. 1975. "Neo-Keynesian Disequilibrium Theory in a Monetary Economy." *Review of Economic Studies* (October).

Clower, Robert W. 1975. "Reflections on the Keynesian Perplex." *Zeitschrift fur Nationalökonomie* 1–2.

———. 1967. "A Reconsideration of the Microfoundations of Monetary Theory." *Western Economic Journal* (December).

———. 1965. "The Keynesian Counterrevolution: A Theoretical Appraisal." In F. H. Hahn and F. P. R. Brechling, eds. *The Theory of Interest Rates.* London: Macmillan.

Darby, Michael, J. R. Lothian, et al. 1983. *The International Transmission of Inflation.* Chicago: University of Chicago Press.

Friedman, Milton. 1968. "The Role of Monetary Policy." *American Economic Review* (March).
_____. 1956. "The Quantity Theory of Money: A Restatement." In M. Friedman, ed., *Studies in the Quantity Theory of Money*. Chicago: University of Chicago Press.
Friedman, Milton, and Anna J. Schwartz. 1963. *A Monetary History of the United States, 1867-1960*. Princeton: Princeton University Press for NBER.
Gordon, Robert J. 1981. "Output Fluctuations and Gradual Price Adjustment." *Journal of Economic Literature* (June).
Hahn, Frank. 1983. *Money and Inflation*. Cambridge, Mass.: MIT Press.
Hicks, John R. 1982. *Money, Interest and Wages: Collected Essays on Economic Theory, Volume II*. Oxford: Blackwell.
_____. 1936. "Mr. Keynes's Theory of Employment." *Economic Journal* (June).
_____. 1933. "Gleichgewicht und Konjunktur." *Zeitschrift fur Nationalökonomie*, Volume XLIII.
Kaldor, Nicholas. 1982. *The Source of Monetarism*. Oxford: Oxford University Press.
Keynes, J. Maynard. 1979. *Collected Writings XXIX: The General Theory and After, A Supplement*. Cambridge: Macmillan.
_____. 1972. *Collected Writings IX: Essays in Persuasion*. Cambridge: Macmillan.
_____. 1971a. *Collected Writings IV: A Tract on Monetary Reform*. Cambridge: Macmillan.
_____. 1971b. *Collected Writings V-VI: A Treatise on Money*. Vols. I-II. Cambridge: Macmillan.
_____. 1936. *The General Theory of Employment, Interest and Money*. London: Macmillan.
Klein, Benjamin. 1978. "Competing Monies, European Monetary Union and the Dollar." In Michele Fracianni and Theo Peeters, eds., *One Money for Europe*. London: Macmillan.
_____. 1975. "Our Monetary Standard: The Measurement and Effects of Price Uncertainty, 1880-1973." *Economic Inquiry* (December).
Kydland, Finn E., and Edward C. Prescott. 1982. "Time to Build and Aggregate Fluctuations." *Econometrica* (November).
Laidler, David. 1982. "Did Macroeconomics Need the Rational Expectations Revolution?" Paper prepared for a conference on "Economic Policies for Canada in the 1980's," Winnipeg, Canada, October.
_____. 1981. "Monetarism: An Interpretation and an Assessment." *Economic Journal* (March).
Leijonhufvud, Axel. 1983a. "Keynesianism, Monetarism, and Rational Expectations: Some Reflections and Conjectures." In Roman Frydman and E. S. Phelps, eds., *Individual Forecasting and Aggregate Outcomes: Rational Expectations Examined*. New York: Cambridge University Press.
_____. 1983b. Review of Robert E. Lucas, Jr., *Studies in Business Cycle Theory*, in *Journal of Economic Literature* (April).
_____. 1982a. "Rational Expectations and Monetary Institutions." Paper presented at International Economic Association Conference on "Monetary Theory and Monetary Institutions," Florence, Italy, September.

——. 1982b. "Constitutional Constraints on the Monetary Powers of Government." Paper presented at Heritage Foundation Conference on "Constitutional Economics: The Emerging Debate," Washington, D.C., November.

——. 1981a. *Information and Coordination: Essays in Macroeconomic Theory*. New York: Oxford University Press.

——. 1981b. "Inflation and Economic Performance." In Gerald P. O'Driscoll, ed., *Money in Crisis: Government, Stagflation, and Monetary Reform*. Cambridge, Mass.: Ballinger Press.

——. 1973. "Effective Demand Failures." *Swedish Economic Journal* (March), reprinted in Leijonhufvud (1981a).

——. 1968a. "Comment: Is There a Meaningful Trade-Off between Inflation and Unemployment?" *Journal of Political Economy* (July/August).

——. 1968b. *On Keynesian Economics and the Economics of Keynes: A Study in Monetary Theory*. New York: Oxford University Press.

Lucas, Robert E., Jr. 1981. *Studies in Business Cycle Theory*. Cambridge, Mass.: MIT Press.

——. 1980. "Methods and Problems in Business Cycle Theory." *Journal of Money, Credit, and Banking* (November), Part 2, reprinted in Lucas (1981).

——. 1978. "Unemployment Policy." *American Economic Review* (May), reprinted in Lucas (1981).

——. 1975. "An Equilibrium Model of the Business Cycle." *Journal of Political Economy* (December), reprinted in Lucas (1981).

——. 1972. "Expectations and the Neutrality of Money." *Journal of Economic Theory* (April), reprinted in Lucas (1981).

Lucas, Robert E., and Thomas J. Sargent. 1979. "After Keynesian Macroeconomics." Federal Reserve Bank of Minneapolis *Quarterly Review*, no. 2.

Malinvaud, Edmond. 1977. *The Theory of Unemployment Reconsidered*. Oxford: Blackwell.

Okun, Arthur M. 1981. *Prices and Quantities: A Macroeconomic Analysis*. Washington, D.C.: Brookings Institution.

Phelps, Edmund S. 1968. "Money Wage Dynamics and Labor Market Equilibrium." *Journal of Political Economy* (August).

Robertson, Sir Dennis. 1954. "Thoughts on Meeting Some Important Persons." *Quarterly Journal of Economics* (May).

Sargent, Thomas J. 1981. "Stopping Moderate Inflations: The Methods of Poincaré and Thatcher." *Economic Policy in the United Kingdom*. Proceedings of a conference sponsored by the General Mills Foundation, University of Minnesota.

——. 1973. "Rational Expectations, the Real Rate of Interest, and the Natural Rate of Unemployment." *Brookings Papers on Economic Activity*, no. 2.

Sargent, Thomas J., and Neil Wallace. 1981. "Some Unpleasant Monetarist Arithmetic." Federal Reserve Bank of Minneapolis *Quarterly Review* (Fall).

——. 1976. "Rational Expectations and the Theory of Economic Policy." *Journal of Monetary Economics* (April).

Sims, Christopher A. 1980. "Comparison of Interwar and Postwar Business Cycles: Monetarism Reconsidered." *American Economic Review* (May).

——. 1980. "Is There a Monetary Business Cycle?" *American Economic Review* (May).

Solow, Robert M. 1980. "On Theories of Unemployment." *American Economic Review* (March).
Tobin, James. 1981. "The Monetarist Counter-Revolution Today—An Appraisal." *Economic Journal* (March).
Tumlir, Jan. 1983. "J. M. Keynes and the Emergence of the Post-World War II International Economic Order." Paper presented at a conference on "Tactics of Liberalization," Madrid, March.

* * *

COMMENT BY BARRY BOSWORTH

Although this is a difficult paper to read, it contains many interesting observations on the current debate on macroeconomics as well as a fascinating diversion into the history of economic thought and Keynes' views on monetary policy. If I might voice a minor complaint, I would question the author's classification of the participants in the debate as either Keynesians or monetarists. I believe it presents an overly rigid view of a rather steady evolution of macroeconomics. Most economists, for example, found the contribution of Phelps and Friedman, concerning the natural rate of unemployment, to be pathbreaking articles, and the whole discussion significantly altered views on the Keynesian concept of rigid money wages, without necessarily converting everyone to monetarists. The discussion highlighted the problems with the standard Keynesian explanation of why markets fail to clear.

I do agree that the new classical economics, the marriage of rational expectations with the classical assumption that underlying markets are continuously clearing, has initiated a much more devisive debate. Professor Leijonhufvud quite accurately draws a distinction between the two elements, since rational expectations can be applied equally well to models of behavior that do not assume continuous market clearing. Some work in this area has been undertaken by Stiglitz and others, based on expectations about quantities rather than prices.

I would categorize the basic issues that delineate the debate over macroeconomics somewhat differently from perhaps Professor Leijonhufvud. First, there have been two competing views of how the basic economy operates: the classical model of auction markets and the Keynesian model in which markets do not clear automatically. The Keynesian model has dominated the analysis in the postwar period, not so much by the strength of its theoretical arguments, but more due to the fact that, at the empirical level, unemployment was an observed phenomenon inconsistent with the classical model. But economists have long been uneasy with the Keynesian reliance on sticky nominal wages as the reason for the failure of markets to clear. Most analyses used a synthesis of the Keynesian model for short-run analysis and the classical model for the longer term. In other words, economists were content to examine the consequences of the failures of markets to clear without delving too deeply into the question of why they did not.

Several events upset this situation during the last decade. First, the events of the late 1960s and the 1970s clearly highlighted the inadequacies of previous models of inflation. That experience, combined with the contributions of Friedman and Phelps seriously damaged the concept of fixed or sticky nominal wages. Second, the unsatisfactory nature of the situation was brought into sharp focus by the effort to develop a consistent microeconomic foundation for macroeconomics.

Third, the new classical economics school has made substantial progress toward developing an integrated theory based on a coherent macroeconomic theory of how markets operate, that is, at least in a general stylized sense, consistent with observed phenomena. It does admit, for example, the possibility of involuntary unemployment due to informational misconceptions and lags. It still does not, however, seem to hold up well to empirical verification.

On the other hand, the Keynesian model lacks an adequate microeconomic foundation. It does not explain why markets do not clear. Certainly nominal wages and prices did not appear to be rigid or sticky in the 1970s, and there has been considerable variation in real wage rates. Thus, the issue that divided macroeconomists is, in fact, a microeconomic dispute about how individual markets operate.

The basic Keynesian *IS-LM* curve analysis can be quickly summarized, as in Figure 1.2, in terms of aggregate demand and supply functions. Under normal conditions, a decline in the price level would be expected to induce increases in aggregate demand; but Keynes introduced two possibilities of a vertical portion of the demand curve: a liquidity trap or an inability to equate saving and investment at a positive rate of interest. The only possibility of an underemployment equilibrium, however, required some curvature to the aggregate supply curve, such as rigid nominal wages. In that case, a higher output level could be achieved through a shift in the aggregate demand curve. Thus, the liquidity trap and the saving-investment inequality were thought of as demand-side problems, and the failure of markets to clear as a supply-side problem. However, the analysis of Friedman and Phelps pointed out that the change in the price level could also be expected to shift the aggregate supply curve upward at the same time, unless wage behavior reflected money illusion. Thus, expansionary demand policies could not generate permanent employment gains if the problem was rigid real rather than nominal wages; yet, there was no good explanation for rigid nominal wages.

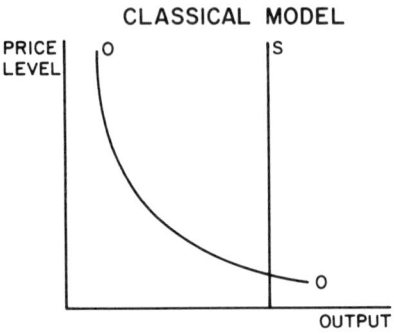

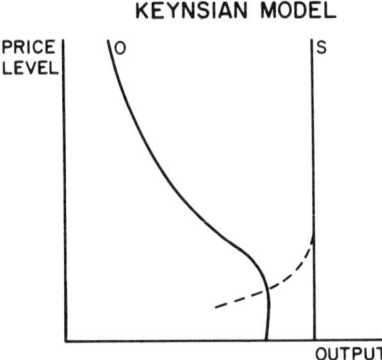

FIGURE 1.2

Professor Leijonhufvud argues strongly against this traditional interpretation of the debate, preferring instead a classification that distinguishes between real and nominal shocks and real and nominal adjustment failures. In his view, sticky nominal wages—a nominal adjustment failure—are not central to the Keynesian model. He seems to find the combination of real adjustment failures in response to real shocks, and he points to a capital market failure (intertemporal substitution) rather than labor markets as the fundamental problem. I found many of his arguments convincing until I got to the section on business cycles. When tracing a Keynesian recession, he refers to a failure of workers to reduce the reservation wage because of informational errors. This sounds a lot like sticky wages to me. Nor could I draw a clear conclusion from the paper about Professor Leijonhufvud's views on whether the underemployment situation he describes represents a stable equilibrium or not. In the standard *IS-LM* analysis, capital market failures lead to an underemployment disequilibrium. Without the sticky wages, the capital market failure would seem to describe a continual downward spiral of demand.

I thought the section of the paper that discussed expectations as an endogenous (Lucas) versus exogenous (Keynes) phenomena was most interesting. Similarly, I enjoyed the discussion of the parallel between Keynes and Sargeant with respect to the effect of changes in policy regimes, even though my ignorance of the history of economic thought prevents any significant comments. In summary, this is an important contribution that covers a wide range of interrelated topics. The author's picture of chaos in macroeconomics is disturbing, but I believe, despite the confusion, that some progress has been made and he may be overly pessimistic.

* * *

COMMENT BY CHRISTOPHER PISSARIDES

Axel Leijonhufvud has offered a typically lucid account of Keynes' views on expectations in the light of recent developments in expectations theory. I am especially encouraged by the fact that he found the macroliterature concerning the controversies about expectations confusing. I also found it confusing. One reason that I think it is confusing is that we are not always clear about the ground rules that we follow when talking about these issues. Sometimes we talk about demand and sometimes we talk about supply; sometimes we refer to prices set by the firm and at other times we refer to "market-clearing" or "non-market-clearing" prices, without being very clear of what the terms mean. For example, the Keynes-monetarist controversy in the 1960s was about demand, that is, what causes changes in aggregate demand. Again more recently, the controversy has moved toward aggregate demand, but this time with regard to the question about balanced budgets and investment and savings. By contrast, the rational expectations controversy is firmly a supply controversy and focuses primarily on labor markets.

Let us then ask: What do we need a good macromodel of the supply side to satisfy? I think the most important criteria of a good model are endogenous prices and some notion of market equilibrium.

The first models that tried to address the question of adjustments within a market equilibrium model were the models of imperfect information and search. The apparent breakthrough of search models was the derivation of quantity adjustments from choice-theoretic foundations, which happened to be consistent with a long-run natural rate. Here, the nominal wage acts as the rigid variable; so although apparently monetarist in structure the models are (according to Leijonhufvud) late Keynesian. In these models, there is a short-run downward-sloping curve in inflation-unemployment space, which summarizes the policy choices available to the authorities.

However, it became clear from the early days of search theory that search models could explain only small deviations from the natural rate, resulting from expectational errors; and more importantly, that these deviations were not Keynesian, in the sense that they did not generate a multiplier effect with second-round employment effects.

Ironically, the most important development in inflation-unemployment theory since then, Lucas' 1972 paper, built on these aspiring Keynesian models, but with an ingenious twist. The shocks, rather than nominal, were a mixture of nominal and real. Neither nominal nor real shocks could in isolation produce an "adjustment failure." But in Lucas' model, agents do not know the nature of the shock, and this is how the maladjustment arises. I would therefore put rational expectations monetarism firmly in one of Leijonhufvud's empty boxes, in the middle row of Figure 1.1. It does not really matter which variable fails to adjust. There is market clearing everywhere given demands and supplies. But these demands and supplies are conditioned on misperceptions. And the reason there are misperceptions is because of mixed shocks.

It would not be an exaggeration to say that Lucas's model provided a "counterrevolution" to the neo-Keynesian models of the inflation-unemployment trade-off, in a way parallel to the "counterrevolution" that Clower talked about a decade earlier, when referring to the demand side of Keynes' model. Lucas showed that an equilibrium model could produce the observed deviations from the natural rate. When Keynesians tried to rationalize Phillips' observations, they thought only a disequilibrium model could do. Of course, equilibrium models with static or adaptive expectations could also produce the same deviations. Moreover, in these latter models policy, even purely monetary policy, would be effective in minimizing the impact of these deviations. The second and potentially more important element of Lucas' theory was the role of monetary regime. We owe it to Leijonhufvud for bringing this out clearly in his paper. Lucas conditions expectations on the monetary regime and derives from it the ineffectiveness proposition.

Keynes devoted a large part of his career to a careful design of monetary regimes, and it appears (from what Leijonhufvud says) that he conditions his theory on the regime in existence. The view that the change in Keynes' writings from the *Tract* to the *General Theory* was merely a "rational response" to change of regime is a fascinating one. It reveals Keynes as a practical theorist who will survive for "relevance" by adapting the ground rules of his theorizing to the policy environment. But it also leaves him open to one of the most important criticisms of RE theory today: the adjustment to RE equilibrium. Thus, the *General Theory* played different rules from the *Tract*, but there is nothing to tell us how the adjustment from one set of rules to another comes about.

I would like to conclude with a note about "involuntary" unemployment and expectations. Like Leijonhufvud I do not think the distinction between voluntary and involuntary unemployment is helpful or that it has helped economic theory or policy in the past. The real question is whether a failure of effective demand to signal a notional demand leads to a multiplier process—or more generally whether it leads to underemployment equilibrium. It seems to me that one of two conditions will ensure that there are substantial second-round effects of a first-round inability to sell. The first is imperfect capital markets. In the extreme, if there are no assets, demand for goods equals income earned; so if income earned is low demand for goods is low too. I believe that many early Keynesians had something like this in mind when discussing the multiplier. For example, relying on a static model with a sequence of dates for multiplier analysis implies absence of some asset markets.

However, this is not the only reason for significant effective demand failures. A second reason could be elastic expectations about quantities. That is, inability to sell today signals a substantially increased probability of failing to sell tomorrow. For example, this is how Barro and Grossman derive the multiplier in their book.[1] This possibility is exciting in the light of today's theory of unemployment because it could lead to self-sustaining underemployment equilibria. The observation of reduced ability to sell leads to a depression in expectations about future abilities to sell, which are in turn fulfilled because of the second-round effects of the depressed expectations. Keynesian theory built along these lines would be stronger with the assumption of rational expectations than without it. Keynes may, after all, have liked rational expectations.

NOTE

1. See Barro and Grossman (1976).

REFERENCE

Barro, Robert J., and Herschel I. Grossman. *Money, Employment and Inflation*. New York: Cambridge University Press, 1976.

COMMENT BY PAUL DAVIDSON

I view my role here as a sort of gadfly. Keynes provided a theoretical revolution, but what is involved in a revolution? It means that you are building a model based on different axioms than were previously used. You cannot start a revolution if you start with the same axioms because if you follow the logic you come to the same conclusions. Currently, almost everyone uses the same basic microanalysis because they start with the same axioms.

The question is how do we get the profession back to dealing with the unemployment problem, with this real world kind of problem, when we are all starting with axiomatic models of a Walrasian system? Robert Clower's answer was that you take the microanalysis and you introduce a constraint. You change an equality here to an inequality. You fiddle with the basic model a little bit because you know where you want to go. You want to show that there is unemployment. And I said, well if you fiddle with it here, they will fiddle with it there and show the opposite.

And look at the war of words: adjustment failures, shocks. The implications of those words is that the economy would normally be at full employment, except for shocks, failures, and collapses. This implies that unemployment is not normal and, if we only let things alone, employment would improve. Now Keynes came along and said that unemployment, rather than full employment, is normal. Now how do we get there? Later I will explain the axioms that Keynes threw out.

Keynes compared classical economists with Euclidean geometry and said that when Euclidean geometrists see parallel lines apparently crashing into one another they rebuked them for not staying parallel. But the solution is, in a non-Euclidean world, to throw out the axiom of parallels. Keynes' next sentence said that for economics today we have to throw out certain axioms that are perfectly alright for the neoclassical world (equivalent of Euclidean geometry) and get into a non-neoclassical (non-Euclidean) world so that when we see apparently parallel lines crashing, i.e., unemployment, we know that it is normal.

The specific point I wanted to make is that the box in which Axel places Keynes is not the Keynes of 1936. Let me explain why. It is absolutely correct that the shock is a shift in the marginal propensity of capital. That was one of the explanations in the business cycle/trade cycle chapter. But on page 142 of the *General Theory*, Keynes specifically talks about vicious confusion between the nominal rate of interest and the real rate of interest. Keynes said that anybody who makes a distinction between ex ante real and nominal interest rates is just confused.

Keynes may have been confused and he may have been wrong about this, but he certainly did not think so. Chapter 17 in the *General Theory* states that the money rate of interest rules the roost—the *money*, not the real, rate of interest. In 1934 Keynes wrote a monetary theory of production. And this is while he was writing the *General Theory*. He said that he desired to write a theory, not about a real-real economy or nominal-nominal economy (to use the Leijonhufvud classification); rather he desired to write a monetary theory of production in an entrepreneurial economy, and he says specifically that in such an economy money affects real output in both the short run *and* the long run; that is, money is *not* neutral. You cannot say anything about the decisions of the agents or the outcome of production without following the money supply from the first step to the last step. Hence Keynes began by arguing that the classical dichotomy is wrong, at least for an entrepreneurial economy.

So I would argue that Keynes started in Leijonhufvud's real-nominal box. I agree with Axel that it was not the rigid money wage that caused unemployment for Keynes. Keynes has a whole chapter called "Changes in Money Wages"; so clearly he did not think his theory had anything to do with rigid money wages. But what he did think was that money is a real phenomenon. And that requires a different (non-Euclidean) axiomatic basis for the theory of monetary, entrepreneurial economics.

* * *

COMMENT BY KARL BRUNNER

I enjoyed listening to what Axel said, and I would like to take up one or two points that puzzle me a bit. I hope I understand you correctly. You seem to say that part of our criticism addressed to the Keynesian analysis involved the lack of microfoundations concerning the assumption of comparative wage inflexibility. Well, frankly, that was never our point. I think the public record is very clear in this respect in terms of our writing.

I never understood the idea of calling comparative wage inflexibility an especially Keynesian phenomenon. The point is that it has been very well established in the tradition of monetary analysis for 200 years. It is very clear in Irving Fisher's works, particularly if one looks at the intervening chapters and not just at the summary chapter. The business cycle literature of the nineteenth century is very clear about the fact of comparative wage inflexibility. Money wages do not fully adjust to all ongoing real and nominal shocks. Keynes was very explicit that this was not his idea but accepted this tradition as a well-established fact. With this fact integrated as a relevant piece into macroanalysis, I cannot accept the specific interpretation of a market-clearing approach proposed by the new classical analysis.

The next point is that Keynesian analysis can hardly be criticized for the lack of microfoundations. This analytic incompleteness was our common fate. The reason was that we had a tradition of microanalysis that denied or neglected crucial aspects conditioning the institution of comparative wage inflexibility. The microfoundation disregarded the role of information and transaction costs. This is most explicitly and beautifully represented in the Arrow-Debreu paradigm. Starting from this paradigm will not get us any kind of monetary analysis except in a very contrived and artificial way. The Minneapolis school represents today in my judgment such a blind alley. Money appears in their models but without rationale for serving any monetary function. It does not function as an information device in the solution of the social coordination game beyond the role of prices.

Our reservation was thus not addressed to the absence of an adequate microfoundation. We objected to the apparent willingness to replace economic analysis in matters pertaining to labor market problems with a sociological adhocery. Such ad hoc sociologizing pervaded Keynesian arguments and most particularly those bearing on the inflation problem.

There are no other issues that we discussed at the time, and I would like to mention them very quickly because they were frequently overlooked. First, we addressed the nature of the transmission mechanism and argued, in this context in particular, that the "islamic" framework was poorly designed to analyze major issues of monetary analysis and policy. Second, there is what I used to call the internal stability problem. Today I prefer to approach it as the problem of the occurrence and relevance of a normal output. Third, we encounter the impulse problem to which Axel referred. Fourth, we have the problems of the money supply process. And last, I should mention aspects of political economy. In terms of the underlying hypothesis about the role and functioning of political institutions, we advanced in this range a very different approach than the Keynesians did. These issues concerned us already 20 years ago and keep on attracting our attention today.

I do agree with Axel however that there has been some subtle shifting on these issues in the last ten years and also reversals of roles in peculiar ways. For example, in 1975, at the March meeting of the Shadow Open Market Committee, we mentioned the impact on *real* and nominal aspects of the OPEC shock as one of the first groups. We emphasized the occurrence of a once and for all permanent effect on the price level, a permanent (negative) effect on output and at the same time a *transitory* effect on inflation. The OPEC shock induced a serious reevaluation of the historical significance of nominal and real shocks in the generation of fluctuations. This reevaluation contributed possibly to the revival of interest in real business cycle theory with its deep ramification for stabilization policy. The theory implies that the observation of fluctuations is not a prima facie case for stabilization policies. Fluctuations in response to real shocks may be an efficient solution. Under the circumstances, attempts at stabilization produce inefficiencies. These are some of the new questions that come up and move us quite a bit away from the old issues that agitated us about 20 years ago.

* * *

REPLY BY AXEL LEIJONHUFVUD

We have been discussing a widespread concern with the microfoundations problem; the fact that from the 1960s onward so many people felt that this was a major concern gave great impetus to the new classical economics, because people thought that the new classical approach might finally solve the microfoundations problem. I think they are half correct in the following sense. The microfoundations problem as I saw it was this tension of a micro theory that had been built up into a macro theory. We took the micro theory of the 1950s and asked what kind of macro superstructure could be built on those foundations. The answer was that you could have Patinkin and you could have Arrow-Debreu, but that was all. And that did not seem to be of any interest whatsoever for macroeconomic theory.

Then there was a separate problem: What kind of microfoundations can you suspend under this Keynesian economics that seems to be suspended in thin sociological air and cannot really be tied down to the base of the Walrasian system? This tension between the two was a big problem. To a very large extent it was motivated by the fact that when I went to school we learned micro on Mondays, Wednesdays, and Fridays and macro on Tuesdays and Thursdays. And the hope was that if you had slept well enough you would not realize how inconsistent the two were with one another. I do not agree with Lucas' approach on this problem. What Lucas and company did was to deny that it is a problem at all. They said that we should do micro strictly according to the book and build from constrained maximization and then take whatever macro theory results. It is a very convenient denial of an extremely difficult problem, and I think we will have to wait for the new classical economics and its variants to run into increasing empirical trouble, which I am sure will be forthcoming.

With regard to the reason for stickiness of the reservation wage, I would like to take it up in the following way. On the one hand we have real wages, and on the other hand we have something called the nominal scalar of the system. In very simple models an exogenous money supply determines the nominal scalar of the system. If we double the money supply, then the scalar will double. In the earlier literature we tend to think of sticky money wages as stickiness of the nominal scalar. Increase the money supply and you will see this stickiness. So when I was talking about stickiness of money wages, in certain kinds of monetary regimes it is rational that people should have a sticky nominal scalar. And that can be true for a lot of different disturbances. The monetary regime with price level stability and the gold standard is one possibility here. That kind of regime will nail down the nominal scalar, and that would be people's rational expectations. When there is a shock to money in such a system, people do not assume that the proper response is to reduce the nominal value of the scalar. After forty years or a hundred years under a system like that, you would expect to find that there is not much action in nominal wages. Suppose the regime then changes to one of completely discretionary tinkering with the monetary base, unrestrained by fixed exchange rates; I would expect in very short order that this stickiness in the nominal scalar would disappear.

So, with sticky reservation wages, and particularly with this intertemporal disequilibrium of excess demand for future goods/excess supply of present goods, you get unemployment. That creates a problem for wage earners. The rate of interest is not low enough for firms to employ enough of present factors to produce future output. What else could be done? Possibly labor could somehow bribe the firm into, nonetheless, undertaking this production, making it profitable for them by reducing the real wage. But there is a moral hazard aspect to that.

Lucas' model does have strange information of the sort that should give you stickiness of reservation wages. You know that the money supply has not decreased; so there is no reason to cut your nominal wage. You also know that your productivity is the same as yesterday, and the marginal product is the same as yesterday; so you see no apparent reason to cut your real wage. Thus there should be only gradual readjustment in the real wage.

Pissarides said that he thinks I have Lucas in the wrong box, that Lucas belongs with the mixed nominal and real shocks, for otherwise the misperceptions do not arrive. I agree. In the paper I argue that one of the reasons we have to take some interest again in the real shock idea is that we cannot explain what appear to be the real consequences of what are otherwise purely nominal shocks. However, with Lucas the real shocks are microlevel shocks, stochastic disturbances that surround individual entrepreneurs, while the nominal shocks are the only aggregative shocks that he entertains. That is the reason I put him in the nominal shock box.

Paul Davidson's remark made me realize that I have done something misleading to connoisseurs of Keynes. In Keynes the money rate of interest rules the own (real) rates of interest of the firms. When I talked about the real interest rate, I meant the Fisherian concept, which Keynes would not have gone along with. I did it because today's audiences are used to thinking in terms of Fisher's real and nominal interest rates, and I wanted to make it clear that I was talking about a real intertemporal relative price.

I think I have already touched on Karl Brunner's comment in one respect. He mentioned the long tradition of comparative relative wage inflexibility in the monetary literature and, of course, I agree with that. What I tried to do in the paper was to put wage inflexibility in the context of monetary regimes. I think the rational expectations view is quite helpful in that respect. It changed the regime to one in which the money supply will be manipulated at will and is manipulated at will. Then you expect much less nominal wage inflexibility.

2

Financial Markets and Macroeconomic Fluctuations

Robert J. Shiller

This chapter addresses two simple theories of speculative markets and something I might call a nontheory due to Keynes. What will be done here is something of an exploratory data analysis. We will examine these really basic and simple theories that represent what different people think they know about the stock market and the bond market.

I have had a little problem at first deciding what it is that people think they know about these speculative markets. There is at least one thing that a lot of people have felt more or less in agreement on. This, our first simple theory, is called the efficient markets theory: the idea is that because smart money dominates markets and because prices efficiently discount all public information, all price movements must be due, ultimately, to new information about future dividends. Loosely, this has been referred to as the "random walk" theory of stock prices, but it asserts more than that stock price movements cannot be forecasted. It asserts that stock price movements can be justified in a certain way by subsequent dividend movements. The 1960s and 1970s have seen the development of an extensive empirical literature testing variations of this efficient markets hypothesis. This literature has inclined many

---

The original version of this chapter was presented at the Conference on Macroeconomics, University of Delaware, January 12-13, 1984. The chapter was revised in July 1984 for the conference volume. Portions of this chapter are taken from the author's paper "Stock Market Prices, Interest Rates and the Business Cycle," which was presented as part of the Conference on Monetary Policy, Financial Markets and the Business Cycle, International Center for Monetary and Banking Studies, Geneva, Switzerland, 1984. This research was supported by the National Science Foundation and the Sloan Foundation. Nigel Wilson provided research assistance.

researchers to take the view that real stock prices are best described as the present value (with a fairly stable discount factor) of optimally forecasted real dividends.

The second theory, which might be called a consumption-based asset-pricing theory, emphasizes the business cycle correlation of stock market prices. Stock prices move up and down as much as they do because of very large swings in the rate at which expected future dividends are discounted into today's price, and these discount rate movements can be understood directly in terms of the hardship (measured by how much people are actually consuming) imposed by the business cycle. This view of the volatility of the stock market prices was formalized by Grossman and Shiller (1981) and LeRoy and LaCivita (1981) in a model that borrows a theoretical framework from the modern "intertemporal substitution" school of macroeconomics, as developed by Breeden (1979), Lucas (1978), and others.

The "nontheory" emphasizes our irrational side. There has always been talk, by those who interpret price changes, of changes in market psychology, of swings of moods between optimism or pessimism among investors, or of other irrational behavior that might affect prices. Keynes, a major spokesman for such a view, doubted that there were any market forces to prevent the psychology of ordinary investors from causing wide swings in market prices:

> It might have been supposed that competition between expert professionals, possessing judgment and knowledge beyond that of the average private investor, would correct the vagaries of the ignorant individual left to himself. It happens, however, that the energies and skill of the professional investor and speculator are mainly occupied otherwise. For most of these persons are, in fact, largely concerned, not with making superior long-term forecasts of the probable yield of an investment over its whole life, but with foreseeing changes in the conventional basis of valuation a short time ahead of the general public. They are concerned, not with what an investment is really worth to the man who buys it "for keeps" but with what the market will value it, under the influence of mass psychology, three months or a year hence.[1]

Although market analysts still make frequent reference to such a view, this Keynesian view of speculative markets has largely disappeared from academic discussions.

We shall look more closely here at the evidence that has been taken as contradicting the Keynesian view of financial markets and as favoring the efficient markets theory. Some of my recent work (1979, 1981a, 1981b) will be discussed, which claims that the volatility of stock market price indexes appears to be too high to accord with the efficient markets model given the observed variability of aggregate dividends.

We shall then discuss what evidence there is that might enable us to evaluate our consumption-based asset-pricing view. This theory might be described as turning the Keynesian view around completely. Keynes and his followers tended to regard the mysterious movements in the stock market as exogenous and as affecting consumption and macroeconomic activity through a "wealth effect." In the alternative view, the stock market is not exogenous but responds to the same factors that cause consumption to vary.

The basic problem that Keynes' view poses for empirical work is that it does not tell us what kind of econometrics we ought to be doing, that is, what kind of empirical regularities we should expect. Although I am attracted to Keynes' view, I am obliged to leave it behind as a sort of residual theory to turn to if the others fail.

EFFICIENT MARKETS AND THE BEHAVIOR OF STOCK MARKET PRICES

Stock prices vary a lot. The value of the entire stock market, as measured by the Standard and Poor Composite Index or the Dow Jones Industrial Average, often changes up or down 20 percent, 40 percent, or even more in a single year. These price changes are very hard to forecast. Moreover, even after a particular price movement, it is hard to say what caused the price to move. What then can be said about these price movements?

The conventional answer is that stock price movements reflect new information about the expected earnings of the companies and ultimately about the dividends that will be paid. We can easily think of examples of individual stocks where news arrived either of imminent bankruptcy or of a new breakthrough. In these examples, the price per share moved a great deal—perhaps to zero in the case of bankruptcy or to a much higher level in the case of a breakthrough. It is tempting to generalize from such anecdotes to the stock market as a whole. But do aggregate stock price movements reflect new information about future aggregate dividends?

Figure 2.1 shows the real Standard and Poor Composite Stock Price Index. The term *real* means divided by an aggregate price index (the consumption deflator for nondurables and services). The Standard and Poor Composite Price Index is a continuation of a series begun initially by Alfred Cowles (1938). He said that the index is intended to represent the behavior of the whole New York Stock Exchange and the series continues to be very comprehensive. One easily sees some familiar events

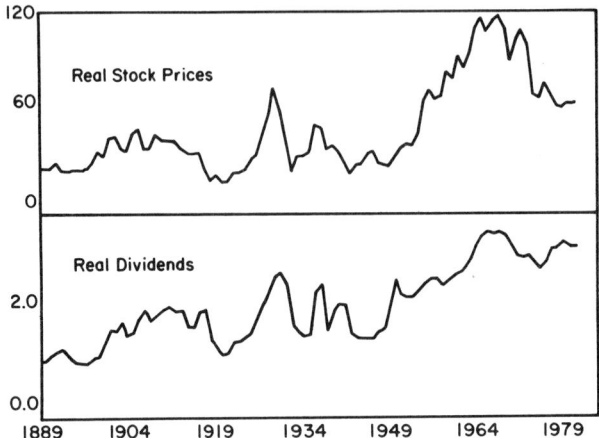

FIGURE 2.1 Real (corrected for inflation) Standard and Poor Composite Stock Price Average, annual average, 1889–1981 (upper plot) and real dividends accruing to Standard and Poor stocks, total for the year (lower plot).
Source: See Appendix.

in the data, for example, the runup of stock prices in the 1920s and the crash in stock prices between 1929 and 1932. One sees the bull market of the 1950s and early 1960s and the notably sour performance of the market since then. In other respects, however, the plot may look different from what one expects. The reason is that the series is plotted in real terms. Because these series are real, the stock market crash of 1929–32 looks smaller than with the nominal series. The consumption price index was falling over this period. By the same token, the decline in the real stock market since the late 1960s was much more dramatic than would be indicated by the nominal series. The consumption deflator rose by a factor of 2.4 from 1968 (the year the real Standard and Poor Stock Price Index reached its highest value ever) to 1981. Thus, by converting a fairly stable nominal index into real terms, a big drop in real value is revealed. The real index, rather than the nominal index, is more interesting from an economic standpoint. The real index represents how much the stock market is worth in terms of commodities rather than in terms of a monetary unit whose value changed dramatically over the sample period.

Also shown in Figure 2.1 are the real dividends accruing to stocks in the Standard and Poor portfolio. In this case *real* means divided by the same price index used to deflate the stock price series. The real dividends, along with capital gains (that is, increase in the stock price), represent the return that investors get for holding stock. Contrary to popular belief, the dividends are the much more important component of total returns on average. The average annual dividend price ratio for the Standard and Poor series for this data over this sample has been 4.8 percent, while the average annual growth rate of real price is only 2.2 percent. The sum, 7.0 percent, is the average real return on the stock market for 1889 to 1981. Thus, most of the return comes from dividends rather than capital gains. This point could be made more dramatically. The total increase in real stock price from 1889 to 1981—92 years—was 140 percent. This was the return one would have made over those 92 years if one threw away the dividends. Some people who have seen certain investments (for example, their houses) rise in value this much over much shorter time intervals will be surprised to see that the market appreciated so little. In contrast, if one reinvested dividends and earned 7 percent a year compounded for 92 years, one would earn an increase in real value of one's portfolio of 50,000 percent! Putting it yet another way, if I plan to hold stock for 30 years and sell it at the end, if my rate of discount is 7 percent and if price grows at 2.2 percent a year, what is the present value today of the revenue from the sale of stock 30 years hence? The answer is only 25 percent of the price today. The rest of the value of the share today must come from the intervening dividends. Thus, the present value of dividends over the succeeding 30 years ought to represent fairly well the intrinsic value of the stock.

The real stock price and the real dividend series look similar in many ways. The eye immediately picks out dramatic comovements. For example, both dividends and prices had spectacular runups in the 1920s and drops in the early 1930s. Both series show dramatic increases in the bull market of the 1950s and early 1960s and a sort of a downtrend since. The series also show a number of differences. For example, the real value of the market since 1968 has fallen more than the real value of dividends. The dividend series looks more stationary around a trend than does the price series; for example, it looks a little more mean reverting. There are several more sharp spikes in the dividend series than in the price series, and the dividend series looks more as if it has the same trend throughout the sample. The price series appears to have no real trend to it. Before World War II the price series shows no tendency to rise. After World War II the price series seems to have a simple inverted U shape.

Is the behavior of the dividend and price series consistent with the efficient markets theory that stock prices are the present value with a constant discount rate of expected future dividends? This is the theory that the expected return on the market is always the same (for example, the expected return equals the discount rate) so that there is no good or bad time to enter the market. We can write it formally in the present value formula:

$$P_t = \sum_{k=1}^{\infty} \left(\frac{1}{1+r}\right)^k E_t(D_{t+k}) \tag{1}$$

where P_t is the real price of a share or the real stock price index at time t, and D_{t+k} is the real dividend of a share or the real dividends accruing to the index k periods after time t. $E_t(D_{t+k})$ is the expectation at time t of D_{t+k} and, because this an efficienct markets model, we assume that this expectation is a true mathematical expectation conditional on all public information at time t.

The real discount rate r is assumed constant here; it does not vary over time. It may seem unnecessarily restrictive to say that the discount rate is *absolutely* constant, but we shall consider here this extreme case for the sake of argument. I think this model is the basic story that many people are talking about. In other words most people would not attribute the volatility of stock prices to changes in the discount rate. At the end of this chapter, we will come back and consider changes in the interest rate as an alternative to this model. The model represented in equation (1) has the property that price changes are attributable *entirely* to new information about future dividends. Much popular discussion would suggest that many people think that price movements could be attributed *almost* entirely to information about future dividends. This model says that any information about future dividends is discounted in this sense into today's price. If you ask economists to interpret a stock price movement today, this paradigm is what they would very likely refer to. They would say something like, "well, if the stock market went up, it must have had some new information, some optimistic information, that suggests that dividends will be higher in the future." The model is an interpretation of the "random walk" theory of stock prices in that the model asserts that evidence that the market is "low" is not evidence that returns on investing in the market will be high or that, when the market is high, returns to investing in it will be low.

Before considering testing the model (1), it is useful to consider a special case of the model: the case in which dividends are a random walk. If dividends are a random walk, then the expectation at time t of D_{t+k} is just today's dividend D_t. Thus, dividends are always expected to continue at their present level forever. Dividends are never thought to be "high" or "low" relative to any long-run path. In this case, we can substitute D_t for $E_t D_{t+k}$ in expression (1), and we find that $P_t = D_t/r$. What is appealing about this special case is that it suggests that plots of P_t and D_t ought to look similar to each other, as we indeed observe. Literally they should look identical except for a scale factor r, and both should be a random walk. Since they are not *identical*, the random walk dividend cum efficient markets theory is not a perfect description of reality. But the theory might yet seem useful as a first approximation.

It may be very reasonable to suppose, as a psychological theory, that people generally tend to expect current dividends to continue. Efficient markets theory, however, requires more than this. They must also be *right* in supposing that dividends are best forecast to continue at their current level. If people think that dividends are a random walk while in fact dividends tend to return to trend, then a profit opportunity in an expected value sense will be generated by their behavior. Whenever dividends (and hence prices) are low, it would be a good time to buy stock, since prices will rise when the dividends return to trend. Low dividends would indicate that the market was low.

It is well known that it is difficult to judge whether a series is a random walk by looking at a plot of a realization of the series. There are, however, formal tests of the random walk hypothesis. One such test, which was reported in an earlier paper (Shiller 1981b), rejected the random walk hypothesis using real Standard and Poor dividend data 1871–1978 at the 5 percent level, in favor of an alternative hypothesis that dividends are a stationary ("AR-1") process around a trend. This test outcome is due to the fact that the observed real dividend series has repeatedly moved rapidly back to trend, as one observes in Figure 2.1. Of course, based on such a test, we cannot prove that the dividends are not a random walk, only that the observed outcome is unlikely if real dividends are a random walk.

Other evidence regarding the random walk hypothesis for dividends of a more judgmental nature might be considered. One must remember that dividends can never be negative, yet the dividend series we observe is not far from zero. It has repeatedly gotten close enough to zero that a couple of big downward movements of the kind actually observed would put it below zero. Thus, if dividends are a random walk, the variance of changes in dividends must decline when dividends are low. A random walk with independent identically distributed increments will pass below zero with probability one. Is it reasonable to suppose then that some of the periods of very low dividends were also periods when one would expect stable low dividends? It may be more reasonable to suppose that when dividends are low there is a substantial probability that dividends will move right back to where they were before. This will generally mean that dividends have an upward bias when they are low, and therefore dividends cannot be a random walk.

Given that real dividends do not seem to behave like a random walk and given that the real price series resembles dividends somewhat, is it in fact true that low prices are an indication that the market will go up? Indeed, it appears that we can forecast stock returns on this basis. Using the data plotted in Figure 2.1, we can compute an annual return series for 1890 to 1978 for the Standard and Poor Index. For each year, this return is equal to the capital gain (from January of the current year to January of the next year) plus the dividend for the current year, all divided by the price for January of the current year. This return was regressed on two variables. The first was the real price of the current year divided by the real dividend of the previous year. The price was divided by the lagged real dividend as a way of correcting for trend in price. The real dividend was lagged since the real dividend of the current year is not fully known in January. The second variable was the change in real price since January of the preceding year divided by the real price in January of the preceding year. The first variable has a coefficient of $-.008$, which has a t statistic of -2.18 that was significant at the .031 level. The coefficient is consistent with the view that, other things being equal (that is, if the price has not increased or decreased a lot recently), returns tend to be low when stock prices are high relative to dividends. The coefficient of the second variable was .14, which had a t statistic of 1.17 that was significant at the .243 level. Although this second variable was not significant, the coefficient did have the sign a naive investor might have expected. If stock prices have been rising then, other things being equal (that is, if prices are not high relative to dividends), returns can be expected to be high in the future.

If it is so easy to reject the efficient markets theory, then why has the impression persisted that the simple efficient markets model is such a good model? I think that the main reason is that, while the t statistics in the regressions may be significant, the R-squared in the regressions are quite small. In the regression reported above, the R^2 was .053. The R^2 is the percentage of the variance of the dependent variable (stock returns) that is explained by the independent variable. Thus, while annual stock market returns are clearly forecastable, they are not *very* forecastable. If we use the R^2 as a metric for the fit of the model, we might conclude that the efficient markets model fits approximately. Moreover, there is some reason to mistrust the data, particularly the consumption price index data. One might well wonder if such small R^2 could be due to data errors. Because people mistrust old data, most researchers tend to confine their attention to the recent data that we know well. Data before World War II are rarely used. It is, however, a basic principle of statistics that one cannot detect small correlations without a lot of data; that is, the power of the t tests is low in short samples. Thus, by ignoring data that are not completely trustworthy, the researchers guarantee that they will not be able to reject efficient markets.

Some of my recent work has been aimed at developing another metric for judging the fit of the efficient markets model, a metric other than the R^2 in regressions of returns on information. Even though the R^2 is very low, the stock price series may depart significantly from the efficient markets theory in other ways. Moreover, other ways of displaying the data may help us better judge how important the data errors might be.

The sense in which stock prices appear to be inconsistent with the simple efficient markets model is that stock prices seem to be too volatile to be justified in terms of new information about future dividends (Shiller 1981a).[2] At the outset, it should be recognized that stock prices can be very erratic and volatile and still stationary, that is, mean reverting, yet the annual return may not be very forecastable. Consider for the sake of argument a stock price that is generated by a stationary "first order autoregressive" or "AR-1" process, a process that has nothing to do with dividends at all. By this, we mean that with annual data the stock price P_t is determined by $P_{t+1} - \bar{P} = a(P_t - \bar{P}) + u_{t+1}$, where a is a constant between zero and one, $\bar{P}$ is the mean price, and u_{t+1} is an error term that is uncorrelated with P_{t-k}, $k \geqslant 0$, and with u_{t-k}, $k \geqslant 0$. Since a is strictly less than one, P_t tends to revert to the mean $\bar{P}$ but also to be shocked away from it by u_t. We assume that u_{t+1} does not represent any information about future dividends. Clearly this example will not produce the similarity between stock prices and dividends that we observe in Figure 2.1, but it will make a different point. If a is close to one, then P_t will look something like a random walk but will still be mean reverting. When P_t is very high relative to $\bar{P}$, then price can be expected to drop in the following period. The optimally forecast change in P next period, ΔP_{t+1}, based on information at time t is always $(a - 1)(P_t - P)$. If a is close to one, then this expected change will be big only when P_t is very large (in which case the expected change is negative) or very small (in which case the expected change is positive) relative to P. When P_t is in the vicinity of $\bar{P}$ the forecast change in P will not be very large relative to the error term u_t, and P will look approximately like a random walk. Suppose, now, to make the example even simpler, that acual dividends are constant, $D_t = \bar{D}$. In this extreme case, with prices jumping around erratically and dividends absolutely constant, the efficient markets model (1) should not look very good. Yet simple regressions of returns on information will still yield low R^2 and will still fail to reject in small samples. If $\Delta P_{t+1} + D_{t+1}$ is regressed on P_t, and a constant, the R^2 is theoretically $(1 - a)/2$. Suppose $a = 0.9$, which would imply that, in the absence of further shocks, price would, if ever away from the mean, return halfway to the mean in seven years. The R^2 in the regression would be .05, and one would not generally find a significant t statistic in small samples. Putting it another way, if one made a 25-year career of exploiting this profit opportunity, one would still not have much evidence from one's experience that one knew how to make money. One would have been predicting speculative booms to end but would probably not observe them end very many times, if at all. One would expect low stock prices to followed by reversion to the mean, but one would not have much experience, if any, with such reversions.

In the above extreme example where dividends are absolutely constant and prices move around erratically, it ought to be possible to reject the model decisively based on *some* statistical test. It makes no sense at all to attribute movements in stock prices to new information about future dividends if dividends never move. Why is it that regression tests of the kind we described above are not powerful enough to reject the model when the model is so obviously wrong? I have discussed the power of regression tests elsewhere (Shiller 1981b). At this point it is sufficient to note that the simple regression tests make no use of the information that price movements must be justified in terms of subsequent dividends.

We may look directly at measures of the volatility of stock prices as a way of testing the model. In an earlier paper (Shiller 1981a), I showed that if the model (1) holds then there is a lower bound to the standard deviation of dividends given the standard deviation of the change in price:

$$\sigma(D) \geqslant \sqrt{2r}\, \sigma(\Delta P) \qquad (2)$$

The right-hand side of (2) is the smallest value the standard deviation of D could have and still be consistent with the observed r and $\sigma(\Delta P)$. Dividends must be at least this variable to justify the movements in price, and if the standard deviation is to be at the lower bound then D_t must be a certain AR-1 process. If r is .07, the $\sigma(D)$ must be at least .37 times $\sigma(\Delta P)$. The standard deviation of ΔP using the data shown in Figure 2.1 is 8.20, which would imply, using $r = .07$, that $\sigma(D)$ must be at least 3.03. In fact, the standard deviation of D with the data shown in Figure 2.1 is only .76. Even if we were to say that we had overestimated the discount rate by a factor of two and thus should cut the discount rate in half, to .035, $\sigma(D)$ must still be at least 2.17. Clearly, the violation of the inequality is robust over a very wide range of r. The standard deviations presented here are simple standard deviations of the data plotted in Figure 2.1 with no trend or heteroscedasticity correction. Such corrections were made in the earlier paper (Shiller 1981a). The corrections themselves became a source of controversy however.

The violation of the inequality (2) means that dividends just have not varied enough over nearly a century to justify the large swings observed in stock prices. We can see what this means in more concrete terms by referring to the depression of the 1930s. Figure 2.1 shows the big stock market decline from 1929 to 1932. How was that justified in terms of the efficient markets model? Should the stock prices have gone down so much? Well the depression *was* coming, and dividends were going to fall. Dividends *did* fall, but they fell for a few years and then came back up again. Dividends really did not change very much in the depression in real terms. At the same time, prices varied a lot. This is the story you see repeatedly.

Any story that might be told to try to save the efficient markets model (1) will inevitably have to imply that, by the luck of the draw, dividends chanced to be exceptionally stable over the last century and that in fact the true (population) standard deviation of dividends is much higher than the observed standard deviation. The random walk story for dividends discussed above is one such story. If dividends are a random walk, then $\sigma(D)$ is infinite. The gradual uptrend we observed over the century (which one might naturally have attributed to the growth of the economy and the policy of reinvesting retained earnings) might by the random walk model equally well have been a downtrend. Moreover, the reversions to trend observed in real dividends that kept observed dividends close to the trend path cannot be expected, if dividends are a random walk, to occur in general. The next century will therefore, by the random walk theory, be expected to show much more erratic behavior of dividends than did the last.[3]

The idea that dividends may be a random walk, or nearly so, has become a central idea in much of the criticism of the variance bounds literature. The most dramatic embodiment of the random walk idea is due to Marsh and Merton (1983) in an argument that was later taken up by LeRoy (1984). Marsh and Merton showed that if the dividend series is a random walk, then if one substitutes sample standard deviations in place of population standard deviations in one of the variance inequalities, analogous to (2) above (which LeRoy, Porter, and I used to reject the efficient markets model), the direction of the inequality is reversed. This was a clever argument but really proves nothing more than the observation already made that the efficient markets model may be reconciled with the variance evidence if dividends are inherently much more variable than they turned out to be over the last century. It has often been overlooked in this discussion that this Marsh-Merton argument applies only to that one inequality, and not to the one used in this chapter.

We spoke above of testing and rejecting the hypothesis that dividends are a random walk. Is it possible to test whether the dividend process is of such a nature that the sample standard deviation of dividends is much lower than the observed standard deviation? One can speak of doing such tests in the context of a specific time series model for dividends (such as an "ARMA" model). Something like this method has been pursued by LeRoy and Porter (1981) and Singleton (1980). Their use of asymptotic distribution theory to infer the small sample properties of their statistics has been criticized by Flavin (1983). We note here, however, that any such tests make sense only in the context of a given model, and also there certainly are alternative models for which their tests would not be valid.

An interesting alternative model is a disaster model. Suppose that a disaster may occur in each year t with a small probability π_t, which we assess at the beginning of the year. The disaster might be nationalization without compensation. If the disaster occurs, then stockholders will no longer receive their dividends. The statistical properties of the dividends are no indication of the likelihood of disaster. That is, there may be no reason to expect that dividends will be low just before the disaster. Dividends might even be constant, as in the extreme example discussed above, and yet the price will still fluctuate in response to news about the probability of disaster in future years. Is there then any way to use statistics to judge whether the fluctuations in price are excessive? Certainly, the true potential variability of dividends received cannot be inferred from the historical variability of dividends in a sample where the disaster did not occur. It would seem to be hopeless to test the model using historical data. However, there is one piece of information about potential disaster that can be exploited. Since we know that stocks have limited liability, dividends can never be negative. The worst dividends can do is become zero. Thus, if price movements are to be justified in terms of information about probability of disaster, then the disaster must have a fairly high probability. We might then infer that the disaster model is unpromising since the disaster has not occurred in the observed U.S. history.

The probability that no disaster occurs between time t and time $t + k$, where the probability is assessed at time t, is $E_t \Pi_{j=0}^{k}(1 - \pi_{t+j})$. If D_t is an underlying dividend process in the absence of disaster that is independent of the stochastic process π_t, then the expected value (given that no disaster has occurred as of time t) of the dividend *received* at time $t + k$ is $E_t\{[\Pi_{j=0}^{k}(1 - \pi_{t+j})]D_{t+k}\}$. Thus, the efficient markets model (1) becomes:

$$P_t = E_t \sum_{k=0}^{\infty} \left(\prod_{j=0}^{k} \left(\frac{1}{1+r}(1 - \pi_{t+j}) \right) \right) D_{t+k} \qquad (3)$$

Thus, the model indicates that price is the expected present values of dividends discounted by a *time-varying* discount factor $(1 - \pi_{t+j})/(1 + r)$.

In terms of the behavior of P_t and D_t, the model is no different from a model that attributes stock price movements to changes in the rate of discount of future dividends. However, this model gives an interpretation to the changes in the discount factor in terms of the probability of disaster. According to the analysis in Shiller (1981a), the data suggest that the one-year discount rate must have a standard deviation of something like .05 (5 percentage points) if movements in the discount rate are to justify the observed variance in stock prices. But if the probability of disaster is to vary so much it must often be high, which leads one to wonder why the disaster has not yet been observed. For example, if the disaster probability were 0.1 each year, then the probability that no disaster occurred in our 93-year sample is 0.00006.

The disaster model thus does not look promising. Since, however, there is no upper bound on dividends like the lower bound of zero, we cannot use the same method to rule out the occurrence of a great good fortune that boosts dividends to a new high plateau. Suppose, to consider an alternative model like the disaster model, there is a small probability π_t assessed at the beginning of year t that a windfall would occur during the year that would cause dividends to rise immediately to a new plateau $\bar{D}$ and to stay at this new high level forever. Suppose again that the probability π_t is independent of the dividend process in the absence of the windfall. Then, the efficient markets model (1) becomes:

$$P_t = \frac{\bar{D}}{r} + E_t \sum_{k=1}^{\infty} \left(\prod_{j=0}^{k} \left(\frac{1}{1+r} (1 - \pi_{t+j}) \right) \right) (D_{t+k} - \bar{D}) \quad (4)$$

The terms $(D_{t+k} - \bar{D})$ in the summation represent a scale factor that can multiply up the effect of the time-varying probability of windfall by an arbitrary amount. Thus, even if the probabilities π_t are sufficiently small that it is not improbable that the windfall did not occur in observed history, it is still possible that new information about these probabilities could account for observed fluctuations in price. All we need is a $\bar{D}$ that is sufficiently high.

The question that remains, then, is do we think that such a windfall is within the realm of possibility? Is it plausible to think that movements in stock prices were due to information about a great windfall with very low probability? Although we have not been formal about it here, our analysis suggests that $\bar{D}$ must be very high indeed. What is the potential source of such a windfall? One could certainly conceive of such a windfall for individual businesses, but it is hard to know what it would be for the stock market as a whole.

THE TERM STRUCTURE OF INTEREST RATES

Keynes proposed essentially the same "psychological" theory for long-term interest rates as for stock prices:

> It might be more accurate, perhaps, to say that the rate of interest is a highly conventional, rather than a highly psychological phenomenon. For its actual value is largely governed by the prevailing view as to what its value is expected to be. Any level of interest which is accepted with sufficient conviction as likely to be durable will be durable, subject, of course, in a changing society to fluctuations for all kinds of reasons round the expected normal.[4]

This is what is known as the liquidity trap story. It says that the monetary authority just cannot move long-term interest rates because these interest rates are determined by some convention. People think this is what the long rate ought to be and they will not budge it.

Like the Keynesian view of stock prices, this view of long-term interest rates has lost favor. Today, one is more likely to hear of a "rational expectations" theory of the term structure of interest rates.

The same model given in expression (1) applied to bonds rather than stocks implies, if the inflation rate is not explosive (that is, is a stationary stochastic process) and is sufficiently stable to allow a linearization, that an approximate expectations theory of the term structure holds. The expectations theory of the term structure says that the long-term interest rate is some weighted average of expected future short rates over the length of the bond. If we use a 30-year bond, for example, then the long rate should be essentially a 30-year average of expected future short rates. This is the old Irving Fisher theory.

Consider a consol (or perpetuity) that pays C pounds per year forever. The real value of the coupon (which corresponds to D_t in expression [1]) is C_t/I_t where I_t is the price index used to deflate nominal values into real values. If the average inflation rate is positive, then D_t for the consol will be steadily decreasing in time, that is, will show a steady downtrend. The real price P_t of the consol will show the same downtrend, but the long-term interest rate $L_t = D_t/P_t$, which is the yield "to maturity" on the consol, will not show any downtrend. Consider then a one-period discount bond at time t that pays a single "coupon" (the principal) at time $t+1$ and nothing thereafter. We will refer to the short-term interest rate S_t as the yield to maturity, which equals its principal at $t+1$ divided by its price at time t minus one. Then using a linearization argument in Shiller (1979), one has:

$$L_t \simeq \frac{\bar{r}}{1+\bar{r}} \sum_{k=0}^{\infty} \left(\frac{1}{1+\bar{r}}\right)^k E_t S_{t+k} \qquad (5)$$

where $\bar{r}$ is the average level of nominal interest rates around which the linearization is made. If the average inflation rate is zero, then $\bar{r}=r$, while if the average inflation rate is higher than zero then $\bar{r}$ will be greater than r. According to equation (5), the long-term interest rate L_t is a weighted average of expected future short-term interest rates S_{t+k}, $k=0,\ldots,\infty$. More weight is given to short rates in the near future than in the more distant future. In form, expression (5) is virtually identical to (1) with L_t replacing P_t and S_{t+k} replacing D_{t+k}. Thus, the long-term interest rate is proportional to the "present value" with constant discount rate of expected future short-term interest rates, just as the stock price equals the present value of expected future dividends. The principal difference in form between (1) and (5) is that (5) is premultiplied by $r/(1+r)$. Premultiplying by $r/(1+r)$ makes the weights sum to one in the weighted average.

Essentially the same arguments can be made against the expectations theory of the term structure that could be made against the efficient markets theory of the stock prices. Because of the similarity between (1) and (5) the same principles outlined above apply to nominal interest rates. The same sorts of inequalities were used (Shiller 1979) to argue that long-term interest rates appear to be too volatile to accord with expectations models of the term structure.

I could have quoted some earlier work to say the expectations model of the term structure works poorly. Hansen and Sargent (1981) have a paper rejecting the expectations model of a term structure. What I wanted to convey is that the expectations theory is really quite wrong, at least as applied to long-term bonds. And it is wrong in the following manner, as clarified in a recent paper (Campbell and Shiller 1984): long-term interest rates have always behaved essentially as a moving average of short rates plus noise. In the period 1953 to 1981 this moving average itself was not terribly at variance with the expectations theory of the term structure. The problem is instead the noise *term*, which has a half-life of about a year. Because of the noise *term*, a lot of short-run volatility is thrown on to long-term interest rate, which makes excess returns forcastable, and this is inconsistent with the expectations theory of the term structure.

The same sorts of arguments carry over about a possible random walk behavior for S_t, and the same lower bound of zero applies to S_t. There is, however, a difference in the application. Since the short-term interest rate is a nominal rather than a real quantity, it is not hard at all to see how a "windfall" could occur that would push nominal interest rates up to astronomical levels. This event has happened repeatedly in countries that experience hyperinflation. Thus, the volatility of long-term interest rates might conceivably be attributed to new information about the probability of such an event. A good example of this is afforded by recent behavior of interest rates, which have indeed far surpassed their former record high. The question is whether it was information about such an event that was responsible for the high volatility of long-term interest rates over the last century. Clearly, it is not possible to use statistical methods to resolve the issue. One cannot hope to test from data in which an explosion of interest rates did not occur whether people were correct to worry about such an explosion.

If one looks at a sample of data in which the "windfall" rise in interest rate did not occur, then one can expect of course to see some "profit opportunities" inconsistent with the model (5). These profit opportunities might ultimately be offset by the great "windfall" or "disaster" on the day that it occurs, but that day is outside the sample. Simple regression techniques that might be used to reveal departures from the model may not give significant results, but if long-term interest rates were excessively volatile and mean reverting then we would expect that high long rates ought to indicate a good time to buy long bonds. Evidence for such a profit opportunity was discovered for a number of sample periods by regressing the difference between the short-term return on long bonds and short bonds on the long-term yield to maturity. As with the regressions discussed in the previous section, the R^2 in the regressions was very low.

A CONSUMPTION-BASED ASSET-PRICING THEORY

The discussion above of the behavior of stock market prices assumed that the real discount rate was constant. In the disaster model a sort of time-varying discount rate was discussed, but the variations in the "discount rate" were really due to changes in the probability that disaster will befall stocks. What about the kind of changes in discount rate that are due to change in the marginal rate of substitution between present and future consumption of the representative individual? These true discount rate movements would not be specific to stocks but would show up in other asset prices, as they reflect economy-wide changes in the "real interest rate."

Recent literature in theoretical finance, notably Breeden (1979) and Lucas (1978), has suggested useful ways of formulating the effects of such charges on asset prices. In a recent paper (1981), Sanford Grossman and I made use of the following theory of stocks or other long-term asset prices:

$$P_t = E_t \sum_{k=1}^{\infty} M_t^{(k)} D_{t+k} \tag{6}$$

where $M_t^{(k)}$ is the ex post marginal rate of substitution between consumption at time t and consumption at time $t + k$. The $M_t^{(k)}$, $k = 1, \infty$ are time-varying discount factors that can cause stock prices to move even in the face of stable dividends. Equation (6) is really straight out of Lucas' "Asset Prices in an Exchange Economy" (1978). It really says that the price of a share should be the expected present value of dividends discounted by the ex post marginal rate of substitution between the time today and the time the dividend is paid. Equation (6) is the consequence of assuming that people maximize the expectation of an additively separable utility function in consumption. The same discount factors $M_t^{(k)}$ apply to all assets; that is, there is no "risk premium" in the discount factors applied to stocks. However, since $M_t^{(k)}$ is an *ex post* discount factor, it is random to someone who has information as of time t. The expectation of the summation in (6) therefore depends on the *covariance* between discount factors and future dividends. The effect of this covariance might be interpreted in terms of a sort of risk premium. Putting it another way, Breeden (1979) showed that the expected return on a stock is, according to such a model, determined by its covariance with the marginal rate of substitution. Such a model may therefore be called a "consumption beta" model to contrast it with the "market portfolio beta" models in theoretical finance in which expected return is determined by covariance with the market portfolio.

Grossman and I (1981) thought that the volatility of stock prices might be attributed to information about variations in the marginal rate of substitution $M_t^{(k)}$ rather than to information about dividends. In simplest terms, the model says that the marginal rate of substitution $M_t^{(k)}$ is low whenever consumption at time t is low relative to consumption at time $t + k$. Thus, stock prices will tend to be low in recessions and high in booms, so long as people perceive the recessions or booms to be temporary. Thus, the model offers an explanation for the business cycle behavior of stock prices that has been noted over the last century. The model is not simply a business cycle model. Stock market prices will also be influenced by longer-run expectations regarding future consumption. It predicts erratic stock price movements too, as new information arrives about future consumption.

According to this model, stock prices are low in a recession that is perceived to be temporary because people do not like to be consuming less. If stock prices did not fall in a recession, people would sell some of their shares to consume the proceeds. But everyone cannot sell shares at once, or else there would be no buyers for the shares. Of course, when some individuals have a "rainy day" on a given day, they can sell some of their stock to someone else who is not experiencing the same trouble. When everyone is experiencing a rainy day on the same day, as in a recession, something must happen that will dissuade people from selling. What happens is that a "profit opportunity" appears. The price of stock becomes so low that it is viewed as a bargain that people cannot pass up. The number of shares outstanding in a recession is the same (roughly) as in prosperous times, and if the present value of future dividends with a constant discount rate is roughly the same, the stock market has roughly the same "intrinsic" value. It would certainly seem that shares would be demanded less in a recession unless stocks were perceived as a good buy. Is it not possible that stock prices might fall 20 percent, 40 percent, or even more in a deep recession before people are willing to hold existing shares? If this is plausible, then we might attribute most of the variability of stock prices to such an effect.

I will try to briefly give you some intuitive feeling for the source of volatility of stock prices that we were getting at. The idea is that it is not really dividends that are causing the stock market to go up and down. It is not that there is new information that Ford Motor Company is not going to sell cars or is going to sell cars. Let us assume that everybody knows that dividends are going to trend up. You could still have big fluctuations in the stock market due to changes in the demand for stocks. The reason why people's demand for stocks changes is because of changing economic conditions. What might cause you to have a low demand for stock is your thinking that there is not much need for you to save now and hold stocks. Conversely, what might cause you to have a high demand for stocks is a feeling that times will be worse, so that you will need savings.

As an example, consider the Great Depression in the 1930s. Imagine that the year is 1932 and you are suffering a lot. Part of the time you have been laid off. If you are the representative person in 1932, your real consumption is 18 percent lower than it was in 1929. What are you going to do with your savings? Well, stocks are supposed to be held for a rainy day. So when you have a rainy day you sell your stocks and use the money to tide yourself over. Now, that would be fine if you had broken your leg or something like that, but what happens during a depression? That is one big rainy day for most people. So everybody goes out and decides that they will sell their stocks since they might be unemployed for six months. But if everybody decides to sell, you cannot find a buyer; so the price has to fall.

Is it plausible that the volatility of the stock market can really come exclusively from such shifts in the demand for stocks? It is really changes in people's feelings of need for saving and ultimately due to their outlook for the business cycle. Grossman and I (1981) did some exploratory work with the stock market that suggested that maybe this was an effect of the right order of magnitude to explain the actual volatility of stock prices, whereas the dividend effect in equation (1) did not seem to be the right order of magnitude.

Rather than present analysis, let us introspect. Imagine again that it is 1932. You are sitting at the dinner table with your spouse. Your daughter is wearing a tattered dress. The house is cold for want of fuel. The paint is peeling off the walls. You say to your spouse, "You know I think this is a good time for us to invest in the stock market." What kind of reaction do you get? So you say that you know John Maynard Keynes, who said in 1932 that this is the chance of a lifetime to buy stocks. He was right ex post. If you bought in 1932, you might easily double your money in a year. But how good a story would it have to be before you could convince your spouse that that was a good idea? Suppose your story was that you think the market will increase 50 percent in value over the next five years, that is, 10 percent a year. That would probably not be a good enough story to convince your spouse to hold as much stock as you have in the boom year of 1929. That is my introspection. It seems plausible that you might require a very large return before you would actually hold as much stock as you did in 1929. Such very variable expected returns would make the market very volatile.

The problem with such an explanation is that it would seem to predict similar movements in all assets that, like stocks, have fairly stable dividends. If people rush to cash in their investment in stocks in a recession, should they not also cash in their investments in bonds, housing, or land? The problem is that there is not much similarity in the behavior of real prices of these assets (Figure 2.2). In looking at the four series plotted there, one notes that two of the series (land and housing) reach local minima in 1917, and two (stocks and bonds) reach minima in 1919.[5] But it is hard to find any other similarities.

The "real dividends" of long-term bonds have, of course, shown a steady downtrend over most of the sample period shown in Figure 2.2, with the principal exceptions of the early 1890s and the early 1930s. The downtrend is due to the fact that the dividend is defined in nominal terms, and the price level has generally been trending upward. Thus, we expect a downtrend in real bond prices rather than the uptrend observed

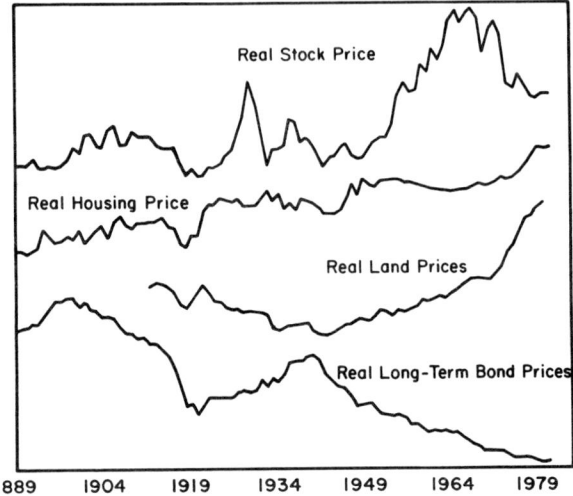

FIGURE 2.2 Real (corrected for inflation) prices of corporate stocks, housing, agricultural land, and long-term bonds.
Source: See Appendix.

in stock prices, and this is what we in fact observe. The trend is sufficiently smooth, however, that we would also expect to see, according to the model (6), that the short-run movements in stock prices should also show up as short-run movements in bond prices. This we just do not observe.

Data on agricultural land and housing are not as reliable as data on stock or bond prices. The reliability of these data are discussed in Shiller (1982). However, the real land and housing prices shown in Figure 2.2 should give some rough idea of the patterns of movements in prices of these assets. Unfortunately, these price series are lacking a corresponding dividend series. We do not have a comparable series on the rents on agricultural land or on housing. Still, it might be reasonable to suppose that the rents on these assets are no more volatile than the dividends on stocks. If that is the case, we might also see some short-run movements in their prices that correspond to movements in stock prices. There does not seem to be any similarity between either of these series and the stock price series. Why, for example, did real values of housing and land show no appreciable change over the period 1929 to 1932 when corporate stock prices fell dramatically? If people were trying to sell their stocks in a pinch, why not also sell their land or their housing? Since we are lacking a dividend series for these assets, it is technically possible that the expected real "dividend" on these assets made an upward jump just at that time, a jump that might then have offset the effects of falling $M_t^{(k)}$. It seems unlikely, however, that the real dividend of housing and land jumped upward dramatically just as the depression began.

Our analysis of these data is exploratory, and there are many special effects pertaining to these various assets that might be held responsible for the lack of similarity. There may yet be an important element of truth to the notion that asset prices do move because of changing rate of discount, but the effect is not robust enough to show up in an analysis at this level of simplicity.

CONCLUSION

This chapter began with a couple of theories and the nontheory of Keynes and others that asserted that there is little hope of finding any economic rationale for most of the regularly occurring large changes in stock market or bond market price indexes. If the other more recent theories considered here were to be rejected, we might then fall back on such a psychological theory.

The simple efficient markets model of stock prices appears to be wrong, since dividends just have not moved around enough in history to justify the movements in stock prices. The popular notion that a particular market decline might be justified in terms of new information about a recession that is just around the corner is clearly wrong. Short-run dividend movements simply are not big enough to justify the stock price movements. The long moving average in the present value relation should smooth out such short-run fluctuations. One might still hope to save the efficient markets model by claiming that dividends are potentially much more variable than they have been historically. A disaster model or a windfall model would do the trick, but neither seemed to be an inspiring answer.

The rational expectations model of the term structure of interest rates was found to be lacking in much the same way. Long-term interest rates appear to be too volatile for their movements to be justified in terms of new information about future short-term interest rates. A "windfall" theory for the volatility of long-term interest rates might salvage the expectations theory of the term structure, but such a theory is still not inspiring.

The notion that stock prices might owe their variability to fluctuations in the marginal rate of substitution between present and future consumption has definite appeal when stocks are considered in isolation. The movements in stock prices are roughly of the right order of magnitude so that they might be attributed to this. However, other asset prices do not seem to behave in a manner that looks encouraging for this theory. The appeal of this notion seems sufficiently strong, though, that one has reason to hope that such a notion will have a place alongside the Keynesian notions described above in explaining part of the variability of stock prices.

APPENDIX: SOURCES OF DATA

The price index used to convert all series to real terms is the consumption deflator for nondurables and services, as described in Shiller (1982), where 1972 = 1.00.

The nominal stock price index is the annual average Standard and Poor Monthly Composite Stock Price Index. The nominal dividend series from 1926 is "dividends per share... adjusted to index, fourth quarter" from Standard and Poor Statistical Service. For 1829 to 1929 nominal dividends are Cowles (1938) series $Da = 1$ scaled to correct for change in the base year.

The long-term bond price is the price of a 5 percent coupon 25-year bond whose yield to maturity is the Moody Aaa corporate bond yield average for the second trading day of the year, from 1936 to 1981, and Macaulay's (1938) railroad bond arithmetic index for 1890 to 1937.

The nominal housing price series was created by linking together a number of series of market prices of homes, except for the brief period of 1949 to 1952 where, since no such series could be found, a construction cost index was used. The series before 1953 can all be found in the 1975 edition of the *Historical Statistics of the United States*; 1890-1934, the Grebler-Blank-Winnick price index for owner-occupied housing (Series N260); 1934-48, the Fister median asking price of houses in Washington, D.C. (Series N261); for 1948 to 1953, the Boeckh construction cost index for housing (Series N121). For 1953 to 1963, the series were the home purchase component of the consumer price index; for 1963 to 1981, the Census Bureau price index of new houses sold.

The land price series is the U.S. Department of Agriculture index of average value of farm real estate per acre. A printout of all data is available from the author on request.

NOTES

1. J. Maynard Keynes, *The General Theory of Employment, Interest and Money* (London: Macmillan, 1936), p. 154.
2. LeRoy and Porter (1981) had earlier made an analogous claim regarding stock prices but used earning series instead of dividends.

3. Even a random walk story is not quite enough to justify the observed variability of price since the dividend price ratio varies in such a way as to make prices even more variable than D/r.
4. Keynes, *General Theory*, p. 203.
5. There was an explosion of inflation between 1916 and 1917, with the consumption price index rising 25 percent in one year. If housing and land nominal prices were "sticky," this might account for their drop in real prices.

REFERENCES

Breeden, D. 1979. "An Intertemporal Asset Pricing Model with Stochastic Consumption and Investment Opportunities." *Journal of Financial Economics* 7 (September):265-96.

Campbell, John Y., and Robert J. Shiller. 1984. "A Simple Account of the Behavior of Long-Term Interest Rates." *American Economic Review* 74 (May) 44-48.

Cowles, Alfred, and Associates. 1938. *Common Stock Indexes*, 1871-1937. Cowles Commission for Research in Economics. Bloomington, Ind.: Principia Press.

Flavin, M. 1983. "Small Sample Bias in Tests of Excess Volatility in the Bond Market." *Journal of Political Economy* 91 (December): 929-56.

Grossman, S. J., and R. J. Shiller. 1981. "The Determinants of the Variability of Stock Market Prices." *American Economic Review* 71 (May):222-27.

Hansen, Lars Peter, and Thomas J. Sargent. 1981. "Exact Linear Rational Expectations Models: Specification and Estimation." Federal Reserve Bank of Minneapolis Staff Report.

Kleidon, Allan W. 1983. "Variance Bounds Tests and Stock Price Valuation Models." Stanford: Stanford University. Mimeographed.

LeRoy, S. 1984. "Efficiency and the Variability of Asset Prices," *American Economic Review* 74 (May):183-87.

LeRoy, S. 1984. "Efficiency and the Variability of Asset Prices." *American Economic Review* 74 (May):183-87.

LeRoy, S., and C. J. LaCivita. 1981. "Risk Aversion and the Dispersion of Asset Prices." *Journal of Business of the University of Chicago.* 54 (October):535-47.

LeRoy, S., and R. Porter. 1981. "The Present Value Relation: Tests Based on Implied Variance Bounds." *Econometrica* 49 (May):1555-74.

Macaulay, F. R. 1938. "Some Theoretical Problems Suggested by the Movements of Interest Rates, Bond Yields and Stock Prices in the United States since 1856." New York: National Bureau of Economic Research.

Marsh, Terry A., and Robert C. Merton. 1983. "Aggregate Dividend Behavior and Its Implications for Tests of Stock Market Rationality," unpublished working paper, Sloan School of Management, MIT, Cambridge, Mass.

Shiller, R. 1982. "Consumption, Asset Prices and Macroeconomic Fluctuations." *Carnegie Rochester Series in Public Policy.* eds. Karl Brunner and Allan H. Meltzer. Amsterdam: North-Holland, pp. 203-238.

———. 1981a. "Do Stock Prices Move Too Much to be Justified by Subsequent Changes in Dividends?" *American Economic Review* (June):421-36.

_____. 1981b. "The Use of Volatility Measures in Assessing Market Efficiency." *Journal of Finance* 36 (May):291–304.

_____. 1979. "The Volatility of Long-Term Interest Rates and Expectations Models of the Term Structure." *Journal of Political Economy* 87 (December):1190–1219.

Singleton, K. J. 1980. "Expectations Models of the Term Structure and Implied Variance Bounds." *Journal of Political Economy* 88 (December):1159–76.

U.S. Department of Commerce, Bureau of the Census. *Historical Statistics of the United States*, Colonial times to 1970, Washington, D.C., 1975.

* * *

COMMENT BY KARL BRUNNER

I am delighted to discuss Bob Shiller's paper. I have followed his work in some detail over the past years. Some of his work was published in the *Journal of Monetary Economics*. Let me make it clear from the very beginning that I disagree fundamentally with him. It should be acknowledged, however, that he has "stirred up the natives" in a very useful fashion. He contributed to the clarification of issues and further development of the analysis. He brought new aspects and dimensions to bear on the issues under consideration. The paper is most appropriate for this conference since it explores a fundamental flaw of a market system emphasized by Keynes.

The stock market proceeds according to Keynes as a multidimensional "Professor Moriarty and Sherlock Holmes game," each trying to outguess the other. What problems does this pose for understanding the stock market and the bond market? And most particularly what does this imply for the social role of the stock market?

The issue is whether we can really explain these observations cast up by the stock market and the bond market. Is it possible to explain these price movements in terms of relevant underlying information and relate them to relevant underlying processes in a systematic fashion? The basic point of Keynes casts doubt on our ability to do so. Such doubts are justified should it appear that the stock market is just a big game without any particular social function.

The issue that Keynes really raised is not an academic exercise. The stock market cannot provide rational guidance to the allocation of resources in his view. The savings investment process suffers, he felt, a fundamental market failure as the prices formed on the stock market could not possibly reflect social circumstances. He concluded at the time that we need state control of investment in order to provide an appropriate level of investment and in particular to prevent the instability of investment that was a major cause, according to his analysis, of the instability of the economy and its low-level trap. I note in passing that by the 1940s he somewhat modified his public policy conclusions.

The alternative view of the stock market, of course, is the efficient market model. The class of efficient market hypotheses asserts that the movement in the stock markets reflects basic informational aspects. It reflects systematic information exploitation about the underlying fundamentals that shape the process. The same idea extends to the bond market. Both markets satisfy, therefore, a major and systematic function in the social coordination and allocation of our resources. Bob Shiller's paper centrally addresses these alternative views of the stock market. He concludes hard and categorically that the efficient market model appears to be wrong. It appears to be wrong because the variability of the stock prices is much too large relative to the underlying fundamentals. Similarly, the rational expectations model of the term structure of interest rates fails for the same reason. He adds, moreover, a very interesting statement. He refutes the popular notion that a stock market decline might be justified in terms of an incipient and anticipated recession based on new information. So we need to examine now the detailed argument supplied in support of this vigorous restatement of Keynes' idea.

The body of his paper is organized into three major sections. The first section covers the efficient market model and the behavior of stock market prices. The second section attends to the rational expectations hypothesis of the term structure of interest rates. Lastly, he considers a variable discount rate approach in the context of a consumption β model.

The first section introducing the efficient market model also offers a detailed description of real stock prices and real dividends over a long period. He properly emphasizes the broad similarity of the movements. He also emphasizes quite correctly that the real dividends do not follow a random walk. This observation raises a question. If real dividends do not satisfy a random walk, and we still observe this broad similarity with real price movements, what should we expect about the behavior of the real stock market prices?

Shiller initially presents an interesting regression based on 88 annual observations of changes measured from January to January in real stock prices. He adds the dividends accruing during the intervening years and divides the result by the real stock price of the initial January. This real return is regressed on the ratio of the real stock price observed in the earlier January to the real dividends in the preceding year. He includes as a second regressor the relative change in the real stock price over the preceding year. He derives a *t* statistic for the first independent variable slightly above two. The *t* value for the coefficient of the second variable is 1.17. Shiller finds that the statistics may be significant. This possible significance suggests the systematic effect of available information on real stock prices.

This regression poses a puzzle. Why would the efficient market model be so widely accepted if it is so easily disconfirmed? But consider the low correlation associated with this regression. The R^2 is slightly more than .05. Shiller emphasizes that is is very difficult to discern systematic but low correlation coefficients in small samples. The actual prevalence of low (population) correlation coefficients biases our procedures in favor of the efficient market model. The low correlation coefficient also means however that there remains a dominant range of random variability beyond what the major contribution of systematic information variables included in the regression show. Public information would still remain a hazardous guide to speculation. But the regression is just an initial step to get our attention. Shiller argues cogently that we need to proceed beyond such regressions.

We have to exploit other aspects and use unexploited observations. Shiller refers especially to the variability of the prices. Does this variability really reflect new information as suggested by the efficient market model? This question is indeed important, and it led him to probe new test procedures expressed by a variance bounds test. This test exploits an important implication of the efficient market model. It implies that the variance of "market fundamentals" imposes a bound on the variance of stock prices. An application of the variance test shows—so the author thinks—that the fundamentals cannot explain the variance of stock prices. The efficient market model must be rejected.

Let us move to the next section, which attends to the term structure of interest rates. Shiller emphasizes the similarity of the valuation formula for the stock market and the long-term rates. This similarity determines the same pattern of variance bounds tests with similar results. The author concludes that the results are inconsistent with the rational expectations model or the efficient market model when applied to the bonds market.

The last section in the paper, the consumption β model, is interesting and ingenious. Shiller demonstrated in a paper presented at a Carnegie-Rochester conference that the variability of stock prices could be explained to a reasonable approximation in terms of the variability of the marginal rates of substitution between current and future consumption. These marginal rates appear as weights in the valuation formula for the stock prices.

The author expresses, however, serious reservation about the consumption β model. This reservation is based on the diverse patterns of stock prices and land and housing prices. I am somewhat troubled by this argument. The model under consideration yields statements about general asset price behavior. It is really a model applicable to an aggregate situation. It is, as I understand it, applicable to aggregate wealth. But it cannot incorporate allocative aspects the way it is formulated. This issue involves crucially allocative aspects of the total aggregate wealth accumulation. We should note at least that the argument is quite loosely related to the structure of the model.

But let us proceed now to an assessment of Shiller's paper. How relevantly does his argument bear on the status of the efficient market hypothesis? There are two elements in his paper, regression and the variance bounds test, that we need to consider.

The evidence from the regression is really singularly weak. This strikes me most particularly in that the author seems to disregard the wide array of radically different circumstances that have been investigated and have yielded supporting evidence. The paper contains no reference, discussion, or comparative evaluation of this evidence. This seems hardly an adequate procedure to judge competing hypotheses. The evidence from the single regression barely matches the accumulated evidence from many separate experiences. But this is brushed aside. Shiller uses data over a long period, but these data still form a comparatively short sample in the context of empirical investigations carried out in this field. The single sample result must thus be treated with some caution. In this respect, the examination of exchange rate behavior executed by my project in Bern offers useful material.

If you look at any particular sample for the Swiss franc exchange rates against any of the major currencies, you could easily conclude that the random walk does not hold. Autocorrelations up to the third order typically prevail. But once you compare different samples, you will find that autocorrelations are quite unstable from one sample to the other. But that is exactly what you would expect if a random walk underlies the process. The single regression is comparatively weak in my judgment compared to the array of evidence that has been accumulated over the last ten years.

A paper prepared by Stan Fisher and Richard Mertin for one of the last Carnegie-Rochester conferences on the stock market should also be mentioned here. The paper contributes to potentially emerging integration of finance and macroeconomics. They found that the stock market price is the best predictor of cyclical variations in the economy. This contrasts very sharply with the statement quoted from Shiller's conclusions about the irrelevance of the stock market prices with respect to incipient recessions—so much for the validity of that statement.

The centerpiece of Shiller's paper, however, is the variance bounds test. Several points should be made here. The argument under consideration involved a typical pattern. The hypothesis actually addressed occurs in conjunction with a complex of auxiliary hypotheses. A range of detailed assumptions, therefore, creeps into the actual execution of the empirical test. We cannot simply jump under the circumstances from the negative results of these tests to one particular item in the joint hypotheses without further investigation.

Shiller's choice of dividends as a representation of the relevant fundamentals exemplifies my point. He emphasizes that the variability of dividends cannot explain the variability of stock prices. But many scholars are very dubious that dividends are the relevant variable for our purpose. They do not reflect the earnings ability of the firm. Earnings, even while they are still manipulated to some extent, seem substantially less managed than dividends. It is thus noteworthy that if you substitute earnings for dividends the results improve substantially relative to the efficient market model. The assumption of stationarity imposed on the "fundamentals" offers another example in the complex of joint hypotheses. Bob Shiller typically assumes stationary processes for the short rate, even for stock prices on some occasions, and for the dividends. Once you accept that some of these processes are really nonstationary, the results change dramatically. It should be noted that the paper offers no evidence supporting the stationarity assumption.

We encounter, however, beyond these nontrivial problems, a serious inadequacy in the use of the crucial test statistic based on the bounded variance procedure. Fortunately, I can exploit two important papers for my purpose. A remarkably lucid and beautifully developed manuscript by Kleido, and another probing paper by Marjorie Flavin, bear immediately on Shiller's test procedure. Both papers are thoroughly convincing. Marjorie Flavin effectively exposes the flaw of the test statistic used in these studies. She demonstrates that the test statistic is biased in small samples. This bias actually favors rejection of the efficient market model.

Some elaboration may be useful. The statistical computation yields two point estimates, one for the upper variance bounds and one for the bounded variance. An asymptotic distribution theory is subsequently applied in order to derive probabilistic statements about these two point estimates. The problem arises if the point estimates are systematically biased or if the asymptotic distributions are a very poor approximation to the finite sample distribution. These aspects are investigated in the papers mentioned above. Marjorie Flavin concludes that the bias affecting the upper variance bounds is more serious than the bias affecting the bounded variance. This statistical fact seriously impairs the significance of the tests that Bob Shiller reported in his paper. If one removes the small bias embedded in these test statistics, we also remove to a large extent the excessive variability apparently revealed by asset prices. The major results developed by Flavin effectively dispose of Shiller's categorical conclusions. The violation of the upper bound for the 10- and 20-year bonds disappears. Moreover, the violation of the upper bound by the holding period yields is not robust with respect to the sample period. Also, whenever violations occur, they remain comparatively small, and so far no evidence supports their statistical significance. Thus dissolve Shiller's conclusions.

My final remarks are addressed to the broader issues of Keynes' "irrationality" hypothesis, which the efficient market model so successfully countered. Shiller's attempt to exhibit the empirical irrelevance of the efficient market model raises some basic questions about the nature and content of the alternative explanation. We encounter in my judgment a fundamental difficulty in the interpretation of the "irrationality" hypothesis. Shiller did not attend to clarify the meaning or empirical content of this hypothesis except that it differs from the efficient market hypothesis. No alternative hypothesis was really offered. Keynes offered a story with obscure implications concerning specific patterns. We do have a hypothesis on the other hand that satisfies some rationality conditions. But we also recognize major exceptions observed repeatedly. Specific observations do occur that have not been successfully subsumed under the hypothesis. It has otherwise exhibited remarkable success. Under the circumstances it appears quite irrational to abandon the efficient market model for an irrationality hypothesis in unspecifiable sociopsychiatric terms.

The precise interpretation of Shiller's paper remains in this context somewhat uncertain in my mind. He may suggest the occurrence of some market inefficiency expressed by his regression. He may also suggest at the same time that this information is not really useful as it explains very little. At this point he needs to fall back heavily on the appearance of excessive variances to interpret the massive unexplained portion in terms of irrational behavior dissociated from fundamentals. Shiller thus offers simultaneously two unrelated and unreconciled stories: markets are inefficient in the sense that public information systematically affects stock prices, and markets are also irrational, which apparently means that we can say nothing about them.

Finally, I wish to comment, beyond Shiller's challenging paper, on the idea originally advanced by Keynes. I was struck by how it has been essentially discarded or emasculated in the formulation and evolution of "Keynesian analysis." But Keynes' "nontheory" of the stock market—to quote Shiller's felicitous expression—poses a problem for any analyst.

The idea would require substantial development and explication in order to yield a potentially useful stage. One possible explication may proceed as follows.

Suppose two groups operate on the market, a professional trader group and the outsiders. The professional traders systematically exploit information and use it efficiently, but they have a very high discount rate. They are consequently not interested in long-term aspects. Again, this can be justified in terms of Keynes' analysis of the long-term aspects with the diffuse and murky uncertainty surrounding long-term assessments. Probability distributions dissolve at this stage into Knight's uncertainty. Outsiders, on the other hand, try to guess what the insiders do, or what they know, or to acquire information from the insiders. The result is highly erratic variability (of the stock market) without apparent sense in terms of any fundamentals. And this determined the policy conclusions that Keynes had drawn at the time.

It is important to note that we find a sharply contrasting story when we turn to Keynes' account of the bonds market. He maintained that the bonds market is anchored by long-term expectations of a normal interest rate. This is supplemented by regressive shorter-run expectations that hold the market around this anchor of a normal interest rate. The patterns attributed to the bonds market and the stock market are thus very different. And one cannot subsume and reconcile them and sew them together into a single nonmoney asset market typically represented by the standard *IS-LM* framework.

So we note that Keynes' view of the stock market disappeared from the standard framework. The latter conveys, in contrast, the impression of a highly determined rate of return on nonmoney assets systematically responding to "fundamentals" specified by the model. It seems to me that if one wants to stay in the spirit of Keynes' view of the stock market and the radically different picture of the bond market, we need an analysis that goes beyond a two asset world. But the basic inconsistency in Keynes' approach to the two financial markets reinforced by the comparative weight of evidence suggests the advantage of the efficient market model as a unified and empirically relevant formulation.

* * *

COMMENT BY PAUL DAVIDSON

Shiller starts with Keynes' nontheory; so let me explain why Keynes' nontheory really is a theory. This goes into the question of what Keynes wanted to do with the *General Theory*. Right at the beginning he says that the postulates of the classical theory (I would add neoclassical, new classical, and neoclassical synthesis theory) are applicable to a special case and not to the general case. Moreover, the characteristics of that special case assumed by these classical and neoclassical theories happen not to be those of the economic society in which we live. The result is that its teaching is misleading and disastrous if we attempt to apply it to the facts of experience.

Keynes then goes on to this Euclidean versus non-Euclidean paradigm distinction, which I have already referred to in my comments on Leijonhufvud. Keynes states that you have to throw out the axiom of parallels or its equivalent to get to a theory applicable to the world in which we live. The reason why Shiller thinks of it as a nontheory and Brunner thinks of it as a psychological, sociological mess is that Shiller and Brunner operate under three basic axioms that Keynes rejected.

Remember what an axiom is. An axiom is, to the faithful, a universal truth. You do not question axioms. You work starting from them. Therefore, the Keynesian revolution is a revolution because you are throwing out what the majority believe are universal truths. You are saying the equivalent of there is no God in a neoclassical world. There is no Walrasian auctioneer. There is no efficient market, and there is no complete bounded information set.

Now, what are these axioms that, following Keynes, we should reject? Keynes did not use this terminology, but the statements that he makes require rejecting the axiom of ergodicity. Ergodicity is concerned with probability theory, and Keynes was, as you remember, an important contributor to the logic of probability theory. Ergodicity is very simple. If you have realizations (in time series analysis) that are generated by stochastic processes, you have a time series over time, and there are *time averages* that you estimate over a single realization. You can calculate the mean and the standard deviation. There are also *space averages* or point-of-time averages that you get from the universe of realizations taken at a point of time. If the stochastic process is ergodic, then the time average of an infinite time realization and the space average of the universe of realizations will coincide. If you are talking about finite realizations, which is all we ever have, time and space averages coincide except for random errors. Thus when you have past information (observations we call them), they are a time series realization. You can therefore calculate a statistical mean, standard deviation, etc. for levels and rates of change, etc. and get the probability distribution for history (the information set) and maybe also something about the current point of time set if you can get cross-sectional analysis. But you can infer that these separate space and time averages "coincide" only if they are generated by an ergodic process. If it is ergodic, then you can project that same probability distribution into the future and make forecasts about future events based on the existing information set.

Now, stationary is a necessary *but not a sufficient condition* for ergodicity. So even if you have stationarity, you need not have ergodicity. For example, limit cycles in physics are nonergodic even if they are stationary. A limit cycle is the equivalent of a Hicks' business cycle. It is a harmonic with constraining floors and ceilings. So if you are going to talk about business cycles with floors and ceilings you are merely dealing with nonergodic situations. The past, therefore, does not yield the best statistical probability for forecasting the business cycle even if the process is stationary.

Keynes was a great believer in nonergodic processes involving certain economic variables—the stock market being one. Efficient markets hypotheses will not help you predict, but it is considered a good explanation. But this is the exact opposite of a nonergodic explanation. What post-Keynesians are saying in accepting nonergodic financial market processes is that people may actually believe that the future is not there to be discovered. The future is there to be created! If that is the case, then you do not have an ergodic system.

If you have what Shackle called crucial experiments, where you cannot replicate the conditions of the system, then you have a nonergodic environment. Shackle gives an example, "There is no use telling Napoleon that 95 times out of 100 the Prussian general is going to be late at the battle of Waterloo." He fights it only once. Unfortunately, he got an "outlier"; the Prussian general comes in on time and Napoleon loses the battle, and he does not have a chance to replicate it. The future is permanently different.

The same thing is true if an agent goes bankrupt. If bankruptcy can occur, then all existence theorems are in jeopardy.

The future is not forecastable in the rational expectations sense. That means that the stock market is going to be a psychological nonseries, if you wish.

The second axiom rejected is the axiom of gross substitution. Keynes denied the axiom of gross substitution, which is a fundamental axiom. All economists believe that everything is a substitute for everything else. We do our nice convex indifference curves, production functions, and so on except for when we do linear programming and the like. This convexity means that we do believe in gross substitution. But Keynes did not believe in gross substitution as a ubiquitous phenomenon. Nongross substitutability is concerned with liquidity and the liquidity trap. Unfortunately, Shiller develops his asset model on the basis of intertemporal substitution. Let me point out that John Hicks, the developer of the *IS-LM* system says in his book *Causality in Economics* that he believes that intertemporal substitution, that is, the association of independent utilities with a consumption plan over time (specific consumptions at specific points of time), is a very poor assumption. What you need to understand with regard to Keynes is that you have a choice of consuming today or making some very general and vague provision for the future, not specific intertemporal substitutability.

I am sure that facts never convince any economist. But statistically and empirically let me give you a fact about intertemporal substitution. In an article in the winter 1982–83 issue of the *Journal of Post Keynesian Economics*, Danziger, Smolensky, et al. from the Poverty Institute investigated the propensity to consume of aged and elderly people. They found that the older that people are, ceteris paribus (adjusting for all kinds of income including government subsidies, money income, and any way you want to adjust income), the lower the average propensity to consume is. Those who are 85 years old, ceteris paribus, have a lower average of propensity to consume than people who are 75 years old. What does that mean about intertemporal substitution? Are these people irrational? It has all sorts of implications for overlapping generations models, but it does suggest that people are, even in their old age, saving for their old age on some general provision of the future. The world where agents act like that may be irrational in the economist's sense—if economists believe in ergodic processes and intempol gross substitution.

Now why do economists deny agents act in accordance with these "irrationalities." They suffer from what I call the economists' disease. Economists always want to be like the natural sciences. Economists believe the hallmark of the natural sciences is precision. They mistake precision for accuracy; there is a difference. Accuracy is correct. Precise is merely a statement about absolutes.

Let me give you an example. Your plumbing breaks this morning— because of the cold weather, at 10:00 in the morning the pipe breaks. You call the plumber up and you say, "come over and fix this right away." Now he can give you a precise answer or he can give you an accurate answer. He can say I will be over at 11:02 this morning, which is very precise, but if I know plumbers, is not accurate at all. Or he can say I will be over before the end of the week, which is very accurate but not very precise. The object should be accuracy not precision, you see.

I had a discussion with Arrow which is relevant here. You might look at something that I quoted from Ken Arrow in the *Economica* 1974, page 454. It is a question of risk versus uncertainty. I'll just quote a bit of it. Arrow says,

> it is interesting that the parts of Keynesian theory which became popular were, as you suggest, a retrogression from Keynes' deeper insights, but this is no accident. One part of the theory was capable of

development, a means to be made precise, even though it was an impoverished version of the whole. The other part, deeper though it was, could not in fact be developed.

In other words, the light is better over there; the problem is over here; so we search over there because we can get precise answers.

Now we will take the third axiom to be rejected, the axiom of reals, and then talk for a few minutes about Shiller and why he has some of these problems. The axiom of reals really is the Joan of Arc axiom. We really get burned at the stake for rejecting this. Basically, the axiom of reals says that agents do not worry about nominal values. Agents will worry only about real values and relative prices and not nominal values. We usually think of rejecting the axiom of reals as accepting the money illusion, but it has nothing to do with the money illusion itself. The axiom of reals states that you make all your economic decisions regarding real things, goods, leisure, and real relative prices only; all that matters is the allocative decision. It is called the axiom of real because money does not matter; money is neutral. Despite what Karl Brunner and Milton Friedman say, they believe in the axiom of reals, and therefore in the long run the real economy goes about its way, and money only affects price levels and has no effect on the real output or the natural rate of unemployment. Keynes specifically denies the neutrality of money (axiom of reals) assumption. Money is not neutral in the short run or in the long run. Therefore, it affects decision makers in all sorts of ways.

Do you really invest in "real" stock prices? I do not think that really is important, the nominal value of the stock dividend by the consumer price index. Let me give you an example of a situation and why it might not occur. I am going to use a firm, but you can think of a household. Imagine that in the next Great Depression a firm has a production process that has a gestation period of one year. By the way, for contract purposes, the one thing that you cannot do in the entrepreneurial economy is recontact without penalty. We organize production efficiently because we use forward money contracts in a monetary economy. That is the essence of a monetary economy, the use of contracts, forward contracts in nominal terms. We do not use forward real contracts, interestingly enough.

So this firm organizes its workers and buys materials all on forward contracts. That is the only way of getting cost controls if you are a good entrepreneur. In business people spend all their time not renegotiating real contracts but negotiating them in nominal terms.

Assume you have all your inputs hired on forward money contracts for the year. Then suppose during the year the consumer price index falls by 10 percent, but the price at which the firm expects to sell its product at the end of the gestation period, as opposed to the price at the beginning when the firm made its contracts, falls by only 5 percent. We would all say in relative real terms that the firm is 5 percent better off. But if that continues long enough, the firm goes bankrupt. Its prices fall, consumer prices fall, and it is locked into a money contract.

Now you would say that in the long run they are going to learn not to enter into money contracts, or else somehow or other they are going to be able to predict inflation and deflation rationally. We have lots of people running lots of regressions, and I do not know of anybody who predicts inflation right each and every year or even on average.

In the other case, suppose you entered a contract, and the consumer price index goes up 10 percent and the firm's price goes up 5 percent. In real relative terms, it is worse off. But in actuality it is better off. Which firm would you rather be the entrepreneur of: the one that is in real relative terms 5 percent worse off but in nominal terms is better off or vice versa? It is money flows that are important in a monetary economy; that is why money matters (unless we get *perfect* forecasts)!

When Shiller looks at the real values, he is looking at a very strange animal. In 1932 you want to look at nominal values and ask your spouse what do you want to do. You also ought to ask because, after all, holding money has got some value as well, if prices are falling in 1932. I do not know of anybody who holds the stock for a hundred years; I am not sure what it means to hold the stock for a century. Even pension funds and all these other people do not buy for keeps—they keep turning over their portfolio. So I think that is what you have to look for.

What is the information set on an efficient market? We talk about these things and we write symbolic I's. We talk about information sets. What is the *exclusive set of information*? Shiller being trapped by the efficient hypothesis, says it is the information about future dividends. If you insist that is correct, then fine, but is that what the efficient market really is all about? Suppose we are Keynesian players of the stock market. After all, Keynes not only had a foot in the economic theory; he had two hands and another foot in the real world financial markets in the "city." So he understood more than most academics do about playing the market. Suppose you believe, as Keynes believed, that the market is like a beauty contest, that what is important in the information set is what other agents believe. That becomes part of the information set; you have got to know about what they believe about the future, and so on.

Let him suggest a new regression analysis for you: the color of Lewis Rukheyser's tie on the TV program *Wall Street Week in Review* suggests what the market is going to do next week. Suppose you believe that other people believe that. If that is the case, then that becomes part of the important information set before you form your expectations. Suppose you find that there is a correlation between tie color and the stock market price level. Now, you see the question is to forecast what tie he is going to wear before you observe the tie; that is the beauty contest. Is that really what happens, or is it that people look at long-term dividends, real dividends, and real values?

Secondly, it is not intertemporal substitution for consumption plans that are important. What is important is that the individual makes two decisions, the Hicks' decisions: you consume today or you make some vague provision for the future; that is what marginal time preference is all about. Then the question is that you have to put that provision for the future into some vehicle, a "time machine," a way of moving generalized purchasing power, not specific purchasing power, to the indefinite future. You do not know when you want dinner or what you want for dinner; maybe you want clothes instead of dinner, or a show, or alcohol, or what have you. Today you do not want to commit yourself. So you need a time machine. Now what are time machines? They are any liquid assets. *Resalability* in a spot market makes an asset liquid. Durability, low carrying cost, resalability in a spot market for nominal units (a nominal unit that is the unit for settling nominal contracts) provide liquidity because that is what you have to sell. So liquidity pushes you into a completely different game. You are not playing Shiller's intertemporal substitution of assets.

Think not of stocks and bonds that have some future income stream. If you are a real neoclassical, future income streams are associated with some technological marginal productivity. Let me suggest to you that postage stamps are just as good liquid assets as stocks and bonds, maybe better. What marginal productivity do all postage stamps have, what dividend yield do they have? Or when we are not on a gold standard, when we know somebody is not rigging the market to peg the nominal price of gold, then gold becomes just as valid a speculative time machine. That is why manias, panics, fads, and so on sweep the market, and if you are going to try to get some efficient market hypothesis, or some other stable stochastic stationary process to explain these manias and fads, I think you are talking about a world that Keynes did not talk about. So I conclude by saying that Shiller is correct in attacking the efficient market hypothesis.

I should point out one other thing; in the National Bureau of Economic Research working paper 1130, Ben Friedman has done some empirical work. Again facts never stop any neoclassical theorist, but the empirical evidence that Friedman obtained is that *gross substitution is not statistically significant* among certain kinds of financial assets. Even among most financial assets where it is significant, the size of elasticity is very small, in the order of .035, which suggests that, even when it is significant, all financial assets are not very good substitutes for each other, which comes a lot closer to the Keynesian game. This raises all sorts of questions about portfolio balance, how expectations are formed in these markets, and so on. This work is good empirical evidence, which means that you end up by asking, "Well, what is the stock market going to do tomorrow?" and you answer, "I don't know."

Now, we ought to know when we do not know. That does not make you less of a scientist. Evolution is a science, we think, unless we are religionist, and yet, we can explain the past. But when you say please forecast what the next species is, you are at a loss. Or if you lived in the dinosaur age and you had to predict whether this little furry thing that was running around on two feet was going to survive, based on your time series realizations, you would have had rational expectations that the dinosaurs were going to win, not the mammals. Keynes once said if economists could consider themselves like dentists, competent, humble people, that would be a great advantage. We are not physical scientists; our science does not permit precision or forecasts—but it certainly can permit accuracy.

Shiller writes D_t/P_t, which is the long-term rate of interest. D_t is the real dividend and P_t is the real price. But if you think about that, D_t is nothing more than his console nominal rate, the console yield over the price level (the deflator), and P_t is the nominal spot price of bonds over the same price deflator, so that the nominal rate of interest will be exactly equal to the real rate. There is no difference between the nominal rate and the real rate if you think of the spot price of bonds as completely reflecting what people expect. And that is, of course, exactly the criticism that Keynes made of the real rate of interest as a separate concept. That is, if everybody suddenly expects inflation, either homogeneous or rationally, then they will immediately change the spot price of an existing securities to reflect that, and the possibility of capital gains will immediately disappear.[1] If people have varying expectations, then obviously they could be wrong. But if the market has rational expectations about the future rate of inflation, the current spot price of securities, which are resalable, this console price will immediately change to reflect the changing rate of inflation. As for Shiller's formula here, although he quotes the real price, I will say that it is equivalent to the nominal price, whereas Shiller states that when the inflation rate is more than zero the nominal rate and the real rate differ. This cannot be the case, unless you are using for the nominal price, before you deflate, the issue price of a bond rather than its current market price, that is true, but the current market price will always reflect inflation.

NOTE

1. See Keynes (1936), p. 142.

REFERENCES

Danzinger, S. et al. 1982-83. "The Life-Cycle Hypothesis and Consumption Behavior Among the Elderly." *Journal of Post Keynesian Economics* Vol. 5, no. 2 (Winter), pp. 202-27.

Davidson, Paul. Review of *Epistemic and Economics: A Critique of Economic Doctrines*, by G. L. S. Shackle in *Economica* Vol. 41 (November), 1974, pp. 452-54.

Hicks, John R. 1979. *Causality in Economics*. New York: Basic Books.

Keynes, John Maynard. 1936. *The General Theory of Employment, Interest and Money*. London: Macmillan.

* * *

COMMENT BY JOSEPH STIGLITZ

There are three remarks that I want to make very briefly. The first concerns the general proposition that Bob has put forward considering the irrationality of the market and the responses that have been given to that. It seems to me that there is a lot of other evidence that one could bring to bear at the microeconomic level to support the kind of view that Bob Shiller has taken. There are numerous phenomena that are difficult to reconcile with a market of rational investors and rational firms. It is often difficult to distinguish those paradoxes where the market "failure" occurs as a result of "irrational investors" from those in which the failure results from non-value-maximizing managers. But there is a lot of evidence that there is either a failure on the part of the managers of firms or on the part of investors.

Let me just give one example, and I think a very important one, which is the so-called dividend paradox. This makes note of the observation that, in the United States if a firm buys back its shares, the shareholders are not subjected to income taxes but are subjected only to much lower capital gains taxation; in contrast, when firms issue dividends, the individuals are subjected to the much higher rates of income taxation. From a general perspective these two are equivalent ways of distributing income from the corporate sector to the household sector. The only difference is in terms of the tax treatment. Smart, closely held companies usually do not resort to extensive use of dividends, except under IRS pressure. But the fact is that a lot of dividends are distributed; I think this is very difficult to reconcile with rational behavior. If you talk to managers of firms, they often assert that shareholders will get upset if they buy back shares; shareholders will not understand that these are equivalent actions. That is an argument for irrational shareholders. The other argument is that managers do not understand the equivalence but do not like to admit it.

Another example that is often cited is the long lag that occurred in the switching from the FIFO to LIFO accounting conventions by U.S. corporations in the presence of high rates of inflation. Again, the corporate sector voluntarily gave billions of dollars to the U.S. Treasury. Whereas in the first case, payment of dividends has the problem that you could not announce that you were doing this to avoid taxes or the IRS might clamp down; in the case of LIFO over FIFO you could explain very clearly that this was a switch that was done deliberately to minimize tax liabilities. There is a whole list of other paradoxes that one can only attribute to a combination of investor ignorance and managerial incompetence including the failure to use accelerated depreciation and the use of stock options in executive compensation packages.

Even if one feels nervous about some of Bob's regressions based on a limited amount of data, there is another category of examples that lend credence to his conclusions. Did views of the prospects of the United States increase 40 percent in the last six months as the stock market went up? Does this reflect a sudden change of information? In the past, when the newspaper would come out with a good report about the economy, the stock market would go up. Recently you hear reports that say the stock market went down because the Commerce Department announced that national income is going up. Is it plausible that the structure of the economy has changed so dramatically that what was good news is now more bad news?

In terms of these general phenomena, one does not have to use regression analysis to support the view that there is just a lot of volatility in the market that cannot be explained. At a deeper level there is a kind of logical inconsistency in the pure efficient markets hypothesis arising from the fact that if markets were perfectly efficient it would not pay anybody to invest any resources to find out what are the stocks that are undervalued. If nobody were investing in information, the only information that would be reflected in the market is free information, and as we all know, that kind of information is not worth very much. There is also an empirical counterpart to this logical inconsistency: though mutual funds spend considerable resources trying to beat the market, there seems a clear track record establishing their inability to do that.

The interpretation that I give to all of this is to a large extent the stock market is a gambling casino for the rich. The patterns of investment one sees in the market are not those that will correspond to any reasonable theory of rational risk averse behavior on the part of investor in the stock market. That is the first general remark.

The second set of remarks—or questions—concerns the interpretation of the volatility patterns that Bob noted, particularly the differences in volatility patterns between different classes of assets. First, to what extent can changes in uncertainty that are particular to particular assets explain these differences in patterns of movements in prices? Second, if you take the view that the capital market is characterized by credit constraints and other kinds of imperfections that are not irrational (that is, these are imperfections associated with imperfect information), then one would expect the implicit interest cost of capital associated with different categories of assets to be different; this too would result in different patterns of price movements associated with different categories of assets. To what extent can the differences in patterns of movements be so explained?

The third question is what implications does the irrationality of markets have for macroeconomic analysis (which is presumably the question of interest here)? (Part of our interest today arises from the fact that Keynes said that the market was irrational, and this is a conference on Keynes and not just in macroeconomics). Surely there is a correlation between the behavior of the stock market and the behavior of the economy. But does one want to make a causal inference? And, if one does that, can once clearly delineate the transmission mechanism between the stock market and the rest of the economy?

Let me try to put forward at least a view about why I think it is important to understand how the stock market behaves. I do not think it is because of the role of the stock market in reallocating investment resources. That is, there is a view that is often put forward, that the stock exchanges particularly like, of the critical role of the stock market in giving price signals. When you read this literature, you get the view that all of the managers of the firms have very little information about the profitability of the firms and their opportunities. When the stock market goes up by 5 percent for AT&T, they say all these smart investors have come to the view that telephones are going to be a wave of the future, and therefore we should increase our investment; then the next day when it goes down by 10 percent, they say, oh well, new information has come to the attention of these small investors that has led them to change their minds. All these people are doing much more thorough research than we could possibly be doing in our little research department. So, now we will scrap those plans; in fact we will cancel some of those telephone poles that we had on the delivery line. I do not think that this is a very accurate description of how most managers behave. They pay some attention, but relatively little, to stock prices.

Secondly, not that much investment is directly financed by issuing shares on the stock market. This in itself does not mean that the stock market is not important. It could be that even though they are not issuing shares, it is providing important information, but as I say, I am skeptical that it is providing that information. It is not, as I say, a major source of capital. If it were, then obviously the price they have to pay to raise new capital would be an important consideration in their investment decision, but it is not very important part of raising capital.

The reason I think that the views of the stock market are important is because the question of how firms make their investment decisions is important in determining the level of investment, and we have to have a view of how those investment decisions are made. Those investment decisions are related to the managers' view of the cost of capital that they faced.

Now, I do not have the time to develop a well-articulated theory of the capital market and the associated cost of capital facing managers. There are two parts of the theory that I would construct if I had the time. The first is that in the presence of imperfect information the banking system will frequently be characterized by extensive credit rationing; in that case, it is not the rate of interest that is relevant, but there is a much higher shadow price of capital that firms may face. Changes in credit rationing by banks is not an explanation of changes in investment; even if they are constrained by the bank, why do firms not go directly to the capital market and raise funds? The second part of our theory answers this question. The answer has to do, in part at least, with the information conveyed by the decision to go to the stock market. When firms do go to the stock market, information about their characteristics is conveyed. There is a subset of firms that makes use of it. The evidence is that, particularly in recessions, the implicit cost of capital on average is very high in using the stock market for raising funds. Those firms that do go to the stock market experience a decline in the price of their shares, a sufficiently large decline that at least some people estimated that the cost of capital is as high as 60 percent. This explains why there is not more extensive use of the capital market. If our analysis is correct, it suggests that the results on volatility of prices may not be of that much concern for macroeconomic analysis.

* * *

REPLY BY ROBERT SHILLER

I actually agree with many of the points raised by the discussants. Brunner emphasized the large accumulated evidence on the efficient markets hypothesis. I think that this *is* a very important body of evidence to help us in understanding these markets, buy we must also be careful in interpreting just what this evidence means. Along with the large amount of evidence that is construed as supporting the efficient markets hypothesis, there is also some evidence that appears to contradict the hypothesis, as Stiglitz also pointed out. I think that a very important example is the literature documenting that the price-earnings ratios predict returns. The simple investment strategy that consists of picking stocks that appear underpriced (in having low price-earnings ratios) does seem to produce higher than average return, as documented by Nicholson and, for risk-corrected returns, by Basu.[1] There are other important examples of evidence contradicting market efficiency. Some of these were collected in a special issue of the *Journal of Financial Economics* a few years ago.[2]

The point I want to emphasize in interpreting this apparently conflicting body of evidence is that the reason most of the tests of market efficiency fail to reject may be that the power of the tests they use may be very low. Even if markets behave just as Keynes described, we may not expect very high R^2 in equations predicting returns. For alternative hypotheses with low R^2, it is well known that the power of ordinary t tests or F tests will be low unless there are very many observations. That is why I used nearly a century of data in the regression in my paper. With all that data I was able to reject the random walk hypothesis. But, of course, defenders of the efficient market hypothesis may question the accuracy of all these data going back a century. Purists may prefer to use recent data

well fail to reject market efficiency in regressions like that in my paper. You just cannot detect a tendency of the stock market to cycle between booms and busts unless you get a number of such booms and busts in your sample, and you clearly cannot do that with only a decade or two of data.

The claims in my various papers that corporate stock prices appear to be too volatile to accord with efficient markets theories represented a sort of exploratory data analysis. Some of the critics of these claims tried to look at these claims as formal tests of a model and tried to size these tests. The problem in doing so is that one must make up additional assumptions, not mentioned in my papers, in order to have a well-structured statistical model that allows such sizing of tests. Exploratory techniques usually keep us away from such endeavors. What we may learn from such exploratory data analysis, without any formal hypothesis testing, is that the data do or do not appear to be consistent with a broad class of statistical models. In this case, we learn that dividends have just followed a fairly smooth trend for as long as we have dividend history and that stock price movements were confirmed in corresponding subsequent dividend movements. We should not get into a debate about whether we have proved that dividends do or do not follow a trend.

Davidson's very philosophical remarks struck a lot of sympathetic chords in me; so I was a little surprised to hear this as criticism of my paper. With regard to his "axiom of ergodicity," I am not sure just what sin I was committing in my paper. I do think that he is right that a lot of investors tend not to think of statistics as interesting. This is actually an important point. They are uninterested in statistics perhaps because they tend to view what they see in markets as a lot of one-time-only events. Statistical inference depends on a grouping of a large number of events as generated by a certain experiment, so that the outcome of the events can be viewed as independent realizations of a random variable. But in real markets there is usually something apparently new going on. Robots are being developed in Japan, North Sea oil has just been discovered, or a liberal U.S. president has just been elected. These things make investors feel that past statistics are irrelevant and that probability theory is of no use to them. It is interesting that this criticism of conventional probability notions comes up in a conference celebrating Keynes. He argued, in his *Treatise on Probability*, that we really cannot quantify our subjective probabilities as probability theorists assumed.

I am sympathetic with a lot of other things Davidson said. I would like to put money in my models of liquidity constraints; I would like to do something in this connection with financial crises and federal policy. Unfortunately, these things are not in my model, and I wish they were. Davidson talks about a false precision with which the profession seems to be enamored. That struck a sympathetic chord in me too. I wish there were not quite such a taboo in the profession against mentioning the possibility that psychology might be influencing the market. That does not mean that most of what we will do in the future will not be building models of rational economic behavior. I think that one lesson might be that we just should not try to model the stock market but should move on to something for which modeling may be more fruitful.

The bottom line of all this work on the volatility of stock market prices is that we keep hearing in the news about movements in the aggregate stock market but not about the big event that might have justified it. Journalists have their interpretations as to what causes market moves, but these are usually psychological theories, not theories based on substantive information about fundamentals. Even after the fact one does not find out what the news event might have been that justified any big market move. If you take even the stock market crash of 1929, and look for the news that might have precipitated the crash, you will find that there was none. News about the crash itself pushed everything else into the background. Efficient markets theory offers an excuse for why newspaper reporters may not know right away what the reason for the crash was, but it does not offer an excuse for why crashes and booms can recur with nothing important ever happening to dividends.

NOTES

1. Francis Nicholson, "Price Ratios," *Financial Analysts Journal* 24 (January–February 1968):105–109 and Sanjoy Basu, "The Relationship between Earnings Yield, Market Value and Return for NYSE Common Stocks: Further Evidence," *Journal of Financial Economics* 12 (June 1983): 129–56.
2. M. C. Jensen et al., "Symposium on some Anomalous Evidence Regarding Market Efficiency," *Journal of Financial Economics* 6 (June–September 1978): 93–330.

* * *

REJOINDER BY KARL BRUNNER

After having listened to Bob Shiller, Joe Stiglitz, and Paul Davidson, I seem to be the only spokesman around here on behalf of a major line of research that I have followed very closely. I cannot elaborate my arguments. I just have to lay it flatly on the table. The point made by Joe Stiglitz puzzled me for some time. It appears, if I understand it correctly, that the notion of an efficient market is inconsistent with the fact of costly information. All acquisition and interpretation of information require an investment of resources. This inconsistency is, however, more apparent than real. This impression may be conditioned by the rhetoric occasionally used in the literature. The basic thrust of an efficient market involves the full reflection of accumulated information in the prices. This need not exclude the fact that the production of information requires an input of resources. The very observation that markets are efficient in the sense defined testifies to the effective operation of resource investment. This investment produces the observed efficiency. We need to be careful however when we speak about efficiency. Whereas *market efficiency* is quite consistent with costly information, much of the literature uses the term *efficiency* to refer to a never-never-land of costless information. Reality is always inefficient under the circumstances requiring clever policymaking.

I also seem to encounter an assertion that a number of phenomena can only be explained in terms of ignorance and incompetence by management. Ignorance, of course, exists. You are all ignorant and I am ignorant, in some respects. I, for example, am totally ignorant concerning the working of my car. My ignorance is, however, quite rational. It reflects my choice of resource allocation. Once we admit incomplete and costly information, ignorance and irrationality are not equivalent. Rational ignorance is on the contrary a pervasive occurrence of our reality. Intellectuals often deny this by imposing their normative judgment on preferences. The following example may be useful.

Most people in the world probably still believe that the sun rotates around the earth. This is quite rational on their part because the cost of changing the belief is very high and the return from changing this belief very small. Why would it affect the average Indian or African farmer? Their operations would hardly be affected. My example also suggests that the extent of partial ignorance changes with the stakes expressed by the balance of costs and returns.

"Incompetence" poses a similar issue as partial ignorance. We should not trust it as a cultural datum but examine it as an endogenous phenomenon emerging in and *persisting* in specified respects in response to particular institutional incentives. Bob properly referred to important anomalies: to the market thinness issue, the end-of-year issues, or the firm's size issue. I might add the peculiarity of the new issue market in Switzerland, which suggests very much that you could get rich very easily. I invite you all to try. I have tried, yet I could not get rich, unfortunately. I did not get poor either. There is a very good reason for what happens because it is a tie-in sale operated by the underwriting banks with their major customers. Again, it can therefore be quite properly analyzed in the context of the efficient market hypothesis. There is no a priori reason to rule out such a possibility for other anomalies. The one still most puzzling is the end-of-year puzzle about the behavior of the stock market. But to reject a hypothesis with a substantial range of confirmation because of observed anomalies and puzzles without any better alternative effectively answering some puzzles is silly. But this seems to be the thrust of Shiller's and Stiglitz's critique.

3

Policies for Reducing the Natural Rate of Unemployment

Richard A. Jackman, Richard Layard, and Christopher Pissarides

INTRODUCTION AND SUMMARY

The greatest blow to the textbook Keynesianism of the 1950s and 1960s was the advent of the idea of the natural rate of unemployment. We accept this idea on the basis of innumerable augmented Phillips curves (which incidentally work much better in Europe than in the United States). It follows that a major issue in macroeconomics is how the natural rate can be altered.[1]

In this chapter five main possibilities are considered: tax-based incomes policy, self-financing employment subsidies and taxes, training programs, trade union reform, and reform of the system of unemployment benefits.

Tax-based Incomes Policy

To analyze tax-based incomes policy, we develop a number of models of wage setting, in some of which wages are set by firms and in others by unions. In each case unemployment is determined at the level that just induces wage setters to choose the same wage that they expect

---

The original version of this chapter was presented at the Conference on Macroeconomics at the University of Delaware on January 12–13, 1984. The chapter draws heavily on work done with George E. Johnson; see G. E. Johnson and R. Layard, "Long-Run Unemployment and Labor Market Policy," in *Handbook of Labor Economics*, edited by O. Ashenfelter and R. Layard (Amsterdam: North-Holland, forthcoming). We are grateful to the Economic and Social Science Research Council for supporting the program of work from which this chapter stems.

others to choose. And in each model an employer-based tax on wage increases above the rate of price inflation (and a corresponding subsidy to lower wage increases) would lower the real wage and increase employment. The scheme would have exactly the same effect as a per capita employment subsidy financed by a proportional payroll tax. Both schemes would be beneficial and both are worth using. The argument for using a wage-inflation tax as well as a simple wage tax is that the link to inflation would, one hopes, introduce an additional psychological influence favoring lower real wage settlements.[2]

Targeted Labor Subsidies

The preceding argument related to any class of homogeneous labor. In addition, we consider the implication of differences between types of labor. Low wage markets may differ from high-wage markets in two main ways. First, the former may be more affected by externally imposed rigidities, such as a minimum wage, making for a greater degree of excess supply. Second, they may be more affected by the "distortions" associated with unemployment benefit and taxation of earnings. As a result the proportional distortion may be greater, and the elasticity of labor supply higher. In either case a subsidy to the low wage market financed by a tax in the high wage market will increase employment, and, on standard assumptions, social welfare. Targeting is not easy, since the relevant groups in need of support cannot always be comprehensively defined. Therefore in many cases the best way to operate a "targeted" tax/subsidy scheme will in fact be to offer a flat-rate subsidy for all types of labor financed by a proportional payroll tax. Subsidies, of course, have a bad name and the best way to implement the scheme would be to restructure existing employment taxes by raising the proportional tax rate and offsetting it by a "credit" per worker. The net change in tax on the average firm could be zero.

Training Programs

Training programs can reduce unemployment by lifting workers out of markets that are more rigid and into markets that are less. Where markets are in excess supply, training programs can have a social return far exceeding their private return.

Trade Union Reform

Models of general equilibrium involving unions often imply that the natural rate could be reduced by reducing union monopoly power. This may be an important possibility in some countries.

Reform of Unemployment Benefit

A reduction of replacement rates (of benefits to income in work) would reduce unemployment in all models, but it is undesirable on equity grounds. However, a tightening of the test of willingness to work would also reduce unemployment and would be desirable in some countries.

There are many policies that could affect the natural rate, for example, policies on public housing, regional aid, and so on. But we cannot discuss everything. In fact we concentrate mainly on tax-based incomes policy and targeted employment subsidies. We treat the other policies in the last section of the chapter.

TAX-BASED INCOMES POLICY

Incomes policy has been tried as a method of reducing the natural rate of unemployment in a number of countries. But, if incomes policy means setting an absolute ceiling to wage growth, it also means castrating the process of collective bargaining, which makes it politically infeasible except in short bursts. It also means suppressing the process of relative wage adjustment, which induces allocative inefficiency. Finally it may be considered philosophically illiberal. Hence the best hope is to try restraining inflationary pressure by taxing wage increases above some norm.

But how exactly might such a policy have its effect? One cannot just write down a Phillips curve equation and then assert that the tax will reduce the constant term. The mechanism must be specified as part of a general equilibrium process determining the natural rate. This requires that we specify who in the economy sets wages and how the tax affects their behavior. For simplicity we shall assume that wages are set either by firms or unions. The natural rate (NAIRU) is then determined as follows. The wages set by firms or unions are influenced by the wages they expect to prevail in the rest of the economy *and* by the level of unemployment. In general equilibrium unemployment must be such that the wages that individual agents set are the same as those they expect all other agents to set. If unemployment is too low, individual agents will want to set wages above what they expect to be the prevailing wage, and vice versa.

To show that a wage inflation tax would work, we have to show that in the new general equilibrium the level of unemployment would be lower. If the aim is to reduce the NAIRU, then an effective policy will have to reduce the real cost of labor to employers.[3] It is no good saying that we do not want TIP to reduce the real wage (relative to productivity). We do. However with luck this would happen without reducing the living standards of workers, for two reasons. First, the higher level of employment will raise the tax base and cut social security payments to the unemployed. Hence it will be possible to reduce tax rates, quite possibly by enough to maintain real take-home pay.[4] Secondly, the higher level of economic activity will raise the level of investment, at any rate during the transition to the NAIRU. There will thus be a higher capital stock, and thus higher real wages.

The tax that we propose is simpler than the original suggestion of Wallich and Weintraub (1971). They suggested that the rate of corporation tax could be varied in relation to the excess of wage growth over a norm. This suggestion is certainly inappropriate for a country like Britain where, due to various exemptions, roughly half the firms pay no corporation tax. But in any case it seems less distorting to operate the tax in such a way that incentives to cooperate are independent of profitability. The Wallich/Weintraub argument for relating the tax to profits was that it was then less likely to be passed on. But this is to misconstrue the problem, since the aim of the tax is not to affect the long-run rate of inflation, but to affect the level of unemployment.

Thus we suggest a norm (n) for the growth in average hourly earnings. The firm then pays a tax (positive or negative) equal to $t(w - w_{-1}[1 + n])N$, where t is the tax rate, w is hourly earnings (nominal), w_{-1} is lagged hourly earnings (nominal), and N is employment. We want the scheme to be fiscally neutral; so we accompany it by a small subsidy scheme by which firms get a per capita subsidy per worker (s) such that ex post in a world of homogeneous workers $s = t(w - w_{-1}[1 + n])$. (We call this the government balanced budget condition.)

The key question is the choice of norm (n). Provided the norm is ex post equal to the rate of price inflation, the scheme amounts to a tax on real wage growth, offset by a small real per capital subsidy. The net real tax per worker is thus $T = t(W - W_{-1}) - S$ where W is real wages and S is the real per worker subsidy. Since it is politically, as well as economically, sensible to set the norm at a level that turns out equal to the rate of price inflation, we assume this is done.[5] We then find that a self-financing scheme with a tax on real wage *growth* at rate t operates exactly like a tax at rate δt on the *level* of real wages (where δ is the relevant discount rate). In each case the scheme has the effect of reducing the level of the real wage. Against this has to be set the cost-increasing effect of the tax payment itself, but this is, of course, exactly offset by the cost-reducing effect of the subsidy. So labor cost falls by the same amount as the fall in real wages. And this is what increases the level of employment.

To show this we have to use models in which wages are set, not by supply and demand, but by agents who have genuine latitude in the wages they can arrive at.[6] In some markets wages are set by employers, in others by unions, and in others by bargaining between the two. For our purpose it is enough to look at the two polar cases since we find that they give similar results.

Wage-Setting Models

In all these models the basic idea is the following. Wage setters choose their optimal real wage (W) in a way that is affected by the wages ($\overline{W}$) that they expect to prevail elsewhere in the economy, by the level of unemployment (U) and by the TIP rates of tax and real subsidy (t and S). Thus

$$W = f(\overline{W}, U, t, S) \tag{1}$$

But in general equilibrium wage setters must all be setting the same wage:

$$W = \overline{W} \tag{2}$$

So the function of unemployment is to make wage setters choose the same wage as they expect others to set. If unemployment is too low, they will choose a higher wage, and wages will spiral upward with each group chasing the wages that others have set.

We thus have (with $W = \overline{W}$) an equilibrium wage equation with a common wage determined by:

$$W = f(W, U, t, S) \tag{3}$$

The actual wage and unemployment levels are determined jointly by this wage equation and the labor demand relation:

$$U = g(W) \tag{4}$$

This is illustrated in Figure 3.1. The role of TIP is to shift down the wage equation and thus increase employment.

Models Where Firms Set Wages: A Quits Model

We will begin by looking at a world where firms set wages. In doing this firms are concerned about the effect of their wage levels on their ability to retain or to hire workers or upon the morale and productive efficiency of their workers.

Consider first the case where the main concern is quitting.[7] For simplicity we shall assume that the marginal product per worker is

DETERMINATION OF THE NAIRU

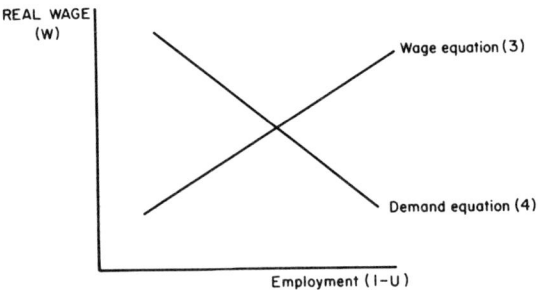

FIGURE 3.1 Determination of the NAIRU

constant (γ) and that free entry ensures zero profits.[8] If a worker quits, this imposes a resource cost $\gamma\phi$ on the firm. The firm's quit rate depends on its wage W relative to the income that a worker not employed in the firm could expect elsewhere, which for simplicity is $\overline{W}(1 - U)$, where $\overline{W}$ is the prevailing wage and U is the unemployment rate. Thus the quit rate is:

$$Q = Q\left(\frac{W}{\overline{W}(1 - U)}\right) \qquad (Q' < 0,\ Q'' > 0)$$

To get a feel for the mechanism by which TIP works, let us start with a simple tax on the *level* of the wage bill (tWN) where N is employment. This is accompanied by a per capita subsidy in which the firm receives SN. The scheme is self-financing.

The firm maximizes its profit per worker, which is:

$$\frac{\pi}{N} = \gamma - (1 + t)W + S - \gamma\phi Q\left(\frac{W}{\overline{W}(1 - U)}\right).$$

The firm chooses W to do this, so that, after setting $W = \overline{W}$, we have the following wage equation:

$$-(1+t) - \frac{\gamma \phi Q'\left(\frac{1}{1-U}\right)}{W(1-U)} = 0. \tag{3'}$$

Second-order conditions imply $Q'' < 0$.

The demand relation comes from the zero profit condition:

$$\gamma - (1+t)W + S - \gamma\phi Q\left(\frac{1}{1-U}\right) = 0. \tag{4'}$$

Eliminating $W(1-t)$ from these two equations we find that

$$Q\frac{1}{1-U} - Q'\left(\frac{1}{1-U}\right)\frac{1}{1-U} = \frac{\gamma + S}{\gamma\phi}.$$

Hence $\partial U/\partial S < 0$.

As the level of subsidy (and tax) is raised, the level of unemployment falls. In terms of the diagram, the demand curve (4') has not shifted, since by definition tW equals S; but the wage equation (3') has shifted down. The lower wages (at given employment) make it profitable for firms to expand employment until the level of quitting has risen enough to bring profits back to zero.

It is interesting that in this model the tax is fully passed back into real wages, since $W(1-t)$ appears as a single variable. Thus the tax as such leaves labor cost unaffected, while the subsidy reduces it. This is a general feature of all our models. It may be a somewhat extreme result, but the basic argument is clear. If wages are taxed, there will be an incentive to reduce wages, and, if there is no net change in labor taxes, this means a fall in labor costs.

We can now use these insights to analyze TIP. The profits of the firm are

$$PV = \sum_j N_j \left(\gamma - (1+t)W_j + tW_{j-1} + S - \gamma\phi Q\left[\frac{W_j}{\overline{W}_j}X_j\right]\right)(1-\delta)^j$$

where δ is the real discount rate and $X = 1/(1-U)$. The optimal choice of wage in the steady state requires that

$$-(1 + t) - \gamma\phi \frac{Q'W}{W} + t(1 - \delta) = 0.$$

Second-order conditions imply $-Q'' < 0$. In equilibrium, all wages are the same (W) so that $Q = Q(X)$ and

$$(1 + \delta t)W + \gamma\phi Q'(X)X = 0. \tag{3''}$$

Also, since competition ensures zero profits,

$$\gamma - (1 + t)W + tW_{-1} + S - \gamma\phi Q = 0 \tag{4''}$$

where W_{-1} is the value in the previous year. We now use the government balanced budget condition that ex post the net tax proceeds are zero ($T = 0$). In addition, we assume for simplicity that there is no economic growth ($W = W_{-1}$), but this could easily be relaxed. In consequence (4'') becomes

$$W = \gamma(1 - \phi Q[X]). \tag{4'''}$$

Thus, substituting for W in (3'')

$$(1 + \delta t)(1 - \phi Q) + Q'(X)X = 0.$$

This determines the natural rate of unemployment, since $X = 1/(1 - U)$.
From this we find that

$$\frac{\partial X}{\partial t} = \frac{-\partial(1 - \phi Q)}{\phi(Q''X - \delta t Q')} < 0.$$

Thus the wage inflation tax reduces unemployment. At the same time it reduces real wages, as can be seen from (4'''). It is easy to check that the same result would follow if the tax/subsidy were levied on workers.

If the discount rate is zero, the tax has no effect. For if a firm raises its wages by £1 this year, it pays an extra £N in tax this year and a reduced £N in tax next year. So only with discounting does the tax work. If the tax is expected to be abolished next period, it will have its maximum impact.

An Efficiency Wage Model

Clearly firms choose their wages with more than quitting behavior in mind. Morale is also important, since it affects productivity. And morale may depend on relative incomes. Thus output per worker might be

$$\gamma e = \gamma e\left(\frac{W}{\overline{W}} X\right) \qquad (e' > 0,\ e'' < 0)$$

Thus unemployment serves as a device to discipline workers (Shapiro and Stiglitz 1984). In this case it is easy to see that the inflation tax will reduce unemployment, even if quitting is independent of wages. Assuming quitting is zero, the firm's present value is

$$PV = \sum_j N_j \left[\gamma e\left(\frac{W_j}{\overline{W}_j} X_j\right) - W_j(1 + t) + tW_{j-1} + S\right](1 - \delta)^j$$

The optimal choice of wage requires

$$-(1 + t)\overline{W} + \gamma e' X + t(1 - \delta)\overline{W} = 0$$

with second-order conditions requiring $e'' < 0$. This is extremely similar in form to the first-order condition for the model with quitting. If it is combined with the zero profit condition and government budget balance ($T = 0$), we find that with $\overline{W} = W$

$$(1 + \delta t)\,e(X) - e'(X)X = 0$$

and

$$\frac{\partial X}{\partial t} = \frac{\delta e}{e'' X - \delta t e'} < 0.$$

Once again the tax reduces unemployment by reducing real wages and making more employment profitable until this reduces efficiency too far.

A Model with Quitting, Hiring, and Vacancies

Finally we can look at firms' behavior in a rather more sophisticated way, with wages affecting hiring as well as quitting.[9] Firms hire by advertising genuine vacancies. That is, they stand ready to fill any vacancy if a suitable applicant applies. And in general they will not wish to employ workers unless there is a workplace for them to work at.[10] Hence the present value of the firm's profits is

$$\sum_j N_j \left(\gamma - (1 + t)W_j + tW_{j-1} + S - \gamma\phi\left[1 + \frac{V_j}{N_j}\right]\right)(1 - \delta)^j$$

where $\gamma\phi$ is the cost per workplace ($\phi < 1$), V_j is vacancies, and $(N_j + V_j)$ is the number of workplaces. Profit is maximized subject to the firm satisfying its flow of labor constraint. For simplicity we shall assume that employment does not change between periods.[11] Hence the firm's quits equal its hires:

$$QN = PV \qquad (5)$$

where P is the proportion of vacancies filled per period. We shall assume, for our present purposes, that quits can be written as

$$Q\left(\frac{W}{\overline{W}}, \frac{U}{V/N}\right)$$

and that the proportion of vacancies that a firm fills is

$$P\left(\frac{W}{\overline{W}}, \frac{U}{V/N}\right),$$

which depends on the relative wage and on the aggregate ratio of unemployed to vacancies in the economy.

Using (5) the firm's maximand is

$$\sum_j N_j \left[\gamma - (1+t)W_j + tW_{j-1} + S - \gamma\phi\left(1 + \frac{Q_j}{P_j}\right)\right](1-\delta)^j$$

If the firm reduces its wages, it reduces its wage bill. But, by reducing its ability to retain and hire labor, it also raises its vacancy rate. The optimal wage involves a balancing of these effects. This requires

$$-(1+t) - \frac{\gamma\phi}{P^2}\left(P\frac{\partial Q}{\partial R}\frac{1}{\overline{W}} - Q\frac{\partial P}{\partial R}\frac{1}{\overline{W}}\right) + t(1-\delta) = 0$$

where $R = W/\overline{W}$, the relative wage. If η_{QR} is the absolute elasticity of quits with respect to the relative wage and η_{PR} is the absolute elasticity of hiring with respect to the relative wage, this implies that (setting $W = \overline{W}$)

$$-(1+t)W + \gamma\phi\frac{Q}{P}(\eta_{QR} + \eta_{PR}) + t(1-\delta)W = 0$$

or

$$(1 + \delta t)W - \gamma\phi \frac{V}{N}(\eta_{QR} + \eta_{PR}) = 0. \tag{6}$$

But zero profit and government budget balance ($T = 0$) imply that

$$\gamma - W - \gamma\phi\left(1 + \frac{V}{N}\right) = 0. \tag{7}$$

Substituting into (6) for W (taken from [7]),

$$\frac{V}{N} = \frac{1 + \delta t}{1 + \delta t + \eta_{QR} + \eta_{PR}} \cdot \frac{1 - \phi}{\phi}$$

Thus

$$\frac{\partial V/N}{\partial t} > 0.$$

Hence a rise in the tax will raise vacancies. It will also reduce real wages (see [7]).

But what happens to unemployment? At the whole economy level, the flow equilibrium condition is

$$Q\left(1, \frac{U}{V/N}\right) = P\left(1, \frac{U}{V/N}\right)\frac{V}{N} = f\left(U, \frac{V}{N}\right)$$

$$(Q_2 < 0, f_1 > 0, f_2 > 0) \tag{8}$$

Hence if vacancies rise, unemployment falls.

The overall mechanism here is quite similar to that in the earlier models. The tax reduces real wages. This makes it profitable to expand vacancies, which reduces unemployment.

Models Where Unions Set Wages: A Wholly Unionized Economy

Some of us come from countries where unions are rather important, and one naturally asks whether the tax would be effective in that situation. We shall show that it would. In fact the effects would be the same whether the tax were levied on firms or workers, but it is more politically feasible to levy it on firms.

We shall assume that the unions fix the real wage, but the firms fix employment. The tax works by altering the trade-off between employment and wages that the unions face. Above the norm a wage increase in the pockets of the union reduces employment more when there is a tax than when there is not—because it raises labor cost by more than it raises wages. Similarly a wage reduction raises employment more with the tax than without it. Hence the tax makes the demand curve faced by the individual union (as a function of the wage paid) more elastic. It thus encourages a higher level of employment.

Let us be a bit more formal. The economy consists of a set of equal-sized firms. Within each of these the union sets the sector real wage, taking the outside real wage as given. In doing so it takes into account the fact that the firm's level of employment (N) depends negatively on the real labor cost $N = N(W + T)$.

In setting wages, unions maximize some objective function, subject to the firm's demand function for labor. Many objective functions have been proposed for unions. Clearly unions care both about wages and about jobs for their members. Since members continually leave, one might expect the unions to raise wages repeatedly to at least as high as the demand price for the surviving members. But this overlooks the fact that unions cannot prevent other members from continuously joining. In fact therefore the union maximizes the interests of a stable but constantly revolving population. This dynamic problem is analyzed reasonably fully in Jackman, Layard, and Pissarides (1983), but here we shall present a much simpler and less rigorous analysis that leads to similar conclusions.

Each union is concerned with the long-run welfare of a group consisting of M people. Of these people N are employed in the union's sector. The remaining $M - N$ are either employed elsewhere in the economy, with probability $(1 - U)$, or unemployed. If employed they get the general wage $\overline{W}$. For simplicity we shall ignore unemployment benefits and assume that utility is linear in income. The objective of the union in period j is thus the expected income of its M members in period j, which is

$$Z_j = N(W_j + T_j)W_j + (M - N[W_j + T_j])(1 - U)\overline{W}_j$$
$$= N(W_j + T_j)(W_j - [1 - U]\overline{W}_j) + \text{constant}.$$

The union thus cares only about the sum of the rents (or surpluses) obtained by its members. (Note that the size of the membership M, which might appear difficult to determine in advance, does not affect the maximization result.)

In the multiperiod context the union maximizes

$$PV = \sum_j N([1 + t]W_j - tW_{j-1} - S)(W_j - [1 - U]\overline{W}_j)(1 - \delta)^j$$

For simplicity, we shall assume that there is no economic growth.[12] It then follows that in general equilibrium (with $W = \overline{W}$), the wage behavior of the union implies that

$$U = -\frac{N}{N'W}\frac{1}{(1 + \delta t)}$$

Since budget balance requires that ex post $T = 0$, this can be written as

$$U = \frac{1}{\eta}\frac{1}{(1 + \delta t)} \tag{9}$$

where η is the firm-specific elasticity of demand for labor.

This analysis makes excellent sense. Unemployment is higher the less elastic the firm-specific elasticity of demand for labor. But if an inflation tax is imposed, this increases the elasticity of labor demand with respect to the wage, since labor cost now rises faster than wages. And this higher elasticity of demand for labor leads to higher equilibrium employment. The story is illustrated in Figure 3.2. The original demand curve is DD and the final one $D'D'$. The equilibrium shifts from E to E' (which has to lie on the original demand curve due to the requirement of budget balance).

A Partially Unionized Economy

A wholly unionized economy may be a reasonable description of Britain but certainly not of the United States. Suppose that only part of the economy is unionized, the wage being chosen by unions. Elsewhere (in the "competitive sector") the wage is determined by supply and demand.[13] The supply of workers at the level of wages prevailing in the competitive sector is elastic with respect to the wage. We consider that part of the population not employed as being unemployed. In these circumstances a rise in the union markup will push workers into the competitive sector, reducing its wage and increasing unemployment. Equally a fall in the union markup will reduce unemployment. But TIP will reduce the chosen markup and thus reduce unemployment.

First we shall show how TIP affects the markup and then how the markup affects unemployment. Let the union wage (W_u) equal the nonunion wage (W_c) times μ. The union maximizes the present value of the expected rents of its members, which, assuming zero growth, is

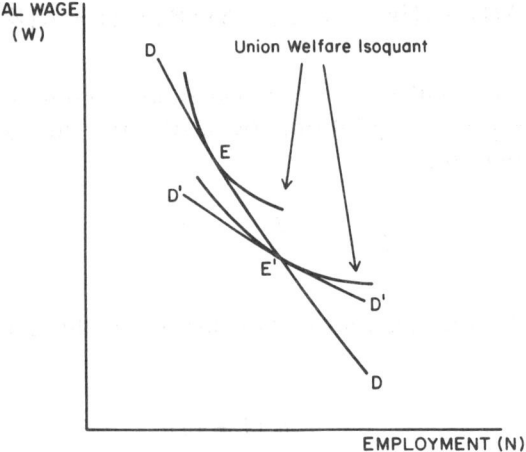

FIGURE 3.2 Sector-specific Employment in a Union Model

$$PV = \sum_j N_j((1 + t)W_c\mu_j - tW_c\mu_{j-1} - S)W_c(\mu_j - 1)(1 - \delta)^j.$$

Assuming a balanced budget, the optimum markup $(\mu - 1)$ is given by

$$\mu - 1 = \frac{1}{\eta(1 + \delta t) - 1}$$

A rise in the tax reduces the markup.

But how does the markup affect unemployment? We assume that the whole population L is willing to work at the union wage. The proportion of them who get work in the union sector is $D_u(W_c\mu)/L$ where $D_u(W_c\mu)$ is demand in the union sector. The number of people who are willing to work at the competitive wage is $S(W_c)$. Of these only a proportion, $1 - D_u(W_c\mu)/L$, supply themselves to the competitive sector, since the rest have jobs in the union sector. Thus equality of supply and demand in the competitive sector requires

$$D_c(W_c) = \left(1 - \frac{D_u(W_c\mu)}{L}\right) S(W_c). \quad (10)$$

From this one can see that a rise in the markup lowers the competitive wage, by flooding the competitive sector with workers. For, from (10),

$$(D_c' - [1 - D_u/L]S' + D_u'\mu S/L)dW_c = (-D_u'W_cS/L)d\mu$$

The resulting change is employment is given by[14]

$$dN = (D_u'\mu + D_c')dW_c + D_u'W_c d\mu$$

$$= \left(D_u'\mu + D_c' - \frac{T}{S}D_c' + [1 - D_u/T]\frac{TS'}{S} - D_u'\mu \right) dW_c$$

$$= \left(D_c'\left[1 - \frac{T}{S}\right] + \left[1 - \frac{D_u}{T}\right]\frac{TS'}{S} \right) dW_c$$

Hence $\partial N/\partial W_c > 0$. Thus, if the markup ($\mu$) rises, the competitive wage falls and employment falls. By using TIP this process can be put into reverse: the markup will be reduced and employment will rise.

Relation of TIP to Taxes on the Wage Level

Before ending our analysis of TIP, we must repeat that, according to the theory, exactly the same results can be achieved by operating a self-financing tax/subsidy scheme in which the firm pays the following tax per worker: $T = tW - S$. The wage tax will have exactly the same force whether it is a tax on wage *growth* or the wage *level*, provided it is accompanied by a substantial per capita subsidy. With TIP the main per capita subsidy element comes from the norm and is represented by the term tW_{-1}. But in each case it is the combination of the proportional tax with the per capita subsidy that produces the twist in the terms on which wage setters make their decisions.

Thus another way to reduce the NAIRU would be to reconstruct employers' taxes on labor so that there was a higher proportional tax, offset by a per capita subsidy (see next section). So is there any point in using a tax on wage *inflation* at all, if the same result could be gotten by a tax on the *level* of wages? There are two arguments for using it. First, we do not really know with any certainty how the natural rate is determined. The models offered above are, we hope, quite well grounded in microeconomic theory. But all we know from empirical observation is that inflation has a tendency to rise when unemployment gets below a certain level. Thus the problem in reducing unemployment *is* inflation. It, therefore, seems natural to address at least one of our policies directly to that problem. It may work by the mechanism we have specified. But, even if all our models are irrelevant, there could be a hope that it would work by some other mechanism.

A second argument in favor of an inflation tax is that it could help not only to reduce the natural rate of unemployment (at constant inflation) but also to reduce inflation (if one wanted to) with less unemployment than would otherwise be required. In practice disinflation normally requires that wage setters set wages below the level at which they expect the general level of wages to be set. It is easy to check in our models that if this occurs (with $W = [1 - \lambda]\overline{W}$ where $\lambda > 0$) unemployment will be higher than otherwise. An inflation tax could offset this. These are good arguments for operating a TIP as well as other measures to maintain employment.

TARGETED EMPLOYMENT SUBSIDIES

Among economists the most common way of thinking about reducing the natural rate has been in terms of structural policies that discriminate between one type of worker and another. These can be justified on two different lines of argument. One is simply that there is a greater disequilibrium in one market than another.[15] For example, suppose there was a minimum wage that was binding in one market and not in another. Then if labor supply in the flex-wage market were completely inelastic (no substitution effect), the optimal policy would be to subsidize employment in the rigid wage market. This could be financed with no efficiency loss by a tax in the flex-wage market. This is illustrated in Figure 3.3.

A second argument for differential treatment arises if there are labor market distortions arising from, say, unemployment benefits and taxes on earnings and these distortions affect the different groups differently (in a sense to be defined later). To take the simplest example, suppose that the high wage group's labor supply was completely inelastic (no substitution effect) in the relevant range, but that the low wage group had a significant substitution response away from work as a result of unemployment benefits and taxes. In the process there is an amount of voluntary unemployment measured as the difference between the total population and those willing to work. This is illustrated in the left-hand panel of Figure 3.4. In this case the efficiency of the economy would be improved by an offsetting subsidy, paid to firms or workers and financed by a tax on high wage labor. In this model both markets clear, but only the low wage market is distorted. The optimal subsidy is at least as great as the preexisting distortion (see Johnson 1980). The mechanism that reduces unemployment is a rise in the relative wage of the unskilled, as in Baily and Tobin (1977).

Clearly one can generalize this model to the case where both types of labor have elastic supplies and both have distortions.[16] We shall find that it would be optimal to tax the high wage group (2) to subsidize the low wage group (1) if

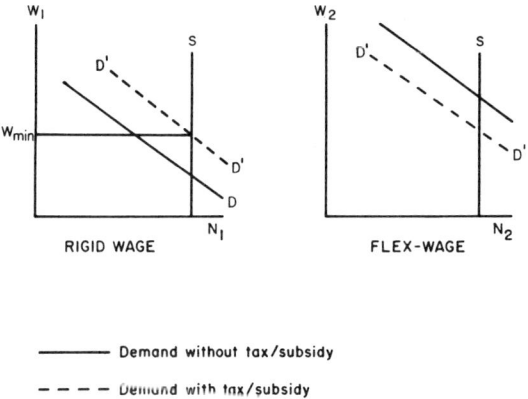

FIGURE 3.3 A Rigid Wage Market and a Flex-Wage Market

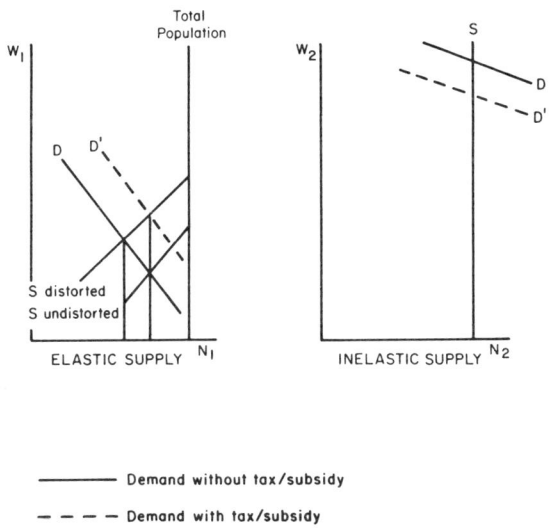

FIGURE 3.4 One Market with Elastic Supply and Another with Inelastic Supply

$$(t + \rho_1)\varepsilon_1 > (t + \rho_2)\varepsilon_2 \tag{11}$$

where t is the proportional tax rate on earnings, ρ is the replacement ratio (of benefits to gross wages), and ε is the elasticity of labor supply. In other words, the low wage group must have a sufficiently high elasticity of supply or replacement ratio or both (in practice these two go together).

To see why this condition holds, we shall start by defining social welfare (Ω). This consists of output, $F(N_1,N_2)$, minus the cost of leisure foregone:

$$\Omega = F(N_1,N_2) - C_1(N_1) - C_2(N_2).$$

If each group of workers pays a proportional tax on earnings t and receives benefits B_i if unemployed, the supply decisions of workers will set $W_i(1 - t) - B = C_i'$, and the decisions of firms will set $W_i = F_i$.

Now consider introducing a small proportional employer subsidy at rate u on the unskilled, financed by an employer tax at rate q levied on the skilled. The change in social welfare is given by

$$d\Omega = (F_1 - C_1')dN_1 + (F_2 - C_2')dN_2$$
$$= (tW_1 + B_1)dN_1 + (tW_2 + B_2)N_2$$

It is thus the changes in quantities weighted by the distortions. The question is under what conditions this is positive.

From the definition of the supply elasticity[17] (ε_i)

$$dN_i = N_i\varepsilon_i \, d \log W_i.$$

If we now subsidize the 1s and tax the 2s, W_1 will rise and W_2 fall, and we need to know the relationship between these two changes. This is given by the factor-price-frontier equation, which implies that for small q and u

$$W_1N_1(d \log W_1 - du) + W_2N_2(d \log W_2 + dq) = 0.$$

But, if the subsidy (u) is wholly financed by the tax (q) and both u and q are very small, then

$$W_1N_1 du = W_2N_2 dq$$

so that

$$W_1N_1 d \log W_1 + W_2N_2 d \log W_2 = 0.$$

Hence we can write the change in social welfare as a function of $d \log W_1$, thus:

$$d\Omega = \left(\frac{(tW_1 + B_1)}{W_1} \varepsilon_1 - \frac{(tW_2 + B_2)}{W_2} \varepsilon_2 \right) W_1 N_1 d \log W_1$$

Since a subsidy will raise W_1, making $d \log W_1 > 0$, the change in social welfare will be positive if

$$(t + \rho_1)\varepsilon_1 > (t + \rho_2)\varepsilon_2$$

In general, groups with high replacement rates will tend to have high elasticities of supply and high unemployment rates. So if we subsidize these high unemployment groups, we can improve social welfare. The gain from stimulating their work effort will exceed the losses from the discouragement of the more skilled group.

One can also examine the condition for employment (rather than social welfare) to increase. This is less demanding and requires only that

$$\frac{\varepsilon_1}{W_1} > \frac{\varepsilon_2}{W_2}.$$

We have discussed the matter so far entirely in terms of the private sector demand for labor. Of course, the public sector should also be encouraged to practice preferential hiring. The simplest method would be to instruct public sector employers to minimize the money cost of public sector output and then pay them the same subsidies (and collect the same taxes) as in the private sector. Alternatively, if they are not paid the subsidies (nor pay the taxes), they need to be given the equivalent shadow prices to use in their hiring decisions.

OTHER POLICIES

Training Programs

Another important policy to reduce unemployment is training. This is most easily seen in the case of the rigid wage model (Figure 3.2). In such a situation any policy that lifted a person from the class of unskilled into the skilled would be efficient, so long as the direct cost of the training was less than the present value of the marginal product of a skilled worker. There is no cost in terms of earnings foregone, since there is a margin of unemployed unskilled people producing nothing.

If we move to the case of Figure 3.3, where markets clear, a policy that lifted a randomly selected group of people out of Market 1 and transferred them to Market 2 would again reduce unemployment in Market 1.

In general individuals will have an inadequate incentive to get trained (see Johnson 1980). To see this, consider the position of unskilled workers in the rigid wage case. The opportunity cost to them of becoming type 2 workers is $W_1(1 - U_1) + U_1 B_1$ where B_1 is benefits. But the social cost is zero.

At this point one should note a conflict of aims between training and employment subsidies that is often pointed out by the enemies of subsidies. If subsidies are used either to reduce unskilled unemployment or to raise the unskilled wage or both, this reduces the incentive to get trained, by raising the opportunity cost $W_1 - U_1(W_1 - B_1)$. Thus employment subsidies and training subsidies should in principle be simultaneously optimized.

Trade Union Reform

We can now look back on our models of Part 1 to see what other clues there are for ways to reduce the natural rate. If unions are important, one obvious candidate is trade union reform. If we could reduce the effective monopoly power of unions (measured by $1/\eta$), we could reduce unemployment. This is so both in a wholly unionized economy and in a partially unionized economy where η determines the markup and thus the unemployment rate.

Reform of Unemployment Benefit

Next there is the rate of unemployment benefit. If we include benefits in our models, we invariably find that unemployment is higher the higher the replacement ratio.[18] However, we do not suggest reducing unemployment benefits as a policy for reducing the natural rate. This is on grounds of equity. But we do think that (in Britain at least) there is a strong case for tightening up the eligibility conditions for benefit. In practice almost no job search test is now applied, and there is evidence that even before 1973 the stringency of the work test was being eroded (see Layard 1982b). A tightening here could be an important way of reducing the natural rate.

Before ending, we should like to pay tribute to that great Keynesian, Abba Lerner, who contributed so much on all these issues. He always believed that we could find a better way.

NOTES

1. There has been much discussion of whether the rate is too high or too low. Most of this has been in the context of a search theory of unemployment. When the average current spell of unemployment, even in the 1970s, lasted half a year in the United States and a year in Britain, it is doubtful whether one should rest one's judgment about the optimality of unemployment exclusively on a theory of job matching. We, therefore, content ourselves with simpler models, which yet enable us to predict the directional effects of policy even if they do not say which direction of change is desirable.

2. We do not discuss administrative issues. These are discussed in both Layard (1982a) and Jackman and Layard (1982). They are also discussed in the report of the Liberal/SDP Commission on Unemployment and Industrial Recovery, *Back to Work*, 1982, which provided the basis for the Liberal/SDP Alliance adoption of the inflation tax as a part of its economic policy.

3. For evidence that employment is affected by real wages see, inter alia, Symons (1985), Symons and Layard (1984), and Nickell and Andrews (1983). If there is imperfect competition, aggregate demand can only alter employment in the short run, but in the long run the level of aggregate demand is constrained to be consistent with the NAIRU.

4. The change in real wages is

$$d(W[1-t]) = dW\left(1 - t - W\frac{dt}{DW}\right)$$

where t is the tax rate and W the gross wage rate. Hence if $dW < 0$, real wages rise if

$$1 = t < W\frac{dt}{DW}$$

Assuming no change in the budget deficit, the government budget constraint is $tWN - (1-N)B = $ constant, where N is employment and B unemployment benefit. Differentiating the budget constraint yields

$$\frac{dt}{dW}W = -\frac{dN}{dW}\frac{W}{N}\left(t + \frac{B}{W}\right) - t.$$

So real wages rise if

$$-\frac{dN}{dW}\frac{W}{N} > \frac{1}{1 + \frac{B}{W}} = \text{(say) } 1.1.$$

Current work at the Centre for Labour Economics gives labor demand elasticities of this order of magnitude.

5. Pissarides (1984) analyzes the general case where this is not necessarily done.

6. Even in a supply and demand world, some self-financing policies can change the NAIRU, for example, a marginal employment subsidy.

7. See Calvo (1979).

8. Allowing γ to alter exogenously over time does not affect the results. Introducing fixed capital and nonzero profits does not lead to substantially different conclusions.

9. For a more elaborate treatment see Jackman, Layard, and Pissarides (1983).

10. If an establishment is very large and employs large numbers of the same type of workers, it may be worth its while declaring more vacancies than it has vacant workplaces, in order to attract more workers, even if occasionally it will have no place where an appointee can work.

11. Strictly the steady state should only be assumed after we have taken the first-order conditions. However, this complicates the analysis without affecting our qualitative conclusions.

12. If we allowed economic growth of the form that $n = N([W + T]/A)$, where A is the level of technical progress, then (9) would still hold, since, if we assume U constant, $(W + T)/A$ must be constant.

13. This model is a modified version of Minford (1983).

14. Since we are assuming zero growth, $T = 0$ in each sector. If we allowed for growth, T would only equal zero in *each* sector if we made the subsidy proportional to wages, rather than a per capita payment.

15. In this section we shall be thinking in terms of supply and demand, as this is the simplest framework within which to make the point.

16. This is based on Jackman and Layard (1980), whose aim was to derive from supply and demand analysis the Baily/Tobin (1977) proposition that changes in relative wages could favorably affect the aggregate unemployment rate.

17. Strictly $dN_i = N_i \varepsilon_i (d \log W_i + d \log[1 - t])$, but if (11) is exactly satisfied, it can be shown that budget balance requires no change in tax rates.

18. If ρ is the replacement ratio, the expressions for the natural rate corresponding to this in the text are as follows. Equation (4) stands but $X = 1/(1 - U(1 - \rho))$. The same applies to (5). In (8) $f(U,V/N)$ becomes $f(cU,V/N)$ where c is the proportion searching per period, which varies negatively with ρ. Equation (9) becomes $U = 1(/\eta[1 - \rho])$. Equation (10) is modified since S becomes $S(W_i,\rho)$ with $S_\rho < 0$.

REFERENCES

Baily, M. N., and Tobin, J. 1977. "Macroeconomic Effects of Selective Public Employment and Wage Subsidies." *Brookings Papers on Economic Activity* 2: 511-41.

Calvo, G. 1979. "Quasi-Walrasian Theories of Unemployment." *American Economic Review* 69: 102-7.

Jackman, R. A., and Layard, R. 1982. "An Inflation Tax. *Fiscal Studies* 3: 47-59.

———. 1980. "The Efficiency Case for Long-Run Labour Market Policies." *Economica* 47: 331-49.

Jackman, R. A., Layard, R., and Pissarides, C. 1983. "On Vacancies." London School of Economics, Centre for Labour Economics, Discussion Paper No. 165.

Johnson, G. E. 1980. "The Theory of Labour Market Intervention." *Economica* 47: 309-29.

Layard, R. 1982a. "Is Incomes Policy the Answer to Unemployment?" *Economica* 49: 219-39.

———. 1982b. *More Jobs, Less Inflation*. London: Grant McIntyre.

Minford, P. 1983. *Unemployment: Cause and Cure*. London: Martin Robertson.

Nickell, S., and Andrews, M. 1983. "Unions, Real Wages and Employment in Britain 1951-79." *Oxford Economic Papers* 35 (November): 183-206.

Pissarides, C. 1984. "Equilibrium Effects of Tax-Based Incomes Policies." London School of Economics, Centre for Labour Economics, Discussion Paper No. 196.

Shapiro, C., and Stiglitz, J. 1984. "Equilibrium Unemployment as a Labor Disciplining Device." *American Economic Review* 74 (June): 433-44.

Symons, J. 1985. "Relative Prices and the Demand for Labour in British Manufacturing." *Economica* 52 (February): 37-50.

Symons, J., and Layard, R. 1984. "Neo-Classical Demand for Labour Functions for Six Major Economies." *Economic Journal* 94 (December).

Wallich, H. C., and Weintraub, S. 1971. "A Tax-Based Incomes Policy." *Journal of Economic Issues* 5: 1-19.

* * *

COMMENT BY BARRY BOSWORTH

This paper shares a common feature with this morning's presentations in that, while it is very interesting to read, it is difficult to discuss because of the diverse range of subjects under discussion. In this case, the diversity comes from the different models that are used to analyze the effect of a tax incentive plan on inflation. The unique feature is that the authors analyze the effect on the equilibrium natural rate of unemployment rather than the rate of inflation per se. I cannot comment on all the models, but they are sufficiently similar that a review of the first carries over to those that follow.

The authors propose a tax on wage *changes* that is rebated to employers on a per worker basis. In the first model employers are concerned with minimizing the cost of quits. Quits are, in turn, inversely related to the unemployment rate. The imposition of the tax reduces the net saving to employers of efforts to raise wages as a means of reducing quits. Thus, employers find it profitable to tolerate a higher quit rate. Since quits are an inverse function of the unemployment rate, the latter can now be reduced.

This argument seems strange to a U.S. economist, who is used to thinking of unemployment as the product of the number of spells, of which quits are a major component, multiplied by the duration of those spells. We often argue that an increase in the quit rate would increase, rather than decrease, the overall unemployment rate. The authors' model appears to conclude the opposite. Implicitly, it must mean that the duration of unemployment is inversely related to the frequency of quits.

I have some questions about the model. First, the authors state that the results have little to do with a TIP (a tax on wage changes) because the same result would hold for a straight wage tax. Essentially that would amount to dropping $t \cdot w_{-1}$ from the equation for the present value of profits. Does this not mean that the maximization of profits in each period is independent of whatever actions the firm took in prior periods? Thus the maximization of profit would seem to be independent of the discount rate; and without a future cost to today's action, the scheme would not appear to work.

Second, the supply side of the model is unusual. The supply of new hires is completely insensitive to the wage rate, but they quit at a rate that is inversely related to overall unemployment and the wage rate. Normally, we would argue that a tax drives a wedge between the cost to the employer and the income to the worker, thus promoting inefficiency. In this model the traditional inefficiencies are ruled out by the absence of factor substitutions.

The second and third models are similar in that, again, the firm is willing to accept a higher quit rate cost in order to avoid the cost of a tax. The authors also present some interesting models of union behavior where the major point is that a tax increases the elasticity of labor demand with respect to the wage rate, reducing the wage rate and increasing employment.

The third section on labor-market distortions leads to some standard results of macroeconomic analysis: there are gains to taxing the good or service with an inelastic supply and applying or offsetting subsidy in the market with an elastic supply. Thus, overall unemployment can be reduced by subsidizing the employment of workers with high propensities to be unemployed and taxing those with low propensities. Such a scheme may have troublesome social implications.

One issue that is brought up near the end of the paper is the commonly articulated view that the unemployment rate, consistent with nonaccelerating inflation, is rising in the United States. Yet, there are good reasons to question that assumption. The period of rapid growth in the labor force is behind us. Unemployment insurance has been cut back to the point that it covered only about 40 percent of the unemployed in the last recession with an after-tax wage replacement rate of 40 to 50 percent. And an increasing proportion of the benefits will be subject to tax in future years. The major factor on the other side is the trend toward dual-income-earning families, which lessens the pressure to seek immediate reemployment. There is no evidence, however, that workers from dual-income families are becoming an increasing share of the unemployed. The unemployment rate for sole earners rose by more than the average in the last recession. It is difficult for U.S. economists to speak in detail about measures to reduce the natural rate when they cannot articulate the reasons that they believe it arose so much in the past.

* * *

COMMENT BY PAUL DAVIDSON

This is a legacy of Keynes. Let me first start by saying that I do not want to tell you what Keynes said, because he is the bible and he is never wrong. I can show you many places where Keynes made errors and was inconsistent in his own work. But what he did do was give us a different way of looking at things. Brunner talks about the Earth being round versus flat, and so on. I think the same thing was true when Galileo found out that the Earth was not the center of the universe. He had no empirical facts and in fact he fudged his data. He really did not do a good study. Given the optics of the telescope that he had, he could not possibly see what he claimed to see. But he knew that the Earth was not the center of the solar system and that meant something. We never went back to believing that the Earth was the center, even though it does not matter to the farmer in Nigeria whether the Earth is the center or not. The important thing is that we do not go back to it. Now Keynes gave us a new way of looking at the general theory of employment (that is one-third of the title of his famous book), but only one or two understand what in the world he was saying and what occurred.

I must say that I was pleasantly disarmed by the Layard-Pissarides paper because they tell us exactly when they are putting the rabbits in the hat, and then when they pull them out there is nothing surprising. They say, for example, that we believe in the natural rate of unemployment as if it really existed, and therefore we are going to show that it really existed. Then they say, and this would have made Sidney Weintraub twirl in his grave, that a "tax-based income policy has nothing to do with inflation; it is the quantity of money that is always the inflationary cause." Such an assertion is merely a consequence of assuming the axiom of reals. Money does not affect the real system; it only affects the price level. If they believe that, then why in the world tax wage income? In fact Layard and Pissarides talk about wage-inflation tax, but it is not wages that are pushing inflation in their model.

What Keynes saw very clearly was that wages are not only a cost of doing business, but also an income-generating demand curve that is shifting force. So you cannot only say what happens when the cost goes up, but also you must specify the change in demand. It is not that you are only pushing the Marshallian supply curve up, but you are also simultaneously shifting out the Marshallian demand curve. The question then becomes what the effect of money wage increase is on the level of effective demand. Bosworth, in a similar context, was asking that question. So we will look for a few moments at what Keynes was talking about.

Figure 3.5a shows expected sales proceeds versus employment. Keynes said that the z function is an aggregate supply function showing alternative hiring levels for each expected sales proceeds level. Keynes used wage units; he did not hold money wage units constant at all. He permitted wage units to vary, but he wanted to see what the effect of such variation was on the aggregate demand and supply functions. You can either measure the Z function in dollars and then you would have a wage bill line, OW (Figure 3.5a), or you could take the dollar wage unit and use it to deflate sales proceeds (Figure 3.5b). Therefore, given technology, and so on, for any given expected level of sales proceeds, there is a certain amount of employment, and we would expect that to be the upward-sloping Z curve in Figures 3.5a and 3.5b. There is nothing strange about that.

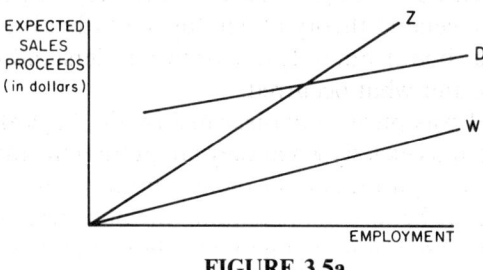

FIGURE 3.5a

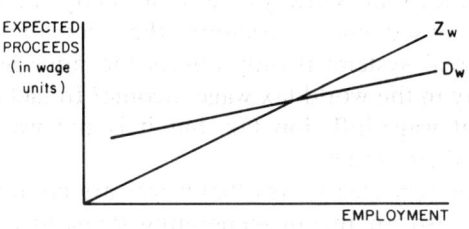

FIGURE 3.5b

Then Keynes said there was an aggregate demand curve (D), which shows expected purchases for every given employment level in Figures 3.5a and 3.5b. We can take the D function as the usual type, which shows desired purchases for levels of employment, and it might be nominal terms (as D in Figure 3.5a) or we can deflate it by the money wage to get D_w in wage terms in Figure 3.5b. Now Say's Law, according to Keynes, said that aggregate demand and aggregate supply coincide (see Figure 3.6a). Increase supply and you increase demand proportionately. Every time somebody works they get X dollars deflated by the money wage, and because work is irksome, the only reason why you work is to get goods, and therefore you spend your whole income on goods, which is what Say's Law was.

Keynes argued, on the other hand, that the aggregate demand curve was not coincidental with the aggregate supply curve (see Figure 3.6b). The unique point of effective demand could be at any employment level. In a Say's Law world (Figure 3.6a), there are an infinite number of equilibriums. In Keynes' world (Figure 3.6b) there is a unique position of equilibrium (E), and that could be at less than full employment.

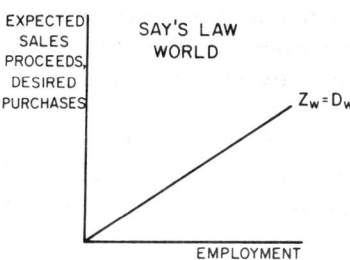

FIGURE 3.6a

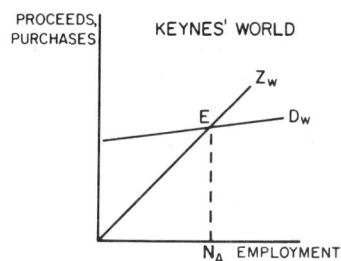

FIGURE 3.6b

There is nothing natural about the natural rate of unemployment. It is, in England, woman-made. Mother Nature is called Margaret Thatcher.

I will give you the Ronald Reagan solution to unemployment if you really believe in the natural rate. Ronald Reagan had a solution for the unemployment problem: you do not have to tax anything or balance the budget or anything of that sort.

But before I give you more on the Reagan solution, we will pursue the first topic a bit. You might think that the short side rules, and Axel in his paper mentions that coordination failures cause unemployment. What do these concepts imply? The natural rate of unemployment is just a full employment solution. The short-side rule is easiest to explain in terms of the Clower-Leijonhufvud model. Purchasing decisions are constrained by actual income rather than notional income. The economy under such a short-side rule is in neutral equilibrium. There is no obstacle to full employment except a failure of the market to signal entrepreneurs that, if they would just hire full employment output, the actual income of workers would be their notional income, and agents would buy the full employment level of output. This is a modern variant of Say's Law. Say's Law did not say that you would automatically get the full employment; it only said that supply restricted demand; increase supply and increase demand *pari passu*. Clower-Leijonhufvud's constrained demand curve would continually march up the supply curve until you got the full employment similar to Figure 3.6a.

If you believe in short-side rationing (as Malinvaud does), or some coordination failure, then you should subscribe to what I call the Ronald Reagan solution to the unemployment problem. In the spring of 1982, Reagan suggested that the unemployment problem could be ended if each business firm in the nation immediately hired one more worker. Since there are more firms than unemployed workers, this solution is obviously statistically accurate. But unless the employment by each of these firms of these additional workers created an additional demand for output at a profitable price, the entrepreneurs would not be able to do it. Now if you believe in a short-side market or a coordination failure, you should subscribe to the Ronald Reagan plan because Ronald Reagan is the coordinator. Reagan says, everybody, go out and hire a worker today, and if you do, everybody would at least momentarily be fully employed. Everybody would go out and spend their notional income. You would get full employment expenditures for output. There cannot be a shortage of aggregate demand because Ronald Reagan is coordinating what would otherwise be a market failure.

Now, when put in these blunt terms, I think even Clower-Leijonhufvud may have a problem with that solution. But that is what natural rates say: do not bother with taxing; get out there and hire people. After all, if the real cost is a lack of real production, we should get everybody out there working, and in the end all will be bought. Believing the axiom of reals, inflation cannot do any permanent harm, although in the short run, it might have some misallocative effects. If you believe Milton Friedman or Karl Brunner, in the long run the real level of output is technologically determined, and money only affects prices, but it does not affect real output!

On the other hand, Keynes would argue that there is currently a lack of effective demand and there is nothing natural about the current unemployment level. It depends strictly upon the two demand components, which he called $D1$ and $D2$, measured in either nominal or in wage units. The nice thing about measuring in wage units, rather than doing it in nominal units, is that you can hypothesize as to the effect of a change in money wages, whether it be subsidies or anything else. The Z_w curve of Figure 3.5b will not shift (by construction). Then you only have to ask yourself what the effect is of this money wage change on the aggregate demand function D_w in Figure 3.5b? Will D_w shift or will it not shift? If it will not shift, you get a unique and unchanging equilibrium despite the money wage change. That is why Keynes, through the first 17 chapters of the *General Theory*, kept measuring in wage units, because he did not want to get in an argument about what changes in the money wage would do to aggregate supply and demand!

What is Keynes' theory of effective demand? I am going to put it in the most irritating terms. I specifically do this because people are creatures of habit, and we are very lazy about thinking about anything new, and we reject things just because they are new. So let me put it in its most irritating form to force you to rethink what the theory of effective demand was about, at least as far as Keynes was concerned. Prior to full employment, the level of spending flow is *never* constrained by income. Spending is only constrained by liquidity and timidity. Say's Law in the Clower sense doesn't hold; the budget constraint is *irrelevant* if liquidity is easily available. That is why the multiplier works, as we have always been teaching in macroeconomics. How else can people spend more than they earn? How can you ever generate more than the current level of income? You are either locked in a Say's Law argument or else you have to say that I cannot spend more! What is usually called autonomous spending is a spending unrelated to earning income now. All I have to do to engage in autonomous spending is somehow get control of purchasing power money in a nominal sense.

What does that mean for supply and demand for labor? The marginal product curve (MP_L) is not the demand curve for labor in Figure 3.7. The marginal product curve is the market equilibrium curve in a

Patinkin sense. For any point of effective demand, for any equilibrium level of employment, there is a real wage associated with that output level. That real wage can be called the marginal product of labor, but it is the net of import costs in an open economy.[1]

The supply curve of labor (S_L) could be backward bending; it could be vertical; it could be upward sloping; it does not really matter. If you happen to be at point K on Figure 3.7, which is the equivalent of N_A in Figure 3.6b, where the point of effective demand is (E), entrepreneurs are just selling what they expect to sell. There is no reason for them to change their hiring decisions, yet the real wage (A) exceeds the marginal disutility of labor (C) in Figure 3.7. That is what Keynes meant by involuntary unemployment, something that cannot exist in the natural situations like Layard's. The involuntarily unemployed would be this group equal to $N_B - N_A$ in Figure 3.7. N_B workers would be willing to work at the real wage of A, and only N_A workers would get offers to work.

Involuntary unemployment has nothing to do with quits. I always worry about using the term *quits*. It implies to me that an unemployed teenager who is trying to join the labor market is told that he is not unemployed because he never quit. If you never had a job, you cannot quit. Are those people part of the labor force? Why are quits so relevant?

I think the answer that I get when I look at this in a very simplified view (maybe you will say simpleminded view) is that we fall into the paradox of manipulating demand and supply curves for labor while assuming the level of aggregate demand is unchanged. I tried very hard to figure out what was happening with all these Ws in the Layard paper. I really could not work it out in terms of a Marshallian diagram. But yet Layard talked about the elasticity of the demand curve for labor, and the question that you ask yourself is: When you have changed the money wage, in a sector, what do you do to the product demand curve? If you

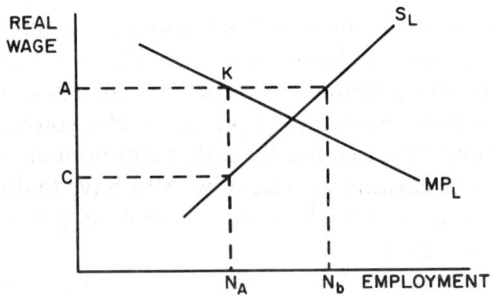

FIGURE 3.7

assume that the product demand curve is unchanged, then the labor demand elasticity depends upon two things. As Bosworth pointed out, it is the productivity of the worker in that sector, but also the marginal revenue you get from moving up and down the marginal revenue product curve on the assumption that the demand curve for the product is *unchanged*; that is, you are just moving a marginal cost curve up and down a product demand curve.

But what Keynes insisted that you had to do was the following: when you let money wages change in some aggregate sense, you not only had to observe in a Marshallian diagram what was happening to the supply curve of the product, but also you had to permit the shifting of the demand curve for the product. Keynes tended to argue that it could well mean that wage changes could raise costs if not offset by productivity changes, but simultaneously they would raise nominal demands at every price because if the wage increase were wide enough you would generate more money income, which would shift the nominal demand curve. I think Layard and Pissarides have to play that kind of game *or* they do not have an aggregate theory. All they have is a theory that asks: *Given the level of aggregate demand*, how can we shift unemployment in this industry by taxing this industry and subsidizing that one and reallocate among the different kinds of industries?

You must ask yourself, if you are a good neoclassic economist, why does anybody work since it is unpleasant. The answer, of course, if you are a good "optimizing type" of economist, is that you only work because you want to earn income. You only want to earn income, not because you like money, but because you like goods. So it concerns the marginal utility of the goods that you buy and the marginal disutility of giving up leisure. So labor, under a Lucas-type supply curve, is nothing more than a proxy for how many goods you are going to get.

There are *four* arguments in this Lucas-type labor supply function. You choose labor versus leisure in this period or labor versus leisure in a future period, and you have an intertemporal substitution problem. People who are unemployed in this period, under a Lucas supply function, voluntarily are removing themselves from the labor force because they expect to get more real income in the next period. Their expectations are rationally derived from the market signals that they get. So their real income in a permanent sense has not changed at all. It is just that they are rearranging things a little over time, and that is perfectly legitimate. That is what the natural rate of unemployment is.

That is not what Keynes would have said, because he had to break Say's Law, while Layard, like Lucas, never breaks Say's Law. If you think about labor supply and the demand for producible goods, you say: What do you mean when you say the marginal propensity to consume is less than one, from not actual income in this period, T_0, but permanent income or income over all the T periods? That would say that over the life cycle of workers, if the marginal propensity to consume is always less than one, they do not just choose between labor and leisure and real reproducible goods. If they did, then leisure would always be voluntary unemployment, and labor supply is always equal to the demand for goods. If workers are working in a neoclassical model, they must have a intertemporal marginal propensity to consume of unity. The more they work, the more they consume either in period T_0, period T_1, or period T_2 over their life. So that, when economists use that Lucas-type labor supply function, they resurrect a Say's Law world. Of course, if that is the case, then any unemployment is natural. People prefer leisure to work, and what is wrong with that? We do not force people to work if they do not want to.

What Keynes would add to this is a fifth argument to the factor supply function. The supply of goods generates a demand, but not necessarily a one-to-one demand for products produced by labor. Or as Frank Hahn put it, when savings have "resting places in nonreproducible assets," Say's Law is broken.[2]

People work not only to have goods and leisure, but also to possess an asset that is not reproducible. In Keynes' world the only assets that are not reproducible are liquid assets. Liquid assets have these very strange properties. He calls them the essential properties—essential properties of interest and money. He says that one of the essential properties of liquid assets is that it is not producible by labor in the private sector. Unemployment develops because people want the moon. If we could only convince people that the moon was made out of green cheese, we could solve the unemployment problem. Then every time people would want "the moon," assets for saving (vehicles to store their savings), or time machines as I call them, just tell them they have to use green cheese as time machines and we will create jobs in the green cheese industry.

If there are things to store savings that are not reproducible, you break Say's Law. So the supply curve of labor has to have these liquid assets, this general provision for any goods, as one of its arguments.

How did Keynes get to this anti-Say's Law solution? He discarded the gross substitution idea, that is, that you do not have intertemporal substitutability among producible goods. This breaks the axiom of reals and money matters.

NOTES

1. See Davidson (1983).
2. See Hahn (1977).

REFERENCES

Davidson, Paul. 1983. "The Marginal Product Curve Is Not the Demand Curve for Labor and Lucas's Labor Supply Function Is Not the Supply Curve for Labor in the Real World." *Journal of Post Keynesian Economics* Vol. 6 (Fall) pp. 105-117.

Hahn, Frank H. 1977. "Keynesian Economics and General Equilibrium" in *The Microeconomic Foundations of Macroeconomics*, edited by G. C. Harcourt. London: Macmillan, pp. 25-40.

* * *

COMMENT BY LARRY SEIDMAN

I just want to raise raise two different points. First, there really are two different motivations for tax-based incomes policy, and you have addressed them in different papers. In this one you are only talking about one. You are talking about what happens after you have disinflated. If you want to make the tax permanent, what would be its permanent effect? Your view is that the permanent effect is not on inflation; it is on the level of unemployment that you can run the economy at and still keep inflation constant. Certainly, many of the people involved in thinking about these policies, including yourself in some of your other papers, are interested in the other problem, which is: If you start with a higher inflation rate and want to disinflate, can a TIP reduce the unemployment and recession cost of the disinflation process, by making sure that wage and price growth move down in step with money growth? Do we have to take the kind of recession that we have taken here and Britain is taking and so forth? So whatever the outcome is of the analysis about the effect on the natural rate of unemployment, that is only one of the two possible motivations you can have for this kind of policy. For example, I still remember that Art Okun at Brookings Institution was not at all persuaded about what the impact of a tax-based incomes policy would be on the natural rate of unemployment. He was very much for it for the disinflation, transitional problem. I would like you to comment on the connection between that transitional use of TIP and the long-term permanent use.

Second, your paper focuses on positive economic aspects: Does it lower the natural rate? How about optimality? I know you have addressed optimality, and Chris Pissarides has certainly done so in some of his work. For example, in your first model, you reduced the natural rate of unemployment. There is a lower real wage equilibrium, there is a higher quit rate in equilibrium and a higher resource cost to firms due to quitting. So it certainly is not immediately obvious, despite the lower natural rate of unemployment, whether the tax is desirable because more quitting is occurring in equilibrium. There is always an additional cost in the vacancy model and so forth.

* * *

COMMENT BY JOSEPH STIGLITZ

I just want to make one remark about the sensitivity of the results to the particular specification of the models. I think the class of models is a very interesting and important class, as I will say more about at another time. Some of the particular results are sensitive to the particular parameterizations and specifications. Let me just mention two of the results that Richard obtained.

One of the results was that ad valorem wage subsidies have no effect, but specific employment subsidies have a beneficial effect. In other versions of the model, one can get the result that the ad valorem wage subsidies do have an effect. In some versions of those, the interesting thing is that an ad valorem wage subsidy may actually increase the unemployment rate rather than decrease the unemployment rate. That makes an important point: policies that from a naive point of view look like they would be good, that is, they encourage employment, actually have a deleterious effect. The reason for that is that the wage subsidy gets shifted, in the usual language that we use in tax theory. A subsidy shifting means that the wage received by the worker is increased. The object was to encourage the employer to hire labor. The net effect, however, depends on how much of the subsidy is absorbed by the workers and how much is left over for the employer. In some of these versions, in general equilibrium, you get the result that the shifting is sufficiently great that unemployment actually increases.

A second example, showing the sensitivity of the results to the specification, has to do with the example concerning the social versus private return to training. This leads to the suggestion that government-subsidized training would be desirable, because the private return is much less than the social return. In some cases the private return is actually negative. Thus one wants to be a little leery about using these models as basis for policy.

The other remark I wanted to make was the answer to the last question that was posed, which is the question of the optimality of the natural level of unemployment. There are very general theorems suggesting that the natural level of unemployment in these models is, in general, not Pareto efficient. Taxes and subsidies exist that could not always, but in general, constitute a Pareto improvement. The problem is that in one model what would be a good thing is a bad thing in another model. Unless you feel fairly confident about the model, one is left to the view that maybe government intervention should not be used. This is not due to the old Arrow Debreu theorem, which I think most of us agree is not very applicable to these kinds of worlds, but because the complexity of the world is such that we are as likely to do harm as good.

* * *

COMMENT BY DAVID COLANDER

I have three comments but will try to be brief. The first concerns terminology. In their papers a number of people use the terms *natural rate* and *non-accelerating inflation rate of unemployment* (NAIRU) interchangeably. I object to this usage, which has real problems. I think that it should be pointed out that the terms signify different concepts of equilibrium. The natural rate suggests that the economy is at a constrained optimal rate of unemployment and that a fully expected increase in aggregate demand, if prices are held constant, would create excess demand; it would not bring forth more output. It involves the traditional frictional, search and wait unemployment. The NAIRU includes that unemployment but also adds what might be called "monopolization unemployment," which results from the existence of generalized monopoly on the sellers' side of the market. NAIRU conveys the sense that the minimum sustainable rate of unemployment obtainable through monetary and fiscal expansion exceeds the quasi-competitive level. Such policies cannot reduce the NAIRU and thus must be supplemented with an incomes policy if full optimality is to be reached.

My second point deals with how to analyze the NAIRU. One way, the way used by Layard, is to look at quit rates and new hires, both of which are a function of excess demand. However, just as in linear programming where analyzing the dual offers new insights into a problem, so too there is a dual to their dynamic analysis, and it too offers new insight. In this case the dual is the speed of adjustment of wages and prices. Whereas in the quantity flow analysis, equilibrium occurs when the quit rate equals the new hires, in the dual, equilibrium in the labor market obtains when the upward pressure on the wage level equals the downward pressure. In both cases the wage level will be constant. The advantage of considering the dual is that it focuses more clearly on the particular variables affected by incentive anti-inflation plans. For example, a TIP tax will decrease the upward pressure on wage adjustments and increase the downward pressure. Put simply, it lowers the NAIRU so that excess demand relative to excess supply is required in aggregate equilibrium.

Let us examine this in greater detail. I have argued elsewhere that our economy operates with continual excess supply, if considered in a supply demand framework.[1] The key elements of the analysis are asymmetries in the monopolization process; supplier coalitions predominate over demander coalitions and push up price in the representative market. I *do not* argue that monopoly causes inflation. Rather, monopoly is itself the result of competition for monopoly and the level of monopoly in a market is determined by the marginal cost, and benefits to monopolization. Monopolization creates excess supply in the representative market (unemployment in labor markets and excess capacity in the goods market); a monopoly excess supply equilibrium exists in long-run steady state because, on the margin, the monopoly rents are being used up in the competition, to gain a monopoly. The equilibrium is stable because the marginal benefit of monopolization decreases, and the marginal cost monopolization increases with excess supply.

If one is to understand the workings of an incomes policy, one must understand how this monopolization process works. An income policy increases the cost of seller monopolization and thereby lessens the amount of steady state equilibrium monopolization, moving the economy closer to a supply/demand equilibrium. Put simply, the incomes policy replaces the excess supply in holding down prices, making the economy more efficient.[2]

The difference between the NAIRU and natural rate views can be seen in Figure 3.8, which represents a stochastic equilibrium in an economy. Possible equilibria are represented by the *EE* line. The distance between the *EE* line and the supply and demand curves represents the excess supply and demand in a market. At each equilibrium some excess supply and demand remain; as price in the market rises, excess supply increases and excess demand decreases.

The natural rate equilibrium is at price P_0 and output level Q_N, where excess demand and excess supply both equal the minimum level of frictional excess demand and supply that can exist $(Q - Q_N)$ given the market institutions.

The NAIRU view is that the natural rate equilibrium is unstable; at price P_0 it is worthwhile for suppliers to monopolize since at the price the marginal cost of monopolization is less than the benefit. Monopolization creates an upward push on the price level. As the price rises the excess supply/excess demand ratio increases. As this ratio increases, the cost of monopolization rises (it is harder to monopolize when there is more excess supply) and the marginal benefits increase. Thus at some level there is a stable equilibrium. That equilibrium I call the NAIRU.

In Figure 3.8, that equilibrium is at price P_1, where the upward pressure on the price level just equals the downward pressure. Unfilled supply, $Q_S^* - Q_E$, exceeds unfilled demand, $Q_D^* - Q_E$, and also exceeds the natural rate level of excess supply by $Q_N - Q_E$. This excess supply is the maximum amount of excess supply that one would want a TIP to remove. A tax-based incomes policy would remove that excess supply by providing a direct downward push on price, increasing the cost of monopolization and thereby moving the NAIRU closer to the natural rate.

The advantage of this approach is that it focuses more clearly on the particular variables affected by incentive anti-inflation plans. Since the plans directly affect the speed of price adjustment, it seems natural to focus the analysis on that adjustment and not on the quantity adjustment. It is much easier to see the role an incomes policy can play if one thinks of equilibrium as that price at which the upward and downward pressure on the price offset each other, and not where supply equals demand or where the flow from the stock of vacancies equals the flow from the stock of new entrants and unemployed. It adds a downward pressure on price, and therefore less excess supply is required to maintain equilibrium. A TIP tax decreases the upward pressure on wage adjustment and increases the downward pressure. Put simply, it lowers the NAIRU so that less excess demand relative to excess supply is required in aggregate equilibrium.

My final point follows from my earlier points and concerns the effectiveness of tax-based incomes policies. In the model presented by Layard, in order to be effective, TIP must affect the real wage, which he interprets as the wage relative to the price level. Such an interpretation, while likely correct if firms are in a static equilibrium, is not necessarily correct and is positively misleading for a dynamic model.

Referring again to Figure 1 and interpreting it as a composite market for all factors of production, if the NAIRU equilibrium is as shown, there will be unemployment in the labor market because of a shortage of aggregate demand. Expanding aggregate demand will not solve the problem since the monopolizing forces will translate that aggregate demand into inflation. Now assume that the composite price is held down but that the wage/price ratio is unaffected. The unemployment level in the market can still be affected by a TIP, contrary to Layard's argument, since less excess supply is needed to equilibrate the aggregate economy. Translated into dynamic terminology, we could say that the TIP affects the equilibrium level of unemployment by changing the reservation wage relative to the market wage. If there is a generalized

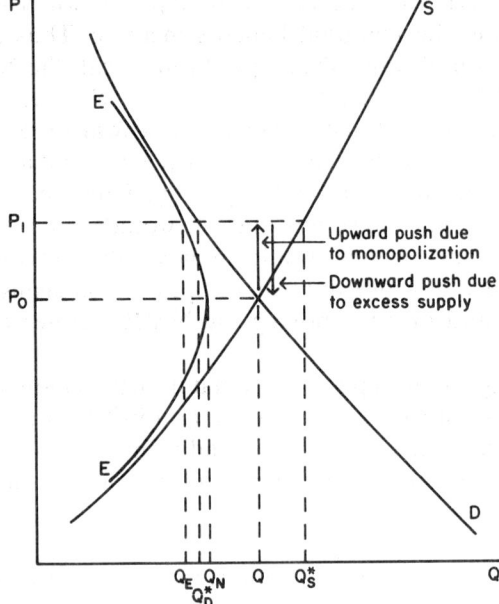

FIGURE 3.8. Labor Market Equilibrium

monopoly in both the product and labor markets, as I believe is the case, this interpretation means that a value-added TIP can be more effective than a wage TIP.

One of the advantages of conferences such as these is that the discussion among participants can help clarify points. In a recent essay, Christopher Pissarides has designed an alternative model to the one presented here.[3] In that model a value-added TIP is more effective than a wage TIP. Such a model, which relies on bargaining and generalized monopoly, is in my view far more consistent with reality than the model presented here by Layard, Pissarides, and Jackman.

NOTES

1. David Colander, "Some Simple Geometry of the Welfare Loss from Competitive Monopolies," *Public Choice* (1985); David Colander and Mancur Olson, "Coalitions and Macroeconomics," in David Colander, ed., *Neoclassical Political Economy* (New York: Ballinger, 1984).

2. For a more complete statement, see David Colander, "Why an Incomes Policy Makes an Economy More Efficient," in S. Maital and I. Lapinski, eds., *Social Conflict and*

Macroeconomics (New York: Ballinger, 1985); David Colander, *Macroeconomic Theory and Policy* (Glenview, IL: Scott Foresman, forthcoming); and David Colander, ed., *Incentive Anti-Inflation Plans* (New York: Ballinger, forthcoming).

3. Richard Pissarides, "Equilibrium Effects of Tax-Based Incomes Policy," in Colander, ed., *Incentive Anti-Inflation Plans* (New York: Ballinger, forthcoming).

* * *

REPLY BY RICHARD LAYARD

Let me take the comments in the order in which they were made. Barry Bosworth started off by saying he felt that the quit model was a funny one. I certainly agree it is a limited one, and I only concentrated on it because it is so simple that one might be able to see what the spirit of these models was. It is illustrative. It is not as ridiculous, I think, as he implied. He seemed to be saying that it was very curious to be aiming at a situation in which you had lower unemployment and higher quitting. It is a fact that quitting is higher when unemployment is lower. This is an econometric fact. They are not inconsistent with each other, because what is happening is not that the people are quitting into unemployment; rather, they are quitting to go to work with other employers. Quitting into unemployment is, particularly in the United States, not a particularly important source of unemployment. But I felt some of the remarks seemed not to have grasped the spirit of what these models are about.

Paul Davidson seemed to imply that because quitting was involved it must in some sense relate to the problem that unemployment was caused by quitting. That is not at all the case. The spirit of the model is that unemployment is concerned with wage setting. How do we find out how wages are set? We must find out what are the things that people are bothered about when they set wages. One of the things that employers are bothered about when they set wages is quitting. We might as well not have quitting in there, but something else affecting wage setting. This is very important because it is a quite different way of looking at the world from the one that most of us used to use; certainly I myself was educated to look at the world differently. It is constantly possible to slip back into the old way of looking at the world, a way that does not have a natural rate at all.

There are two models, I think, between which Paul is hovering, as if they were the only two that you could have. One is the model with no natural rate. Or, if there is a natural rate, it must be supply and demand, because he kept on coming back as if I had been talking in terms of supply and demand. However, I think there is involuntary unemployment and a natural rate. We are in dispute as to how the median-term level of unemployment is determined.

He and Frank Hahn believe that it could be anywhere and it could be given a big push and then end up somewhere else. I am saying that if you look at the series you can see that it does not just go anywhere. It has some tendency to come back to somewhere or other. That is point one. That is the main reason for believing in the natural rate. It is an observation, insofar as it is true, that it tends to come back. In Europe it does not actually look very much as though it comes back. So the other ground for believing in the natural rate is that you can estimate a Phillips curve. It appears that the natural rate in that European Phillips curve has got a hell of a drift on it. It still is a Phillips curve. As far as I can make out in Paul's way of thinking, there is nothing remotely like a Phillips curve. I may say incidently the Phillips curve works better in every other country than in the United States. Most economic relationships work better in other countries than the United States.

There is a tie-up between the Phillips curve as an adjustment process and these theories of the natural rate. The fundamental reasons for believing in the natural rate is that there is some tendency for things to come back, and insofar as they have moved off, you have the Phillips curve. To think about this we have to use models in which, basically, unemployment is in there because it affects wage setting.

Let me come back now to Barry's other main comments. Labor supply is missing. There is nothing fundamentally out of sympathy between the approach that I was adopting and the approach in which the supply is variable. Then, of course, you have to take into account the suppliers' response to a different wage level.

Is it true that labor supply is more elastic in the low wage markets? I think that is the chief foundation for the theory of manpower policy, as it has traditionally been practiced. That is a basic rationalization you could offer for the Baily-Tobin analysis of manpower policy. I think there is some evidence for this. I think empirical econometric evidence is less strong, probably, than one's priors. The kinds of empirical estimates I am thinking of are ones in which people have tried to explain unemployment duration by wages for given benefits and tested for the consistency of the elasticity over the range of wages and found no reason to reject that. That means that when unemployment is very low, the response of unemployment and therefore of employment to a wage change is very small. When unemployment is higher and wages are lower, you are getting a bigger response. This applies more in a system in which you have a flat rate unemployment benefit than one in which you have a proportional unemployment benefit. It applies also where you have a general assistance floor or something like that. You would expect the elasticity of labor supply with respect to wages to fall off as you get away from the floor.

I have made my main comments on what Paul Davidson had to say already; so I will now address the remarks of Larry Siedman. He said the nicest thing about tax-based incomes policy is that it would help you over the transition in a disinflationary period, rather than over the natural rate. What the analysis shows is that for any given value of unemployment you could have less inflationary pressure. The way it works is exactly the same during the disinflation transition as it is at the natural rate. I have noticed that there is a tendency for a big difference between U.S. and European economists as to whether they are worried about a natural rate. A lot of U.S. economists feel that we have had two oil shocks, and that pushed up inflation and the problem was getting it down. Once we got it down, we do not mind what the economy looks like. It will be alright. That is not at all the view that is held in Europe. I will provide the current forecast of the European Economic Community for 1984 and 1987. Unemployment in 1984 is 10.5 percent. The forecast in 1987 is 10.5 percent. Inflation in 1984 is 5.5 percent. The forecast for 1987 is 5.5 percent. You can see that we have got a problem that is one of the natural rate, not just of the transition.

The other point Larry raised is related to optimality. As Joe Stiglitz said, you can persuade yourself, according to which model you choose, providing it has an explicit utility foundation, that the natural rate is too high or too low. I do not think that from theory so far we have gotten a lot of help as to whether the natural rate, in the absence of any "distortions from the government side," is too high or too low. However, in fact, we of course have a massive distortion from the government side. We have gotten unemployment benefits, which in my view have raised the level of unemployment enormously. It depends on how you measure unemployment. If you go to countries where there is no social security, there is very little total unemployment. It does not exist, practically, because people would be starving, apart from the social security provided by the family. So anybody who says that in the absence of social security the natural rate would be half a percent lower is making an underestimate. It obviously has had a major effect, and I think it is a thoroughly beneficial program. I am totally in favor of it. Given that it is a distortion, it seems to me to establish a very strong prima facia for trying to reduce the natural rate, but not by removing that particular distortion.

Joe Stiglitz mentioned that you can get effects going in the opposite direction, and he quoted a model in which you could get the subsidy actually increasing unemployment. I think he had in mind there a model where you subsidize employment in the high wage market. These results are fairly sensitive to the setup of the model.

David Colander raised the question of a TIP applied to capital income as well as labor income, which is a MAP. Those of you who have gone into this will know how extraordinarily complicated this is. There are two arguments in favor of it: one, that it looks nondistortionary and, two, that it looks evenhanded. The arguments against it are absolutely overwhelming. We are not going to get any of these policies unless we keep the issue incredibly simple. A wage increase tax also has to be very crude. In my view it has to be simply based on average hourly earnings regardless of skill or anything like it. I think economists have got to be prepared to compromise in order to get things through.

4

Theories of Wage Rigidity

Joseph E. Stiglitz

It is widely recognized that the assumption that wages are rigid is central to Keynes' explanation of the persistence of unemployment.[1] Indeed, in the fixed price (temporary equilibrium) models, which are currently so much in fashion in Europe, it is the rigidity of wages and prices that provided the sole explanation for unemployment in the economy.[2]

These theories have, however, simply assumed that wages and prices are rigid; they have not attempted to explain the rigidity. This has left these models open to charges of adhocery and inconsistency: why should firms that are assumed to act in such a rational, profit-maximizing, competitive manner with respect to production and employment decisions not act in a similarly rational, profit-maximizing, competitive manner when it comes to decisions concerning wage and price determination? Worse still, the models may not provide an adequate basis for policy analysis: even if wages and prices are fixed in the very short run, might they not be affected by policies, such as the level of unemployment compensation?

This chapter addresses two sets of theories that attempt to explain the observed rigidities in wages.[3] The first set, which I shall refer to

---

The original version of this chapter was presented at the Conference on Macroeconomics at the University of Delaware, January 12–13, 1984. Financial support from the National Science Foundation is gratefully acknowledged. This chapter was completed while I was a Visiting Fellow at the Hoover Institution, Stanford. I am indebted to R. Arnott, C. Azariadis, G. Akerlof, J. Butkiewicz, Russell Cooper, O. Hart, S. Grossman, B. Greenwald, A. Hosios, John Pencavel, A. Weiss, J. Yellen, and D. Newbery for helpful discussions.

generically as *implicit contract theories*, explains wage rigidity as a consequence of implicit insurance provided to risk-averse employees by their employers. The second I shall refer to generically as *efficiency wage theories*; this set holds that workers' productivity depends on the wage that they are paid; firms may not lower wages, even in the presence of unemployment, because to do so would lower the productivity of their labor force. The basic thesis of the chapter is that the former set of theories does not provide a convincing explanation of the kind of wage rigidity that is associated with cyclical unemployment, while the latter theories do.[4]

This discussion is not intended to be a survey of what has developed into large literatures, but rather to provide a critical assessment of the central issues associated with each of the theories.

WHAT NEEDS TO BE EXPLAINED

A theory of unemployment must explain not only the level of unemployment, but its form and composition. For instance, workers may be put on short weeks as well as get laid off. If individuals have quasi-concave indifference curves, they prefer work sharing to having some probability of working a full week, and some probability of not working at all.

There are two easy explanations of the prevalence of layoffs in the United States (in Europe, work sharing seems to be more common). The first concerns unemployment compensation: an individual who is on half-time cannot collect the public subsidy associated with unemployment compensation. There are two basic objections to this "explanation." First, given the limitation on the number of weeks that individuals can collect unemployment compensation (and the fact that there is only a one-week waiting period for collecting it), firms should rotate individuals who are laid off. The argument for job rotation is even more compelling if the marginal utility of leisure diminishes significantly, the longer the individual is unemployed.[5] Moreover, the phenomenon of unemployment predated the extensive provision of unemployment insurance factors.

Another explanation for layoffs is that technologies require individuals to work eight hours a day, but this can similarly be dismissed: in most production jobs, the economies of time-scale seldom extend beyond the day and certainly not beyond the week or month.

It is not, however, enough to explain why firms might lay off individuals: one must explain why other firms do not rehire them. Unemployment arises when layoffs exceed hires. Most of the implicit contract theories have called themselves theories of unemployment simply by *assuming* that there is no labor mobility; in that case, obviously, any worker who is laid off is unemployed. But even in the midst of the Great Depression, there was a high job accession rate, but not high enough to compensate for the even higher layoff rate. Unemployment cannot be explained on the basis of the behavior of a single firm, but only by the analysis of the market as a whole. Any implicit contract theory that purports to explain unemployment must, therefore, be a part of a theory of the market.

Finally, any theory should be able to explain not only why certain shocks give rise to unemployment (an increase in layoffs relative to hires), but also why the unemployment should be concentrated within certain parts of the labor force.

Furthermore, any theory that we construct should be consistent with certain other characteristics of economic fluctuations: among these are (1) those who are unemployed often look very much like those who are employed; individuals with similar qualifications seem to be treated very differently; and (2) those who are unemployed are, for the most part, unhappier than those who remain employed. For the most part, individuals prefer not to be laid off. (However, as we note below, there are a few instances where this is not true.)

Of course, even if we were able to explain why there are layoffs, and why those laid off are not rehired, we would not have a complete explanation of economic fluctuations. We would still need to explain what the sources of the disturbances to the economy are. Our task here is the more limited one of explaining why certain shocks might lead to unemployment, why the adjustment mechanisms, which in traditional competitive analysis lead the economy to full employment,[6] seem to fail so frequently.

IMPLICIT CONTRACT THEORIES OF WAGE RIGIDITY

The Basic Theory

The basic hypothesis of implicit contract theory[7] is that workers are risk averse and have limited access to capital markets. They would like to obtain insurance against fluctuations in their income but cannot obtain such insurance from conventional insurance companies.[8] Their employers, however, are less risk averse and have greater access to the capital market. As a result, employers provide some form of wage and employment insurance as part of the employment package. To put it another way, a firm that offered such insurance as part of its employment package would be able to attract workers at a lower (average) wage than a firm that did not provide such insurance.

Simple Implicit Contract Theory May Explain Wage Rigidities but Not Unemployment

If all states of nature are observable (and verifiable), then the implicit contract would specify the amount of labor and the wage to be paid in each state. In such circumstances, though there may be relatively little fluctuations in wage (incomes), the implicit contract would not give rise to unemployment: the marginal rate of substitution of each individual between income and leisure would be equal to the marginal rate of transformation, and there would be no layoffs.[9] Recall that our original objective was to find an explanation of wage rigidity that could help explain unemployment; the implicit contract theory may provide us with some insights into the movement of wages but (at least in the simple version) does not explain movements in employment.[10]

This can be seen most easily if we think of the firm as having two departments, an insurance department and a production department. The production department pays workers the ordinary "Walrasian" (spot) wages, which may fluctuate considerably. Workers then take this wage to the insurance department; the insurance department agrees to supplement their income in bad states, in return for a premium (payable only in good states.) This results in the workers' take-home pay (their wage plus or minus payments to the insurance company) varying much less than their Walrasian wage. What we observe, of course, is the take-home pay; but what enters into the analysis of the production decision is the Walrasian (shadow or spot) wage, and since the Walrasian wage is perfectly flexible, there is no unemployment.

(If the marginal rate of substitution were less than the marginal rate of transformation in some states of nature, so that the amount individuals required to be compensated for an increase in work by an hour was less than the value of the extra amount of output they produced, then it would pay the firm to ask employees to work the additional hour and increase their pay accordingly. If the individuals are risk averse, and the utility function is separable in consumption and leisure, they will increase their take-home pay equally in all states.[11] More generally, assuming that the firm is risk neutral, the increase in pay will be spread among states to equate the workers' marginal utility of income.

The result that implicit contracts do not give rise to unemployment fluctuations[12] should not come as a surprise. It has long been recognized that insurance contracts (recall that implicit contracts are really nothing more than insurance contracts provided by the employer) improve the functioning of competitive economies.

Indeed, one of the basic results of Arrow and Debreu was to show that a competitive economy would be pareto efficient if there were a *complete* set of risk markets. Subsequently, Borch showed that the absence of insurance markets may make all individuals worse off.[13]

Market Equilibrium Is Not Constrained Pareto Efficient

More relevant for our purpose is the question of the consequences of providing employment-related insurance in economies in which there is not a complete set of insurance contracts. As we have argued, under the conditions given above, such implicit contracts will be associated with full employment (in which the marginal rate of substitution of each individual is equal to the marginal rate of transformation); they are "locally" efficient, in the sense that, given the distribution of prices, employers' expected profits (or expected utility of profits) are maximized, subject to the constraint that workers obtain a particular level of expected utility. But the economy is not a constrained pareto optimum; that is, given the limited set of insurance markets, there are feasible interventions on the part of government (say, taxes and subsidies on employment or output) that will make some individuals better off without making others worse off (Newbery and Stiglitz 1984).

Our interest here, however, is more in the descriptive implication of implicit contracts than in its welfare consequences. But again, we would have thought that, particularly if individuals have limited access to the capital market and their consumption is constrained by this, that the provision of employment-related insurance would have smoothed out variations in consumption and hence would serve to dampen, rather than to exacerbate, the cyclical fluctuations of the economy.

There have been several attempts to modify and extend implicit contract theory to derive conditions under which such contracts might give rise to unemployment.

Unemployment Compensation and Voluntary Unemployment

The first, and most obvious, of these attempts is a consequence of our system of unemployment compensation: given that this is provided not on an actuarially sound basis, it pays firms to devise employment strategies to take advantage of the public subsidies. In the limiting case where the payments of the firm are not related at all to the experience of its employees, the firm would lay off workers in all states in which worker's productivity is sufficiently low. The precise condition depends on whether firms supplement the unemployment compensation of individuals. Then the laid off workers are, in a sense, all voluntarily unemployed provided that leisure is normal: the level of utility that they get from leisure together with the unemployment compensation exceeds the level of utility they would have obtained if they worked (see Appendix A). Most, or at least many, of those who are classified as unemployed do not fall within this category. The problems of unemployment with which we are concerned here antedated the spread of unemployment compensation and welfare systems with more than subsistence level of payments.

Further evidence that there is more at issue is provided by the fact that the pattern of unemployment does not conform to that which would arise if layoffs were simply a result of firms attempting to take advantage of unemployment compensation. In particular, one would expect to see more extensive use of job rotation, ensuring that no individuals exhaust their unemployment benefits.

The Theory of Insurance and Implicit Contracts

A more fundamental approach is to ask what the generic problems associated with insurance contracts are, and implicit insurance contracts in particular, and if any of these problems manifest themselves as what might look like involuntary unemployment.

There are at least six problems that are relevant for our analysis:

1. The observability problem. The insurance contract can only cover events that are observable to the insurance company.
2. The verifiability problem. Even if the event can be observed, to enforce a contract through legal means requires that a third, outside party must be able to verify its existence.[14] This is an example of a wider class of problems that we refer to generically as:
3. The enforcement problem. Whenever the "trade" between two individuals does take place simultaneously, there must be some method of ensuring that the party that has agreed to make the later delivery lives up to its promise. This problem may be particularly acute, as we shall see, with implicit contracts.
4. The complexity problem. Any insurance contract usually covers not a single event (state of nature) but a range of events. Thus writing contracts so that each contingency that should be distinguished from other contingencies is so distinguished is a difficult if not impossible task. Usually, several different contingencies are covered by the same set of clauses, though in the absence of "transactions costs" each would be treated differently.
5. The moral hazard problem. The provision of insurance often affects the likelihood that the event that has been insured against

occurs. To avoid the resulting inefficiencies (individuals failing to take due care against the occurrence of the accident), insurance firms frequently insist on co-insurance clauses.

6. The adverse selection problem. When a group of individuals is offered a given insurance policy, those among the group with the highest (subjective) probability of the occurrence of the accident are most likely to purchase the policy. The insurance firm may attempt to design contracts that separate low-risk individuals from high-risk individuals, for example, by offereing policies with high deductibilities, limited coverage, and so on.

Each of these problems has its manifestation in the provision of employment-related insurance (implicit contracts.) Surprisingly, it is only the first of these problems which has received much attention in the literature; and it does not, in my view, provide a convincing explanation of unemployment.

The Observability Problem

The contracts we described above had hours and wages (income) depending on the state of nature, which we assumed was observable to both the firm and the workers. What happens if the state of nature is observable to the firm, but not to the workers? The firm will not, in general, have the incentive to tell the truth. Consider the case discussed earlier, where individuals have utility functions that are separable in consumption and leisure. The optimal contract entailed equating consumption in all states, but varying hours, with the individual working more hours in the good state than in the bad. Clearly, the firm has an incentive to announce that it is the good state, regardless of what the true state is: what it pays the workers is the same, but the amount of work it extracts from them is greater in the good state.

It is easy, however, to design a contract that induces the firm to tell the truth. We restrict the choices of the firm: if it announces that it is a good state, we compel it to make the workers work more than they would in the Walrasian perfect information equilibrium and to pay their workers more. The extra output produced by a firm in the good state is much larger than that produced by one in the bad. For firms in the good state, the extra output is enough to compensate for the increased wages that they pay. For firms in the bad state, the extra output is not enough to compensate for the increased wages they would have to pay if they falsely announced it was a good state. Such a contract introduces two inefficiencies relative to the first best contract (with perfect information.) Workers have to bear risks, and in the good state there is overemployment.

Assume, in contrast, that firms are very risk averse while individuals are risk neutral. Then the optimal contract would entail workers providing insurance to the firm; in the bad state, they would accept a wage below their marginal product, while in the good state, they would be paid more than their marginal product. In that case, firms might have an incentive to announce that it is a bad state, to get workers to accept a low wage, when in fact it is a good state. Again, firms can be induced to tell the truth by restricting their choices. Now we curtail the amount of employment that they can undertake in the bad state, relative to the Walrasian equilibrium. The "cost" of this reduction is greater in the good state than in the bad. Indeed, if we sufficiently curtail the maximum level of employment that we allow, the loss in profits in the good state exceeds the gains that it obtains from having lower wages, and thus it will pay the firm to tell the truth.

Thus, the "theory" may explain either under-or overemployment. Which phenomenon occurs depends on the specific assumptions concerning the utility functions of workers and risk aversion of firms. The assumptions under which overemployment occurs seem more plausible to me than those under which underemployment occurs, but we do not have to resolve the matter here. The theory can be dismissed on other grounds, as we shall see later.

First, however, we turn to a more detailed analysis of the conditions under which over- or underemployment results. Which occurs depends whether, in the first best equilibrium with complete observability, the firm would, in the good state, prefer the hours and wage associated with the low state, or vice versa. To ascertain which occurs, we need to examine in greater detail the structure of implicit contracts.[15]

The Structure of Implicit Contracts

To examine the structure of implicit contracts, we assume that there are only two states, each occurring with a probability of 0.5. We shall denote the good and bad states by superscripts and subscripts 1 and 2 respectively. We represent the individuals utility function by $U = U(y,h)$ where y is income and h is hours worked. The worker's productivity in state i is denoted by θ_i; so firm profits per worker, ρ^i, are:

$$\rho^i(h_i, y_i) = \theta_i h_i - y_i. \tag{1}$$

We begin our analysis by assuming that firms are risk neutral and that individuals have a reservation expected utility level of U.

Formally, we can characterize the implicit contract with complete observability as the solution to the following problem:

$$\max \rho^1 + \rho^2 \tag{2}$$

$$\text{subject to } U^1 + U^2 = 2U \tag{2'}$$

the solution to which satisfies the first-order conditions:

$$\theta_1 U_y^1 + U_h^1 = \theta_2 U_y^2 + U_h^2 = 0 \tag{3}$$

$$U_y^1 = U_y^2 \tag{4}$$

The first two conditions simply state that the marginal rate of substitution equals the marginal rate of transformation (the full employment condition), while equation (4) is the provision of complete insurance (in the sense that the marginal utility of income of the worker is equated in the two states). This follows from the risk neutrality of the producer; it would not be true, as we shall see, if the producer is risk averse.

We have represented the equilibrium in Figure 4.1a, in which ρ^1 represents a constant profit line in state 1 (that is, $\theta h - y$ = constant) and ρ^2 in state 2. As we have drawn it, the firm makes a positive profit in state 1, but a loss in state 2. For any given level of profits, the hours-income package is efficient; that is, $E_1 = (h_1, y_1)$ is the point where the worker's indifference curve is tangent to the iso-profit line, and similarly for E_2. (Equation 3 is the mathematical representation of this tangency condition.) (We have not yet explained how the levels of profits or losses in each state are determined. These are given by the solutions to (2'), (3), and (4). The diagram is useful only in portraying certain conditions that the implicit contract must satisfy.)

There are three possible patterns that can emerge. Figure 4.1a illustrates the case where profits in state 1 are higher with E_1 than E_2, that is

$$\rho^1(h_1, y_1) > \rho^1(h_2, y_2) \tag{5}$$

and profits in state 2 are higher with E_2 than E_1, that is

$$\rho^2(h_2, y_2) > \rho^2(h_1, y_1). \tag{6}$$

Equations (5) and (6) are referred to as the *self-selection constraints*, and in Figure 4.1a both are satisfied.

On the other hand, in Figure 4.1b, in the good state the firm would prefer E_2 to E_1, while in Figure 4.1c, in the bad state the firm would prefer

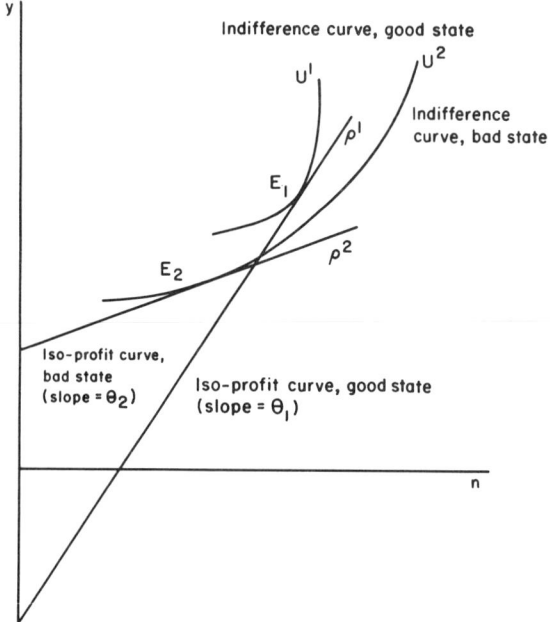

FIGURE 4.1a Self-selection constraints are satisfied in first best equilibrium.

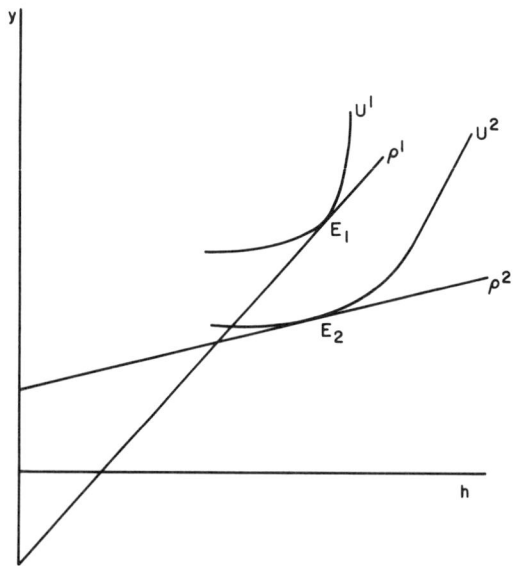

FIGURE 4.1b Self-selection constraints are not satisfied in first best equilibrium. In the good state, the firm would prefer E_2 to E_1.

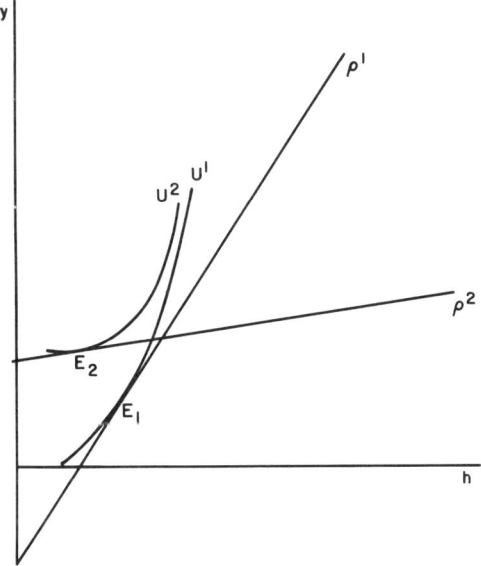

FIGURE 4.1c Self-selection constraints are not satisfied in first best equilibrium. In the bad state, the firm would prefer E_1 to E_2. Note that individuals are better off in a bad state.

E_1 to E_2. In these cases, if the state of nature is not observable, firms cannot be relied upon to tell the truth. The contract must be modified to recognize this.

The Implicit Contract with Unobservability

The implicit contract with unobservability is the solution to the following problem:

$$\max \rho^1 + \rho^2 \qquad (7)$$

subject to $U^1 + U^2 = \bar{U}$, utility constraint and subject to (8)

$$\left. \begin{array}{l} \rho^1(h_1, y_1) > \rho^1(h_2, y_2) \\ \rho^2(h_2, y_2) > \rho^2(h_1, y_1). \end{array} \right\} \text{self-selection constraints.} \qquad \begin{array}{r} (9) \\ (10) \end{array}$$

This problem is identical to the previous one, except that we have appended the self-selection constraints. Under fairly standard conditions, one, and only one, of these constraints is binding. Which one is binding depends on whether, in the absence of the constraint, firms would have lied, claiming it was a bad state when it was good, or a good state when it is bad. Before turning to this, let us note diagrammatically what the self-selection constraints imply. When in the absence of the self-selection constraint, the firm would have said it was bad when it was good, then the firm can be induced to tell the truth by limiting the amount of labor that he can hire in the bad state. Thus, in Figure 4.2a, the contract $\{E_1, E_2'\}$ satisfies the self-selection constraint but entails underemployment in the bad state. (In the good state, the firm is just indifferent between E_1 and E_2'.) Similarly, in Figure 4.2b, we show the equilibrium when the firm would have announced that it was a good state when it was bad. As we argued earlier, truth telling is induced by requiring the firm to hire additional hours; the contract (E_1', E_2) induces truth telling. Note that this contract entails overemployment: the marginal rate of transformation is less than the marginal rate of substitution.

Over- versus Underemployment

We now ask which we expect to occur: over- or underemployment? To help fix our ideas, consider first the case where utility functions are separable in hours and income:

$$U = u(y) - v(h) \tag{11}$$

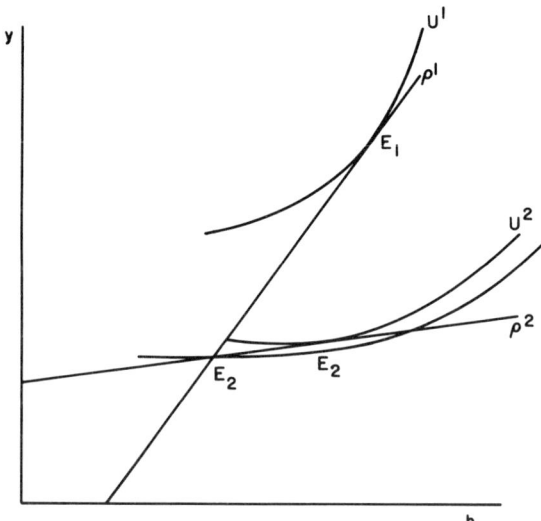

FIGURE 4.2a Contracts E_2 and E_1 satisfy the self-selection constraints, but there is underemployment in the bad state (to force truth telling, employment is restricted in bad state).

THEORIES OF WAGE RIGIDITY / 165

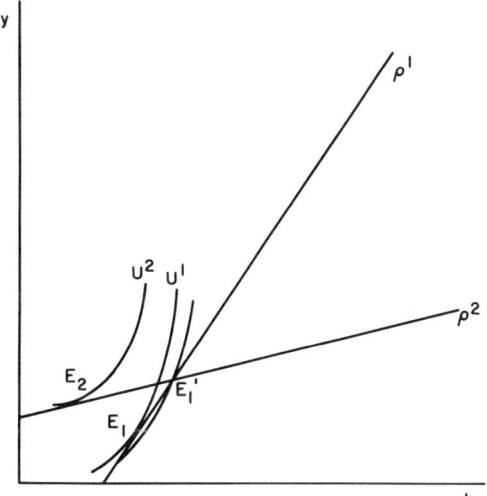

FIGURE 4.2b Contracts E_2 and E_1 satisfy the self-selection constraint, but there is overemployment in the good state (to force truth telling, employment is expanded in good state).

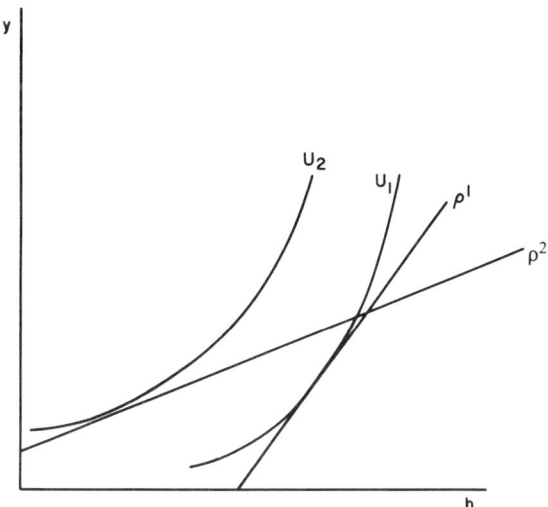

FIGURE 4.3 If $U_{yh} = 0$, there will always be overemployment.

Thus, equality of marginal utility implies that $y_1 = y_2$; this, together with (3), implies that $h_1 > h_2$, and firms always want to declare that it is a good state (to educe more effort). The equilibrium is always characterized by overemployment (see Figure 4.3).

The result holds, a fortiori, if $U_{hy} < 0$: since increasing the number of hours worked decreases the marginal utility of income, individuals in the good state receive less than in the bad state. Thus a necessary condition for implicit contracts with asymmetric information to give rise to unemployment equilibria is that leisure and consumption goods are strong Edgeworth substitutes.

In Appendix B we establish a somewhat stronger and more general result:[16] if firms are risk neutral and the two states of nature are near each other, then there is under- or overemployment as leisure is an inferior or normal good. A sufficient condition for there to be overemployment or full employment is that leisure is a normal good. (Thus a necessary condition for underemployment is that leisure is inferior.)

On the other hand, the overemployment equilibria have the unattractive feature that individuals are always better off in the bad state than in the good state (see Figure 4.1c).[17]

Risk-Averse Firms

We argued in the preceding section that, with risk-neutral firms, there is a strong presumption that implicit contracts either entail full employment or overemployment, but not underemployment. One attempt to obtain underemployment from the implicit contract theory entails assuming risk-averse firms.

Consider the limiting case where firms are infinitely risk averse and individuals have a finite degree of risk aversion. Then, in equilibrium their profits in the two states must be the same, as depicted in Figure 4.4. It is immediately obvious that with infinitely risk averse firms, equilibrium will always be characterized by unemployment.

In Appendix B we show that there is still a presumption that there will be overemployment rather than underemployment. We show that a necessary condition for underemployment to result is that the firm's degree of risk aversion be large. In the case of separable utility functions, the critical value increases with the workers' risk aversion and decreases with the workers' elasticity of marginal disutility of labor.

Curiously enough, while implicit contract theory began as an explanation of wage rigidity in which risk-neutral firms provide insurance for risk-averse workers, in this new version, underemployment only results when firms are very risk averse.

Though the hypothesis of risk-averse firms seems inconsistent with a

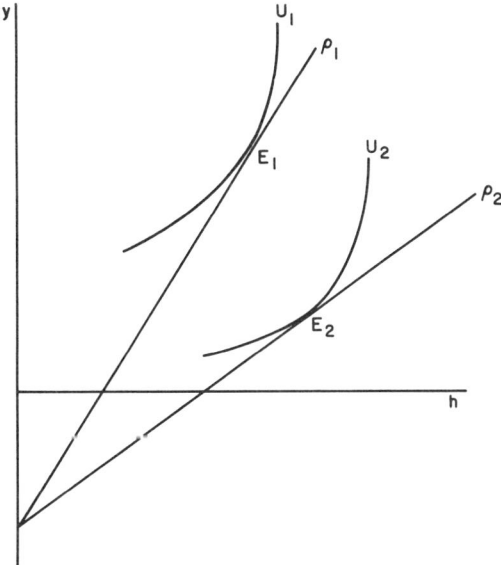

FIGURE 4.4 With infinitely risk-averse firms (and finitely risk-averse individuals) in the good state, the firm always prefers E_2 to E_1.

well-functioning capital market, in the new theory of the firm, in which shareholders are imperfectly informed concerning the actions of the managers, firms do behave in a risk-averse manner. The question is whether they behave in a sufficiently risk-averse manner.

Some Special Examples

This section presents some simple utility functions, for which the first best equilibrium can be easily calculated. For these utility functions, it can easily be ascertained whether there will be under- or overemployment.

I. *Separable utility functions*
We have already noted that if the utility function is of the form

$$U = u(y) - v(h)$$

then, if firms are risk neutral, there will always be overemployment. If firms are risk averse, the condition for underemployment (if the two states are near each other) is:

$$A\alpha v > (1 - \alpha) R$$

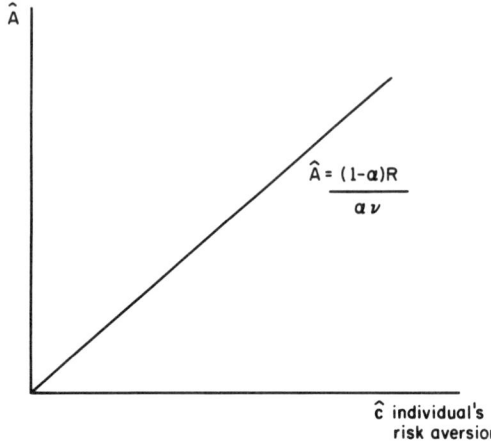

FIGURE 4.5 Critical value of firm relative risk aversion (Â), below which the only equilibria entail overemployment or full employment. Increasing workers' elasticity of marginal disutility of labor and reducing the workers' degree of risk aversion make underemployment equilibria more likely.

where the critical value (see Figure 4.5) is determined by

$A = A(\theta h - y)$, the firm's measure of relative risk aversion

$R = -U_{yy}y/U_y$, the individual's measure of relative risk aversion

$\upsilon = U_{hh}h/U_h$, the elasticity of marginal disutility of labor

α = share of labor.

Since h_1 increases with θ_1, if the two states are far enough apart, we will obtain overemployment or full employment (see Appendix B).

II. *Infinite elasticity of substitution between leisure and consumption*
In this case, the utility function is of the form

$$U = u(y - ah), \; h \leqslant 1, \; \theta_2 < a < \theta_1, \qquad (12)$$

and income and leisure are perfect substitutes. This peculiar utility function gives rise to corner solutions, where individuals either do no work or work to capacity. With this utility function, the self-selection constraints are *never* binding if firms are risk neutral, as illustrated in Figure 4.6a. (Note that equating the marginal utility of income means that

$$y_1 - ah_1 = y_2 - ah_2,$$

THEORIES OF WAGE RIGIDITY / 169

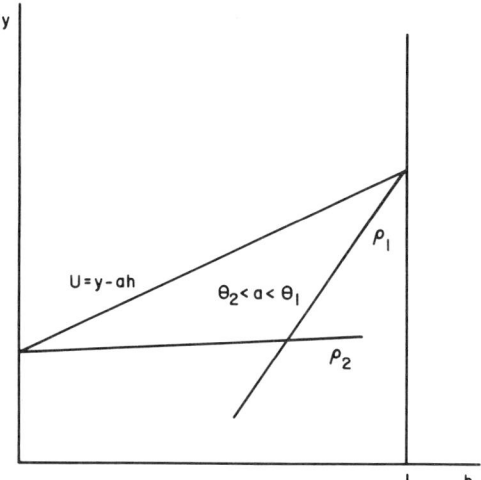

FIGURE 4.6a If leisure and consumption are perfect substitutes and firms are risk neutral, self-selection constraints are always satisfied in first best equilibrium.

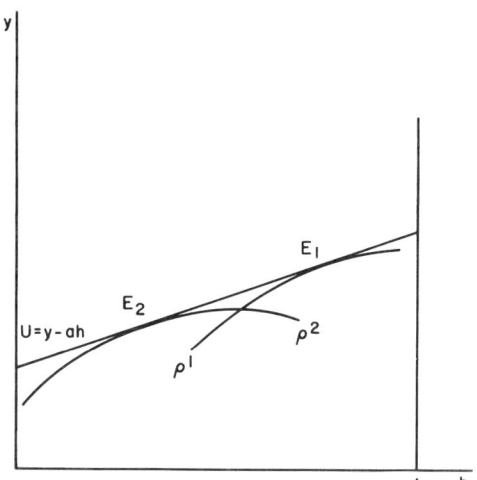

FIGURE 4.6b The self-selection constraints are not binding, even with a nonlinear technology.

the individual's utility in the two states is equalized.) This result does not depend on assuming a linear technology, as Figure 4.6b illustrates.[18] The unconstrained implicit contract is described by the tangencies of the iso-profit curves to the worker's indifference curve. The iso-profit curve for the good state is assumed to be always steeper than the corresponding iso-profit curve through the same point for the bad state. (Because of diminishing returns, the extra income that the firm can pay to a worker who works more diminishes the more the individual works). It is clear that the self-selection constraints are always satisified if $h_1 > h_2$.

When firms are risk averse, the marginal utility of income of workers in the two states will not be equalized. The implications of this can be seen in Figure 4.6c for the utility function (12). Assume first that the firm has a linear technology. Then again, it is easy to show (Figure 4.6c) that the self-selection constraint is always satisfied.

If, however, we assume diminishing returns *and* risk-averse firms, then, as Figure 4.6d illustrates, it is possible that, in the good state, a firm will announce that it is in fact the bad (E_2 lies on a higher iso-profit function for state 1 than does E_1; E_2 entails fewer hours and less income than does E_1, but the decline in pay is greater than the loss in output).

III. A slight generalization

If the individual has a utility function of the form

$$U = U(y - v\,[h]),$$

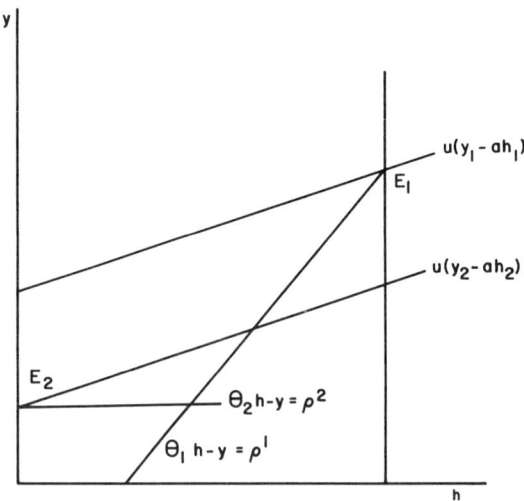

FIGURE 4.6c Self-selection constraints are still satisfied if firms are risk averse.

THEORIES OF WAGE RIGIDITY / 171

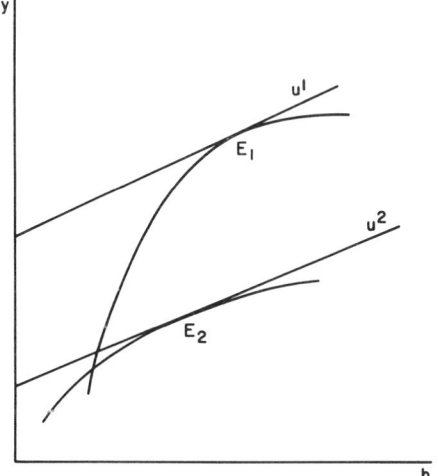

FIGURE 4.6d If firms are risk averse and there are diminishing returns (to the number of hours worked by each worker), then there *may* exist an underemployment equilibrium.

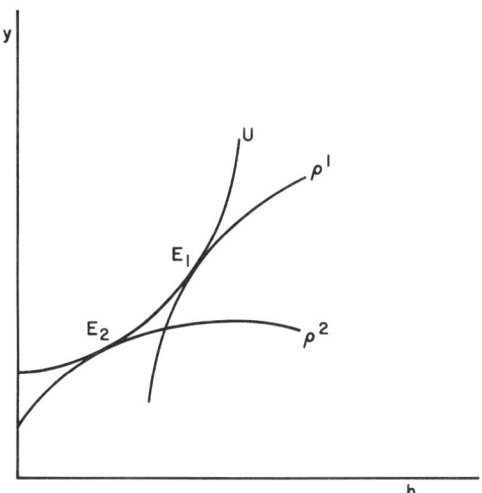

FIGURE 4.6e If individuals have utility functions of the form $U = U(y - v[h])$ and firms are risk neutral, then the first best equilibrium always satisfies the self-selection constraints.

the indifference curves between income and leisure are no longer straight lines; however, the results obtained in the previous section still hold. This utility function has the property that leisure is neither normal nor inferior. In the first best equilibrium, with risk-neutral firms,

$$U'_1 = U'_2$$

(where $U'_i = U^{i'}(y_i - v[h_i])$)

so the individual is on the same indifference curve in both states. Hence, so long as the iso-profit curves satisfy the single crossing property, the self-selection constraints are satisfied in the first best equilibrium (see Figure 4.6e).

IV. *Risk-neutral individuals*

If individuals are risk neutral, then the objective of a long-term contract is not to provide insurance to the worker. (Nor is it plausible to think of the function of the insurance contract as a mechanism for insuring the firm.) For a variety of reasons, long-term contracts may save on transactions costs. Though the reasons that workers and employers engage in long-term contracts may have little to do with the provision of insurance, attitudes toward risk play an important role in the design of efficient contracts, in the presence of asymmetric information.

With risk-neutral individuals and firms, contracts that satisfy the self-selection constraint are easy to construct. All we require is that

$$\theta_1(h_1 - h_2) > y_1 - y_2 > \theta_2(h_1 - h_2).$$

Clearly, if the difference in productivity in the two states is low, differences in income will be low. Note that in the case where hours worked in the bad state exceed that in the good state, income paid in the bad state must exceed that in the good state.

With risk-neutral individuals, there is either full employment or underemployment.[19] Identical results obtain if there is a third party providing insurance to the firm and workers are risk neutral.[20]

The hypothesis of low, effective risk aversion on the part of workers is not as implausible as it might seem at first glance. Our analysis has assumed that workers' consumption is equal to their wage payment; that they cannot save or borrow (or do not receive implicit or explicit unemployment compensation). In fact, most fluctuations are sufficiently small so that it is easy for individuals to tide themselves over without any significant reduction in their consumption. (There is some recent econometric evidence suggesting that there is very limited variability in consumption, as opposed to the purchase of consumer durables.) If that is correct, then the model we have just presented seems more appropriate than one in which the worker is risk averse. As we emphasized here, workers are not entering long-term contracts to have firms provide insurance, but to save on transactions costs. If firms are also risk neutral, the efficient contract gives rise neither to unemployment or overemployment.

If the motivation of long-term contracts is to save on transaction costs, then simple contracts have a great advantage over complex contracts; the simplest contract is one that prespecifies wages and hours.[21] The welfare loss (relative to the Walrasian equilibrium) can be shown to be of the order of magnitude $(\theta_1 - \theta_2)^3$.

The welfare loss relative to the self-selection equilibrium is clearly smaller, and hence, provided the fluctuations in productivity are not too large, it is plausible that a rigid wage-employment contract dominates the self-selection contract.

Though in the absence of enforcement problems (as we have assumed thus far) such fixed wage-employment contracts cannot explain unemployment, once we introduce enforcement problems, they may easily give rise to unemployment.[22]

Interpretation

The conditions that we have derived show, at the very least, that the asymmetric information theory of implicit contracts does not provide a robust explanation of unemployment: whether underemployment exists is sensitive to special assumptions concerning the nature of the utility function and the degree of risk aversion of firms.

The theory has several implications: first, it is reasonable to assume that different individuals and firms differ in their utility functions and attitudes toward risk. Thus, if the theory provided *the* explanation of unemployment, one should expect to find different firms attracting different classes of workers. Risk-neutral firms that experienced limited risk would always be characterized as having overemployment in good states and full employment in bad; risk-neutral firms that had underemployment equilibria would have workers with special attitudes toward risk. Firms whose behavior (in other respects) seemed to indicate high degrees of risk aversion should experience underemployment in bad states.

Notice too that when there is a dispute about how bad circumstances are, unions try to persuade the firm to hire more workers at the given wage. Unions do not say to management, "we will be willing to accept a further wage cut if you prove that the state of nature is so bad, by throwing more of us out of work," but rather, "we will be willing to accept a further wage cut if you reduce your planned level of layoffs." If these statements are to be taken at anything like their face value, they suggest that what is at issue is not a question of inducing truthful revelation of the state of nature.

Notice that the theory of asymmetric information implicit contracts has reversed the original theory of implicit contracts. While the original theory was based on risk-averse workers and risk-neutral firms, an essential part of the new theory is that firms are risk averse. While the original theory was used to explain wage rigidities (and was successful in this, but not in explaining unemployment), the new theory entails *greater* fluctuations in employee's income than in the Walrasian equilibrium.

Though these observations lead me to the view that this extension (or reversal) of implicit contract theory does not provide an adequate basis for understanding macroeconomic fluctuations, there are other, perhaps less contentious, grounds on which to object to this version of the implicit contract theory as an explanation of unemployment.

Further Objections to the Asymmetric Information Implicit Contract Theory

There are several further objections to the theory. The first concerns what is observable. The theory assumes both too much and too little. The theory assumes that the firm's hours and wage decisions are observable to the worker, while the state of nature (or other surrogates for the state of nature) is not. Though there is some presumption that workers know the amount of their own work and wages (though even here, there may be ambiguities arising from changes in jobs and the complexity of compensation packages), workers are unlikely to be informed concerning total employment. The way that the underemployment contracts "force" the firm to tell the truth is to restrict the amount of labor the firm can hire. If profits depend on aggregate employment, then the firm can evade the force of these restrictions by hiring outside workers. The analysis, as presented, only applies if the firm cannot hire workers (or if there are significant fixed costs per worker so that the restriction in hours worked per old worker is costly).

Not only are workers likely to be uninformed about the total number of employees, but even if they were informed, it would not convey all the requisite information. First, the firm is concerned with the effective labor supply, and it can increase that keeping the number of employees unchanged by increasing the quality of the labor force; secondly, the boundaries of the firm are often ill-defined. The firm could—and would have an incentive to—sell some of its underutilized assets to a subsidiary. Distinguishing such transfers from "legitimate" transfers would seem a difficult task for the average blue collar worker.

Nonobservability of hours (employment) and state of nature. If hours (employment levels) as well as the state of nature are not observable (and there is nothing else relevant upon which to make wages contingent), then the implicit contract will entail a fixed (wage, employment [hours]) contract. Clearly, if workers cannot be bound to stay with the firm, and their productivity at different firms is perfectly correlated, they will leave whenever their wage is less than their marginal product; but in those states when they work for the firm, their average marginal product (plus any insurance premium paid initially) must equal their wage. Thus, if there is no initial insurance premium, the only viable markets are spot markets. (Insurance premiums may take the form of the firm paying individuals less than their marginal product during the initial period after they are hired.) Conversely, if firms cannot be bound not to fire workers, they will do so whenever the workers' marginal product is less than the wage, and again, the only viable labor market is a spot market. When opportunity costs are not perfectly correlated with the workers' productivity in their current firm, then there will exist a set of states of nature in which the workers will not quit and the firm will not fire them (see Hall and Lazear 1982). With bilateral asymmetries of information, with hours worked and state of nature not observable, with imperfectly correlated shocks, and with contracts in which employment levels are not enforceable, *implicit contracts can give rise to unemployment.* Critical to this result is the hypothesis that implicit contracts that specify wages are enforceable, while those that specify employment levels are not; the reasonableness of this hypothesis is addressed in the section on the problem of enforcement.[23]

Contingent contracts. In the previous paragraphs, we have argued that the standard asymmetric information implicit contract theory assumes that variables that are probably not observable really are. It also (implicitly) assumes that variables that are observable are not.

Though the state of nature is not perfectly observable, there are many good surrogates: consider the recent recession in the car industry; sales of automobiles (of each firm), inventories, and foreign imports are readily observable. Moreover, aggregate variables, like unemployment, money supply, and the rate of inflation, and so on, which may be relevant to the demand facing an industry or firm, are also readily observable. Direct indications of profits are observable. Though audited profits and true economic profits may well differ, and making wages contingent upon audited profits would result in incentives to distort audited profits, there are ways around this problem. First, wages may be made contingent upon profits of other firms (thus eliminating this "moral hazard problem," except if the firms collude together). Second, wages may be made contingent upon the market value of the firm. In a well-functioning capital market, these will reflect true profits, and not audited profits, and,

176 / KEYNES' ECONOMIC LEGACY

again, there will be no incentive for small investors to alter their market valuation because of the wage consequences. Third, compensation plans may exist in which workers are paid partly with the shares of the firm, where the incentives for distorting behavior on the part of firm managers may be mitigated. The fact of the matter is that relatively few firms have (explicit) contracts employing such contingencies as part of wage determination. (The difficulty with implicit contract is that, since the terms are never explicit, one might claim that such contingencies implicitly exist.) Of course, even if such information were employed, there would still be a residual of imperfect information concerning firm-specific shocks (states of nature). Thus, it is conceivable that the under- or overemployment contracts described above would still be employed. The question remains, of course, of the extent of the unemployment that can be so explained.

Enforcement Problem

A second, and equally damaging, criticism of the theory concerns the problem of enforceability, as we noted earlier. The contracts described are one-period contracts; yet the essence of the earlier (symmetric information) implicit contract is the long-term relationship between the employer and the employee. Although the older theory slid quietly over the issue of how such contracts were to be enforced, we can no longer do so. The contracts described above make sense only as *one-period explicit contracts*, not as multiperiod implicit contracts.

The distinction between explicit and implicit contracts is related to the enforcement mechanism. Explicit contracts are primarily enforced through the legal system (or the threat of resort to the legal process). Implicit contracts are enforced through two mechanisms: firms that violate their implicit contract lose their reputation and find it difficult to recruit additional workers; and workers within the firm who feel that they have been cheated may reduce their effort (or act in other ways that reduce the firm's profitability). It should be emphasized that one enforcement mechanism does not dominate the other: to enforce a contract through the legal system requires that the alleged breach of contract can be verified; both sides may really know that the contract has been breached, but the side that has breached it may also know that the other side cannot establish that fact to the court. In that circumstance, the firm may still lose its reputation, and reputation may be an effective enforcement mechanism.

On the other hand, when interest rates are positive, firms must balance the gains from cheating (violating the implicit contract) with the losses (say, from the loss of reputation); in sufficiently bad states, it may pay them to cheat, to violate the implicit contract. More accurately, the implicit contract must take into account the fact that certain contract provisions that could (under appropriate conditions of verifiability and observability) be enforced through the legal mechanism cannot be enforced by a reputation mechanism. The view of implicit contracts we are putting forward is that they represent perfect equilibrium (wage, employment) strategies in a repeated game between employers and employees.[24]

What do equilibrium contracts (implicit or explicit) between workers and employers engaged in a long-term relationship look like? The answer depends on what is observable, what the rate of interest is, and what the structure of the shocks to the economy is. Consider, for instance, an infinite period contract with no discounting, in a world in which the probability during each period that the state of nature is good is 0.5. Then by standard arguments it can be shown that employers can be forced to tell the truth (almost) all of the time. In the long run, unless they announce that the state of nature is good half the time and bad half the time, they will be severely punished. And if they must announce that it is good half the time and bad half the time, they would announce good when it is good and bad when it is bad. Morever, the optimal contract under such circumstances entails full employment. Once again, implicit contracts (even under asymmetric information) have explained wage rigidity but failed to explain unemployment.[25]

Though the structure of the optimal multiperiod contracts with positive interest rates has not received detailed analysis, what is known about multiperiod self-selection problems suggests that their structure (entailing elaborate interperiod contingency provisions) will be even more unlike what is observed than the one-period structure.[26]

Implicit contracts as perfect equilibria. One difficulty with analyzing implicit contracts as perfect equilibria is that it appears that there may be a superabundance of such equilibria. We are particularly interested, however, in ascertaining whether there are equilibria that entail wage rigidity and unemployment. If contracts ensuring that wages do not vary can be enforced, why cannot contracts that ensure full employment be enforced? Let me suggest a tentative answer: recall earlier that we distinguished two reputational enforcement mechanisms, one based on the reaction of potential employees, the other of current employees. If the firm believes that it will be some time before it wishes to hire workers again, the present discounted value of the loss of the "outside" reputation may be relatively low. Yet the firm may still be very concerned with the goodwill of its present employees, a central part of the efficiency wage hypothesis presented later in the chapter. Thus an equilibrium contract may require that the firm pay all retained employees a fixed wage, which entails a subsidy in all states; if the state is bad enough, the firm will reduce its losses by firing (laying off) a fraction of its workers.[27]

Layoffs and Contract Complexity

The version of the implicit contract theory with asymmetric information we have presented explains *at best* work reductions (work sharing) but not layoffs, and not unemployment. Those versions of the theory that attempt to explain layoffs usually simply assume it: the worker is assumed either to work or not to work, so that reductions in work can only show up as layoffs. As we argued earlier, whether with asymmetric or symmetric information, efficient contracts should entail work sharing. Moreover, since they do not provide an explanation of job hiring, knowing the determinants of job layoffs provides an explanation of unemployment only when it is *assumed* that labor is immobile.

A final unattractive feature of most versions of asymmetric information implicit contracts is their complexity. If there are many states of nature, the efficient contract will entail specifying, for each set of observable variables, an hours-wage schedule. Each schedule will have many points on it; the schedule is likely to be highly nonlinear. (Specifying the contract as explicit seems hard enough; knowing whether an implicit contract had been broken would seem nigh impossible.)

In the next two sections, two models are presented that remedy these two deficiencies.

Complexity of Contracts

So far, we have not been able to elicit out of the implicit contract theory a convincing basis of a theory of unemployment. The explanations provided in this and the next section are, I think, more convincing.

The first is based on the problem noted earlier on the complexity that can be encompassed within a contract (whether explicit or, a fortiori, implicit). The contracts described earlier resulting in full employment required wage payments and hours to vary from state to state. If we restrict this even a little, we obtain the possibility of unemployment equilibria. For instance, Newbery and I have considered a simple macroeconomic model in which the "shock" to the economy is the variability in export prices. All contracts are made contingent upon the export price. We show that with any linear indexing rule *even when the level of indexing is optimally chosen* there may be unemployment. Similar results obtain with other simple (log linear, quadratic, and so on) rules.

Theory of Moral Hazard and Labor Turnover

Layoffs represent a nonprice response to a market disturbance: rather than lowering wages in the face of a decrease in demand, employment is rationed. It is thus natural to look for an explanation for this in other instances where markets are characterized by rationing. It is by now well known that insurance markets in which adverse selection and moral hazard problems arise are, in general, characterized by quantity rationing (see Rothschild and Stiglitz 1976; Wilson 1977; Stiglitz and Weiss 1983; Arnott and Stiglitz 1982).

Earlier we argued that a theory (of implicit contracts) that purports to explain unemployment must not only explain layoffs but must also explain why those who are laid off are not rehired. In general, the shocks facing different firms are not perfectly correlated. If information were costless, individuals who are at firms where the value of the marginal productivity of those workers has decreased would move to other firms; labor would be reallocated, until the value of the marginal productivity of all workers at all firms was the same. Note in this case that the optimal contract would not require the firm to provide any unemployment insurance; individuals would never be unemployed; the only insurance required would be wage insurance, and it need not be provided by the firm.

Now assume that information (search) is costly and the process of gathering information is stochastic, so that some individuals who search are unsuccessful. The risk that is to be insured is not just that the firm has a bad state; it is the risk that the firm has a bad state, that the individual searches, and is unsuccessful in finding a job.[28]

If the firm provided complete wage and employment insurance, the individual at the low productivity firm would have no incentive to search. The more complete the insurance provided is, the less incentives for search, and the less efficient the resulting resource allocation. The firm, of course, is not interested in the efficiency of the societal resource allocation; but by inducing individuals to move elsewhere in bad states, the firm saves the subsidy that is implicit in the wage contract in those states. If search were observable, the optimal contract would provide for unemployment compensation that was conditional upon the level of search. But search is not observable, and this is what gives rise to the moral hazard problem.

There are two instruments that are available to the firm for inducing search; one is to lower the wage of individuals who are retained, and the other is to lay off workers. In general, Arnott, Hosios, and Stiglitz (1983) show that both instruments will be employed. The nature of the search process (the individual either does or does not obtain employment) introduces a natural nonconvexity into the problem, which implies that, even if all individuals are identical, it pays to lay off some workers; it is not optimal to rely simply on work sharing. But, in addition, some workers are better than others, and for a number of reasons (both information, equity, and institutional) it may not be possible to differentiate wages among them. Lowering wages results in a differentially higher quit rate among the high quality workers; layoffs do not have a corresponding adverse effect on quality.

On the other hand, when individuals differ in their search costs, reduced wages have an advantage over layoffs. When wages are reduced, those with lower search costs will be induced to search for a better job (where they are more productive); layoffs force both high and low search cost individuals to search.[29]

This model thus has accomplished what the other theories of implicit contracts could not do: it has provided an explanation of the simultaneous occurrence of wage reductions and layoffs (of on the job and off the job search), and it has provided a model of the labor market in which there is an equilibrium level of unemployment. (The theory is, of course, not inconsistent with the theories of implicit contracts with asymmetric information, that is, the structure of the implicit contracts discussed by Arnott, Hosios, and Stiglitz. The specification of wages, hours, and layoff rates in good and bad states, depends on whether the state of nature is observable by workers.)

Patterns of Unemployment

We noted earlier that a "good" theory of unemployment should explain not only the presence of unemployment, but also its pattern. Thus it should explain layoffs as well as work sharing. Our model does this. It should also explain which workers get laid off. To some extent, our model does this too. It is consistent with the use of the seniority system of layoffs; younger individuals may have both lower costs and greater benefits from search. But it does not seem to explain why certain groups, like women and minorities, should experience more cyclical unemployment than do white males. The model presented in the section on efficiency wage theories does provide an explanation both for the use of layoffs and for the concentration of layoffs among certain groups.

The Paradox of the Preference for Being Laid Off

The model has one other failing: it does not provide a satisfactory resolution of the seeming paradox that arises in many implicit contract theories, in which the workers who are laid off are better off than those who are not. Consider, for instance, the case of a separable utility function. With full insurance, and no opportunities for being rehired, the pay of those laid off must be the same as that of those retained, but since those laid off enjoy more leisure, their total utility is higher. All workers would be petitioning to be laid off.[30]

If (1) there is some probability that a worker[31] will be rehired, (2) we ignore the effect of unemployment benefits on search, and (3) the firm cannot monitor whether the individual is rehired and so must set its unemployment benefit as a fixed payment, then the payment will be set to equate the expected marginal utilities. That is, if we assume a separable utility function, and let y_r be the individual's income if he is retained (in the bad state), b be his layoff benefit, and y be his income if he is rehired (a random variable), then b is set so that $Eu'(y + b) = u'(y_r)$.

Whether the expected *utility of income* is greater or less for the laid-off worker than the retained worker depends on the shape of the utility function, that is, on whether utility is a concave or convex function of marginal utility. While with a quadratic utility function the retained worker is better off, a necessary and sufficient condition for the worker to be worse off is that there is decreasing absolute risk aversion. (It is straightforward to derive more general conditions with nonseparable utility functions under which retained workers are better off.)

Now we must take into account the fact that, in the bad state, the pay of laid-off workers affects their propensity to quit. By assumption, the firm is subsidizing workers in the bad state and thus would like to encourage them to leave. Thus, the firm lowers the pay of the retained workers. This strengthens the presumption that retained workers are worse off than laid-off workers.

We have established the fact that workers who are laid off may be rehired means that it is *possible* that retained workers may be better off than laid-off workers, under the plausible condition that leisure and consumption are complements or independent.[32] But whether retained workers are better off remains dependent on specific properties of the utility function, and plausible utility functions still lead to the seemingly paradoxical results.

Our argument in favor of lowering wages for retained workers, to encourage them to search, ignored the effect of lowering wages on their productivity. This is not the first instance in which we have noted indirect effects of current wages on the costs that face firms. Earlier we referred to the fact that to the extent that firms had to rely on reputation mechanisms to enforce contracts, firms had two motivations for paying high wages: to ensure the productivity of their current workers and to lower future recruitment costs.

These are but examples of a more general phenomenon, which we refer to as the efficiency wage hypothesis, which provides an alternative, and we believe more plausible, basis of the theory of unemployment than the implicit contract theory.

EFFICIENCY WAGE THEORIES OF UNEMPLOYMENT

The Basic Argument

The basic hypothesis of the efficiency wage theories of unemployment is that the (net) productivity of workers is a function of the wage paid. If that is the case, then firms may be reluctant to lower wages, even in the face of an excess supply of labor; to do so might lower the productivity more than proportionately, so that total labor costs are actually increased. Competitive equilibrium is thus consistent with a situation in which there is an excess supply of laborers. The law of supply and demand has been repealed.

Moreover, since the relationship between productivity and wage may differ from industry to industry, wages (for similar laborers) may differ across industries. The law of the single price has also been repealed. (Thus, there may exist in equilibrium some sector in which these efficiency wage considerations are not relevant, in which a conventional competitive wage is paid, while in some other sector(s), higher wages are paid. These higher paid jobs are obviously rationed, and queues for these jobs may serve as equilibrating mechanisms,[33] a substitute for the adjustments in wages that do not take place because of the effect of wages on productivity.)

It is important to note that the economy is not always characterized by unemployment, only that it may be. (The repeal of the law of supply and demand is thus a selective repeal.) And changes in the economy (the destruction of some capital, the change in technology, and so forth) may move the economy from a full employment regime to an unemployment regime or may change the equilibrium level of unemployment in the economy.

Alternative Explanations of the Wage-Productivity Relationship

There are at least five different explanations of this phenomenon that have been discussed in the literature.

The earliest, noted in the development literature, was based on the hypothesis that, at least at low levels of nutrition, individuals' productivity depended on their nutrition, which depended in turn on their pay. A productivity-wage curve of the form depicted in Figure 4.7 was

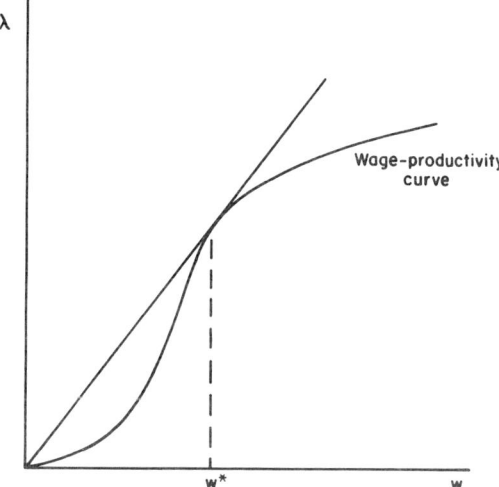

FIGURE 4.7 The efficiency wage is w^*. Wage costs per efficiency unit are minimized at w^*.

hypothesized by Leibenstein (1957) and subsequently analyzed in greater detail by Mirrlees (1975) and Stiglitz (1976b). If $\lambda(w)$ is the efficiency of a worker receiving a wage w, the firm chooses a wage that minimizes the wage costs per efficiency unit,

$$\min w/\lambda(w) \tag{13}$$

the solution to which entails

$$\lambda'(w^*) = \lambda/w^*. \tag{14}$$

The term w^* refers to the efficiency wage and is depicted in Figure 4.7 as the tangency between a line through the origin and the wage productivity curve.

Assume the aggregate production function of the industrial sector is of the form $Q = F(\lambda L)$, where L is the number of workers and λ is their efficiency. Let output of the sector be our numeraire; firms in the sector will pay a wage w^* and hire workers up to the point where

$$\lambda(w^*)F'(L\lambda[w^*]) = w^* \tag{15}$$

the (value of the) marginal product equals the real wage. Let $L^D(w^*)$ be the solution to (15). If $L^D(w^*) < L^S$, the supply of workers to the industrial

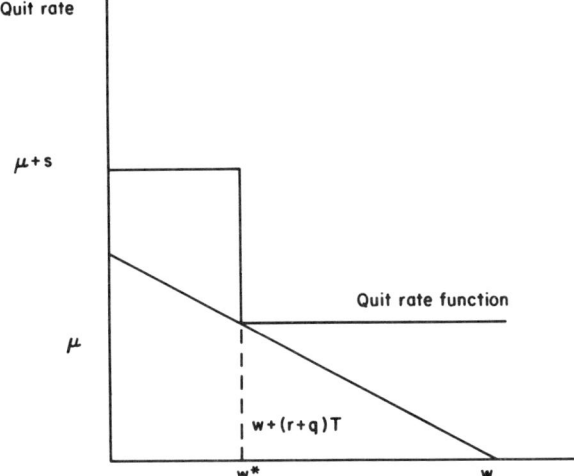

FIGURE 4.8 The efficiency wage is w^*. Total labor costs (including turnover costs) are minimized at w^*.

sector, there will be unemployment: no firm will have any incentive to lower wages.

This version of the theory is useful in helping to bring out the basic structure of the argument, but nutritional considerations are of limited relevance for wage determination in more developed countries.

The second theory is based on labor turnover (Phelps 1970; Stiglitz 1974b, 1982a): the lower the wage is, the higher the rate of labor turnover; so long as the firm must bear some part of the turnover costs,[34] this lowers the net productivity of a worker.

This can again easily give rise to unemployment. To see this most simply, assume that individuals leave firms for two reasons: they die, at an exponential rate, μ, or they quit, to obtain a higher paying job. Assume, for simplicity, that they make s searches per unit time and assume that all firms paid the same wage w^*. Then any firm that paid a wage greater or equal to w^* would have a quit rate of μ, while any firm that paid a wage less than w^* would have a quit rate of $\mu + s$ (since every firm that the searcher sampled would be paying a wage in excess of the lower wage). The quit rate appears in Figure 4.8. The labor costs of the firm (per unit time) are $w + (r + q)T$, where r is the rate of interest, q is the quit rate, and T is the training costs. (The term $[r + q]T$ represents the amortization of the training costs.) Clearly, these are minimized at the wage w^*. Thus, if the economy experiences a shock (a war that decreases the capital stock) and there is not a *coordinated* wage reduction, unemployment will develop. It does not pay for any firm to lower its wage, even in the presence of unemployment (because the unemployed workers, though thankful now to get a lower paid job, will continue to search for a still better job.)

This model can easily be enriched to include individuals differing in their attitudes toward nonpecuniary characteristics of the firm and searching for a good match between themselves and the firm. While in the simple version presented in the preceding paragraph, there is always some full employment equilibrium (although many unemployment equilibria), in a more general theory the only equilibria may entail unemployment.[35]

The third theory (Stiglitz 1976; Weiss 1980; Nalebuff and Stiglitz, forthcoming) is based on imperfect information concerning the characteristics of workers (and/or an inability for legal or sociological reasons to differentiate wages among individuals whose characteristics differ). The quality mix of applicants depends on the wages offered (and the quality mix of those who quit a firm depend on the wages paid to its current employees). In general, by paying higher wages, one obtains a higher quality labor force.[36]

The fourth theory is based on imperfect information concerning the actions of workers: due to the costs of monitoring them, firms must have some method of inducing "good behavior," some threat against workers that are caught shirking. If there were full employment, any worker who was fired would immediately find another job (at the same wage). To induce workers not to shirk, firms thus attempt to raise their wages relative to that paid by others. This has two consequences. If all firms were identical, then they would not raise their wages relative to each other, but as they raised wages, their demand for labor would decrease, and unemployment would increase. So long as the level of unemployment compensation is less than the market wage, the period of unemployment serves as a discipline device. The equilibrium level of unemployment is depicted in Figure 4.9. Assume there are only two levels of effort $(0, e)$ and that the unemployment compensation level is fixed. It seems plausible that the lower the level of unemployment, the higher the wage the firm must pay to make it worthwhile for an individual not to shirk. This no-shirking wage is depicted as an upward sloping curve, increasing with the level of employment. The demand for labor (assuming that workers do not shirk) is the usual downward-sloping function of the wage. The equilibrium is the intersection of the two.[37]

The major objection to this theory is that there are other methods of providing discipline to the labor force, for example, forcing them to post bond. The limitations on these mechanisms are well known (see note 36), but it is worth noting that firms do employ indirect forms of bonding to

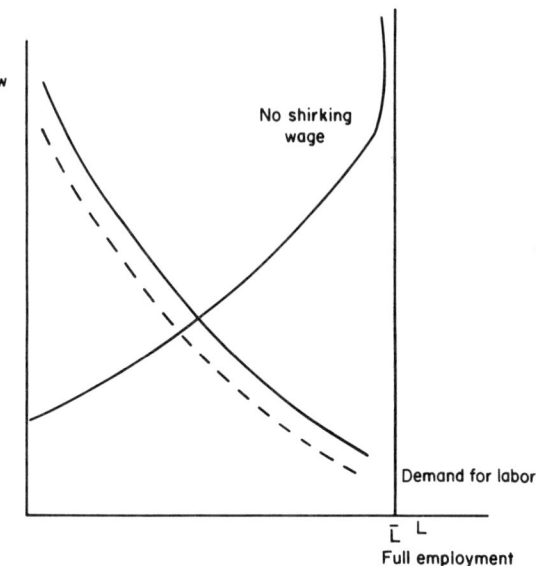

FIGURE 4.9 If monitoring is costly, the only equilibria entail unemployment. A decrease in the demand for labor will result in lower real wages and more unemployment.

some extent. Hall has noted that unemployment rates are highest among groups who, because of limited resources, are least able to post bonds.

The difference between the last two models and the standard competitive paradigm should be noted: the latter assumes that all individuals are paid strictly on a piece rate, that their actions can be perfectly monitored. If they perform the action contracted for, they get paid; if they do not, they will not get paid. In fact, most individuals have at most a small fraction of their compensation depending directly on performance; in many cases, individual performance cannot be directly observed; at best, group performance can be observed, and then only with a lag. Firms do care about the quality of their labor force; they are worried about providing incentives to their workers (in the competitive paradigm, the firm could not care less whether some workers decide to work or not since there is a competitive supply of workers readily available to perform any service; workers who do not do what they have been contracted to do are replaced by ones who will).

The fifth set of theories comprises the sociological theories recently propounded by George Akerlof (1984). Though many of the patterns of behavior that he describes might equally well be described by one of the theories we have provided here, there are some that are not. In particular, he notes that individuals' performance depends critically on whether they

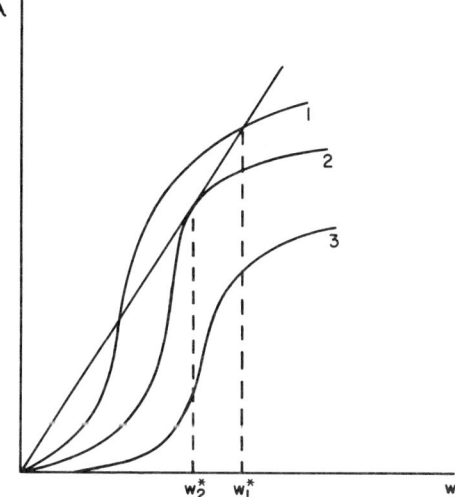

FIGURE 4.10 Consequences of differing wage productivity functions: some groups will be fully employed (group 1), some partially employed (group 2), and some completely unemployed (group 3).

believe they are being treated "fairly." We shall return to this observation later.

Though the five theories differ in a number of important respects, they have a common mathematical structure: the net productivity of a worker at the ith firm is a function of the wage paid by the firm, w_i, the wage paid by other firms, w_j and the unemployment rate (or, more generally, the expected duration in the unemployment pool) $\lambda_i = \lambda_i(w_i, w_j, u)$. The equilibrium level of unemployment and the wage structure may be derived, and the consequences of various policy changes investigated, for alternative specifications of λ.

Patterns of Unemployment: A Further Implication of the Efficiency Wage Model

The efficiency wage models are not only consistent with there being unemployment in a competitive market equilibrium; they also provide some insights into the patterns of observed unemployment. If groups differ in their relationships between wage and productivity, as illustrated in Figure 4.10, equilibrium will be characterized by some groups being fully employed, other groups being partially employed, and still other groups being rationed out of the market. Changes in the aggregate demand for labor will have very large differential effects on the employment of different groups. (This is in contrast, for instance, to the standard theories, where the wages of different groups might be affected differentially, but there is not reason to expect, once wages have adjusted, differential unemployment rates among different groups.)

The Consequences of Policy Changes

The policy consequences may differ markedly depending on the explanation of the dependence of productivity on wages. Consider, for instance, an increase in the unemployment compensation. In the "shirking" version of the efficiency wage model, this results in firms having to raise their wages in order to induce workers not to shirk (the penalty for being caught is smaller at any fixed wage and unemployed level). This in turn results in a higher equilibrium unemployment rate and a higher real wage. On the other hand, in the quality-efficiency wage model, an increase in unemployment compensation may have a differential effect on the search intensities of individuals of different abilities and thus shift the wage-productivity curve facing different firms. If low productivity workers' search is reduced relative to the high productivity workers, then the applicant productivity-wage curve may shift up, as in Figure 4.11, with a consequent change in the wage (which may either increase or decrease) and increase in the demand for labor. In Figures 4.12a and 4.12b we have depicted a case where there are low and high productivity individuals, but the number of individuals of each productivity type who search for a job is affected by the level of unemployment compensation. In Figure 4.12a the mean ability of those applying at high wages is increased; the wage is unchanged, but the demand for labor increased. While in Figure 4.12b the mean ability of those applying at high wages is decreased sufficiently that the optimal wage is lowered (and unemployment is consequently eliminated).

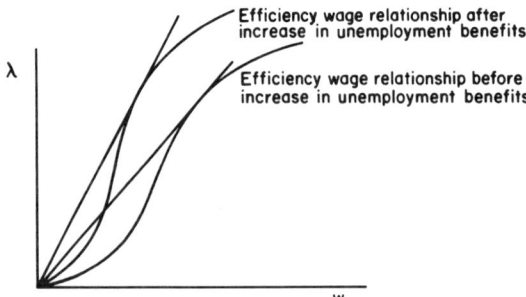

FIGURE 4.11 An increase in unemployment compensation may change wages and the demand for labor.

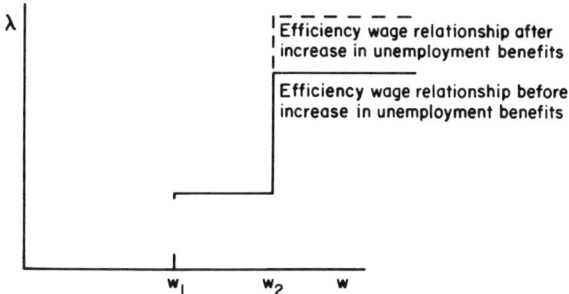

FIGURE 4.12a Two-group case: an increase in unemployment compensation leaves wages unchanged but reduces unemployment.

All of these models should be contrasted with the policy implication of the naive fixed price model, in which an increase in unemployment compensation would be unambiguously desirable, since wages and prices are (by assumption) unchanged, while the unemployment compensation increases aggregate demand.

Thus, though the structure of the equilibrium with the efficiency wage model and the fixed price model may look very similar (real wages do not respond to the presence of unemployment), and a careful general equilibrium analysis of an economy with efficiency wages would entail the same kind of detailed analysis of spillovers and constraints that have characterized the fixed price literature, the comparative statics analysis

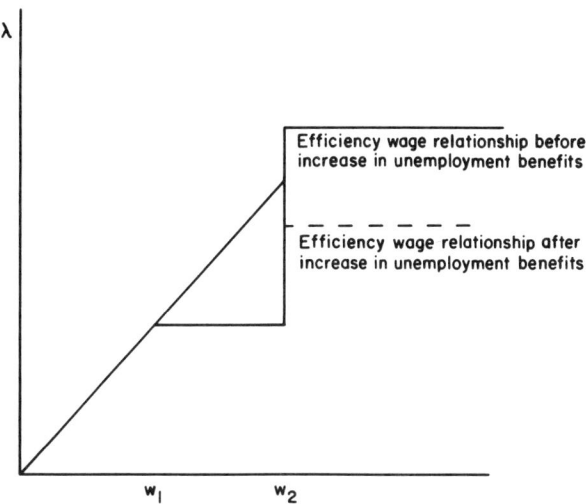

FIGURE 4.12b Two-group case: an increase in unemployment compensation lowers the wage and reduces unemployment.

The Efficiency Wage Hypothesis and Cyclical Fluctuations

We have seen in the previous section how the efficiency wage model can give rise to an equilibrium level of unemployment. Changes in the economy, in, say, the level of productivity of workers, in the capital stock, or in the level of unemployment compensation, give rise to different levels of equilibrium unemployment. Thus, one approach to seeing whether (or the extent to which) the efficiency wage model provides insights into cyclical fluctuations is to ascertain the extent to which we can identify parameter changes that would result in a change in the equilibrium level of unemployment.

For instance, it is easy to show that a lowering of the demand curve for labor in Figure 4.9 (for instance, as a result of the destruction of some of the country's capital stock) will result both in lower wages and a higher unemployment rate.

But the insights obtained from the efficiency wage hypothesis extend beyond those directly obtained from this kind of equilibrium analysis. Even if equilibrium were characterized by full employment, the economy's adjustments to disturbances may be such as to result (frequently) in unemployment.[38]

The argument may be seen most simply by considering the labor turnover model presented above. We noted there that there exists a full employment equilibrium, in which all firms pay a wage, w^{**}, at which the demand for labor equals the supply. Assume that some of the capital stock has been destroyed, so that there is a new full employment equilibrium with a lower real wage.

Consider now what happens if there is *any* friction in the wage-setting process. Assume, in particular, that all contracts last for two periods (seconds, days, years) and that some contracts come up for renewal in even periods, others in odd. Assume further that firms can hire within a period. Then, given even this slight amount of friction, the only equilibrium entails the real wage remaining unchanged, with the resulting increase in unemployment. (If the firms that have the option of lowering their wage did so, they would find that they experienced a higher quit rate, and lower profits.)[39]

The argument is, of course, more general than this simple example. Since the optimal wage at one firm depends on the wage at the other firms (and the unemployment rate), given that (some firms) do not adjust, it does not pay others to adjust to the full equilibrium levels. Adjustments may occur, but they occur slowly.[40]

Furthermore, the private losses from not reducing wages in the efficiency wage model are of second order, while in the standard competitive model, they are first order. That is, if we write the profits of the firm as a function of its wage, the wage paid by other firms, the amount of labor hired, and a vector of other parameters,

$$\rho = \rho\,(w_i,\,w,\,L,\,\eta_j)$$

in the efficiency wage model, the wage is set so that $\rho_w^i = 0$. In the standard competitive model, however, the wage is always the lowest wage at which the firm can obtain workers. Assume now that some parameter η_j has changed and that the wage at which a firm can obtain workers is lowered. In the efficiency wage model, the wage will be lowered

$$dw_i/d\nu_j = -\,\rho_{w\eta}^i/\rho_{ww}^i$$

but the change in profits from this change in wages is zero (since $\rho_w = 0$). But in the standard competitive paradigm, if firms can obtain workers at lower wages, their profits are strictly increased.

As a result, one might expect some "almost rational" firms not to fully adjust their wages in response to disturbances they face (see Akerlof and Yellen 1983). Such distortion in the behavior of one agent in the economy has, of course, its general equilibrium consequences, for example, on prices elsewhere in the economy. But these are in the nature of pecuniary externalities, and were the economy initially at a pareto efficient allocation (where rationing did not occur, e.g., because of efficiency wage considerations), the economy would still be pareto efficient. But under the circumstances described here, there are real welfare consequences of these failures on the part of some firms to adjust their wages.[41]

Nominal versus Real Rigidities

There is a widespread belief among macroeconomists that it is nominal rigidities, not real rigidities, that are to be explained. The evidence on this matter is not completely convincing. The few experiments on fully neutral monetary changes—the change from old francs to new francs—suggest that such changes may have relatively few real effects. Other forms of monetary injection are never uniformly distributed among the population, and it is easy to construct (not necessarily plausible) models in which nonuniform monetary injections will have real effects. Moreover, economies that have practiced extensive indexing (so money wages are not rigid) have experienced episodes of unemployment just as economies in which indexing is not so widely practiced.

Still, it is worth noting that two versions of the efficiency wage model may give rise to rigidities in money wages. In the labor turnover model, we noted an indeterminancy of equilibrium. If all firms were paying a wage w, it would pay them to continue to pay that wage, in spite of a change in the demand or supply of labor. The critical wage could be set in money or real terms. If each firm believes that all others are going to leave money wages unchanged, it would not pay any firm to change its (money) wage. In an economy that has not experienced rapid rates of inflation in the past, it may be natural to "fix" on the money rate, while in other economies, where indexing is more prevalent, it may be the real wage that is rigid.

The second explanation is based on Akerlof's sociological theories of the efficiency wage. If individuals come to believe that money wage reductions are unfair, then it does not pay firms to reduce their money wages. At one level, such an explanation seems unsatisfactory: why should individuals come to view nominal wage changes of any consequence? But if workers exhibit such irrationalities, it pays for firms to reflect those irrationalities in their wage-setting policies. Such a theory may have some degree of plausibility for the short run, in an economy that has had little experience with inflation, but it is unconvincing in the long run. But then do we have much evidence of nominal wage rigidities in such economies?

CONCLUSIONS

Those of us brought up in traditional Keynesian macroeconomics were taught the importance of the assumption of wage rigidity. This was described as a fact of life, explained by vague reference to certain institutional factors. If wage rigidity is as central to the explanation of unemployment as many modern renditions of Keynes seem to suggest, surely we need to explain this wage rigidity. The objective of this chapter has been to investigate two important classes of explanations.

The first approach, the implicit contract theory, has had a long, but sad, history.[42] The simpler models put forward a decade and a half ago provided an explanation of the lack of variability of real wages, but not an explanation of unemployment. The more complicated asymmetric information models were found unconvincing: they more easily gave rise to overemployment than underemployment, and the forms of contracts to be expected, if asymmetric information considerations were paramount, are not observed. Other versions of the asymmetric information implicit contract model, explicitly long term in nature, may give rise to full employment. Two versions of the implicit contract model did, in fact, give rise to unemployment: those with limitations on the complexity of the contracts that could be designed and those in which search was costly and could not be monitored. Though these may provide part of the explanation of the observed patterns of wages and unemployed, of who becomes unemployed and why unemployment takes the form of layoffs rather than work sharing, additional insights may be obtained from the second approach, the efficiency wage models. These not only provide an explanation of the existence of unemployment equilibrium in competitive economies; they also provide part of the explanation of the observed patterns of unemployment, of who becomes unemployed and why unemployment takes the form of layoffs rather than work sharing. They provide an explanation for why different firms may pay similar types of workers different wages. They explain both forms of wage stickiness: why firms may not lose much if they fail to adjust their wages, and why, when they adjust their wages optimally, they adjust them slowly.

The two theories are, of course, not mutually exclusive: employer-employee relationships are frequently long-term relationships; what affects the quality of the labor force attracted to a firm, or the effort that workers exert, is not just the wage at the moment, but their lifetime prospects.

The issues we have raised, concerning the nature of insurance, the presence of asymmetric information, the limitations of enforcement mechanisms, and restrictions on the degree of complexity of feasible contracts, are all relevant in the design of the contract. They must all be taken into account in explaining cyclical movements in wages, hours, and employments. Our argument is that, while simple efficiency wage models can provide a plausible explanation of unemployment, simple versions of the implicit contract model (with or without asymmetric information) can do so only under highly restrictive and implausible conditions and have some important counterfactual implications.

We have just begun the exploration of the full implications of these efficiency wage models. In the end, they may prove as unsatisfactory as the earlier versions of the implicit contract theory; empirical predictions of the theory may be shown to be inconsistent with the observed facts. But for now, they seem to provide the most fruitful direction of research, in extending our understanding of wage rigidities, this central element in the Keynesian legacy.

APPENDIX A

Proof that laid-off workers are better off than retained workers, under hypothesis of normality of leisure.

We assume that firms provide supplementary unemployment benefits.

The optimal contract maximizes profits, subject to workers obtaining an expected utility of U; that is, it maximizes

$$\int_A (\theta h - y) f(s) + s \int_{A'} f(s) ds \tag{A.1}$$

subject to

$$\int_A U(y_1 h) f(S) dS + \int_{A'} U(S + b_1 \theta) f(S) \, dS > (<) U \tag{A.2}$$

as a function of their income, y, and hours worked, h; and $\theta(s)$ is the productivity of an individual in state S. It is straightforward to show that the solution to this entails U_y = constant; individuals obtain perfect insurance, in the sense that their marginal utility of income in all states is the same. Differentiating (A.1), we obtain

$$dy/dh = -U_{hy}/U_{yy} \tag{A.3}$$

thus

$$dU/dh = U_h - \frac{U_y U_{hy}}{U_{yy}} < \text{ or } > 0 \text{ as leisure is } \begin{cases} \text{normal} \\ \text{inferior} \end{cases}$$

APPENDIX B

The optimal contract (without self-selection constraints) must satisfy

$$\theta_2 U_y(h_2, y_2) + U_h(h_2, y_2) = 0 \tag{B.1}$$

$$\theta_1 U_y(h_1, y_1) + U_h(h_1, y_1) = 0 \tag{B.2}$$

$$\frac{p^{1\prime}}{p^{2\prime}} = \frac{U_y(h_1, y_1)}{U_y(h_2, y_2)} \tag{B.3}$$

Without loss of generality, we let $y_2 = y_2^*$.
Then from (B.1), $h_2 = h_2^*$, where

$$\theta U_y(h_2^*, y_2^*) + U_h(h_2', y_2') = 0.$$

Let $U_y(h_2^*, y_2^*) = U_y^*$. Totaling differentially (B.2) and (B.3), we obtain (letting $\rho'/\rho = A$)

$$\begin{Bmatrix} \dfrac{U_{hh}}{U_h} & \dfrac{U_{hy}}{U_h} \\ -\theta_1 \left(A - \dfrac{U_{yh}}{U_h} \right) & \dfrac{A - U_{yy}}{U_y} \end{Bmatrix} \begin{Bmatrix} dh_1 \\ dy_1 \end{Bmatrix} = \begin{Bmatrix} 1 \\ Ah_1\theta_1 \end{Bmatrix} \dfrac{d\theta_1}{\theta_1}$$

Let

$$c = \dfrac{-U_{yy}}{U_y}, \quad b = \dfrac{U_{hy}}{U_h}, \quad a = \dfrac{U_{hh}}{U_h}.$$

$$\theta_1 D = \dfrac{dh_1}{d\theta_1} = (A + c) - bAh_1\theta_1 = A(1 - bh_1\theta_1) + c$$

$$\theta_1 D = \dfrac{dy_1}{d\theta_1} = \theta_1 aAh_1 + \theta_1(A - b) = \theta_1 A[ah_1 + 1] - b\theta_1$$

where

$$D = (A + c)a + b\theta_1(A - b)$$
$$= A(a + b\theta_1) + ac - b^2\theta_1$$

Define

$$S_i = \theta_i(h_1 - h_2) - (y_1 - y_2), \ i = 1, 2$$

$$\dfrac{dS_1}{d\theta_1} = h_1 - h_2 + \dfrac{1}{D}[c + b - A(bh_1\theta_1 + ah_1)]$$

$$\dfrac{dS_2}{d\theta_1} = ([\theta_2/\theta_1] - 1)(A + c - Abh\ \theta_1) + (c + b - A[bh_1\theta_1 + ah_1])$$

Direct calculations verify that

$$\dfrac{dh}{dI} = \dfrac{(b + c)}{\theta(c + 2b) + a} > (<) \ 0 \text{ as } b + c > (<) \ 0$$

$$\dfrac{dC}{dI} = \dfrac{a + b\theta}{\theta(c + 2b) + a} > (<) \ 0 \text{ as } a + b\theta > (<) \ 0$$

where C = consumption. Hence, at $\theta_1 = \theta_2$

$$\frac{dS_1}{d\theta_1} > (<) \; 0 \text{ as } \frac{\alpha A}{1 - \alpha + A\alpha} < (>) \; \eta$$

where α = share of labor = $y/\theta h$
and $A = A(\theta h - y)$ = firm's measure of relative risk aversion
$\eta = -y(d\ln h/dI)$ = income elasticity of labor supply.

It immediately follows that if $A = 0$, the individual works more hours in the good state than in the bad ($h_1 > h_2$). It also immediately follows that for states near each other, whether there is over- or underemployment simply depends on whether leisure is normal or inferior. Moreover, if leisure is normal, and firms are risk neutral, one always obtains either full employment or overemployment, since $h_1 > h_2$.

SPECIAL CASES:

(1) SEPARABILITY

Separability ensures normality, and $dh_1/d\theta_1 > 0$. The condition for $dS_1/d\theta_1 > 0$ can now be written (at $\theta_1 = \theta_2$)

$$(1 - \alpha) \nu - A \alpha \nu < 0$$

where

$C = U_{yy}Y$ = worker's relative risk aversion
$\nu = U_{hh}h/U_h$ = worker's elasticity of marginal disutility of effort

(2) $$U = U(y - \upsilon[h])$$

This utility function has the property that $b + c = 0$.

$$a + b\theta = a - c\theta = \upsilon''/\upsilon' > 0$$

but since $b = u''/u' < 0$, $dh_1/d\theta_1 > 0$, and if the two states are far enough apart, there will be full employment (the constraint $S_2 \leq 0$ is never violated, since $dS_2/d\theta_1 < 0$).

NOTES

1. We shall follow the well-honored tradition in Keynesian analysis of obfuscating whether it is the rigidities in real or nominal wages that are crucial for the analysis. Most of

the theories discussed in this chapter are concerned with rigidities in real wages. Alternative explanations of the rigidity of nominal wages are discussed in the latter part of the chapter.

2. Among recent expositions are two books by Malinvaud (1977, 1980) and one by Grandmont (1982). Earlier studies include those by Solow and Stiglitz (1968) and Barro and Grossman (1971). Although most studies in this tradition place primary emphasis on the rigidity of wages and pricies, other rigidities may give rise to unemployment. For instance, Neary and Stiglitz (1983) analyze the consequences of rigidities in the rate of interest.

3. Elsewhere, I have addressed the question of price rigidity (Stiglitz 1984).

4. As I note below, the two theories are not mutually inconsistent: a full theory will need to incorporate elements of both approaches.

5. There is, moreover, considerable evidence that being without work for an extended period of time is extremely disruptive to individuals and their families; the loss of income is only partially responsible; the loss of sense of worth from not being gainfully employed, the loss of respect from others, and the fear of this loss are probably even more important. Beyond some point, leisure appears to have negative value.

6. Variations in economic circumstances may lead to variations in hours worked or to some individuals deciding not to seek work, even in a Walrasian economy. We wish to explain why variations in employment are apparently greater than they would be in a Walrasian equilibrium.

7. The standard references for the implicit contract theory are Azariadis (1975), Gordon (1974), and Bailey (1974). For two recent surveys, see Azariadis (1979) and Azariadis and Stiglitz (1983).

8. Most of the literature has not addressed the question of why individuals cannot or do not purchase wage and/or employment insurance companies. Arnott, Hosios, and Stiglitz (1983) provide a brief discussion; noting the central problems of moral hazard (to be discussed below), they observe that the employer has an informational advantage over other potential suppliers of insurance.

Similarly the standard implicit contract models do not provide a good explanation of why access to the credit market is limited or why it is more limited for individuals than for firms. One explanation of credit rationing in competitive markets with imperfect information has recently been provided by Stiglitz and Weiss (1981, 1983). Because the firm is more informed about its employees' future income potential than, say, a bank, it has a natural advantage in serving as an intermediary in the provision of (possibly implicit) credit.

9. Except if some individuals would have remained voluntarily unemployed in the corresponding Walrasian equilibrium, because their marginal role of substitution exceeded their marginal rate of transformation at zero work.

10. Even its implications for the movements in real wages may not be totally convincing. If workers' utility functions are separable in consumption and leisure (a case we shall discuss at greater length below), and if workers have no access to the capital market (so consumption and income at each date are identical), then consumption of all those retained throughout the business cycle should be constant; that is, real wages should move inversely to the number of hours worked. If leisure and consumption are complements, then real wages should increase even more in a recession.

11. That is, the optimal contracts entail equal pay in all states; without separability the level of pay depends on the level of work in each state.

12. This view of the implicit contract, and the corresponding implication that implicit contract theory did not give rise to unemployment, was set forth in Stiglitz (1978). See also Azariadis and Stiglitz (1983) and Akerlof and Miyazaki (1980).

13. For general results on the constrained inefficiency of competitive economies with an incomplete set of markets, see Greenwald and Stiglitz (1983), Hart (1975), Newbery and Stiglitz (1981, 1982) and Stiglitz (1973, 1982). For a proof that competitive economies with implicit wage contracts are inefficient, see Newbery and Stiglitz (1984).

14. A closely related problem is referred to as the valuation problem: even when it is possible to ascertain that some loss has occurred, it may be difficult to assess its magnitude.

15. Implicit contracts with asymmetric and incomplete information have been analyzed by Arnott, Hosios, and Stiglitz (1983), Azariadis (1983), Chari (1983), Cooper (1981), Green and Kahn (1983), Grossman and Hart (1981, 1983), Grossman, Hart, and Maskin (1983), Hart (1983), and others. For a partial survey, see Azariadis and Stiglitz (1983).

16. These results extend results independently derived by Cooper (1983).

17. This result does not depend upon any property of the individual's utility function, other than quasi-concavity. Though there are some instances in which workers complain about being forced to work more than they would like, the result that workers are better off in the bad state suggests the inappropriateness of the model for explaining overemployment. One should not conclude that, therefore, the relevant equilibria are those entailing underemployment, but rather that the model itself is at best of only limited relevance.

18. Though the results that $h_1 = h_2 = 0$ clearly do.

19. For the case where the two states are near each other, the result follows directly from the calculations of Appendix B. More generally, with risk-neutral individuals, the optimal employment contract is described by the solution to the problem

$$\max \rho^1(\theta_1 h_1 - y_1) + \rho^2(\theta_2 h_2 - y_2)$$

s.t.

$$U^1 + U^2 \leq U$$

and s.t.

$$\theta_1 h_1 - y_1 > \theta_1 h_2 - y_2$$

$$\theta_2 h_2 - y_2 > \theta_2 h_1 - y_1$$

Letting λ_1 and λ_2 be the Lagrange multipliers associated with the self-selection constraints, we obtain

$$\rho^{1\prime} \theta_1 + \lambda_1 \theta_1 - \lambda_2 \theta_2 + \mu U^1 h = 0$$
$$\rho^{2\prime} \theta_2 - (\lambda_1 \theta_1 - \lambda_2 \theta_2) + \mu U^2 h = 0$$
$$\rho^{2\prime} - \rho^{1\prime} - 2(\lambda_1 + \lambda_2) = 0$$
$$\rho^{1\prime} - (\lambda_1 - \lambda_2) + \mu U_y^1 = 0$$
$$\rho^{2\prime} + (\lambda_1 - \lambda_2) + \mu U_y^2 = 0$$

Subtracting the last equation from the next to the last equation, we obtain

$$\rho^{1\prime} - \rho^{2\prime} = 2\lambda_1 + \mu(U_y^1 - U_y^2) = 2\lambda_1$$

under the hypothesis that $U_y^1 = U_y^2$. Hence, if

$$\lambda_1 = 0, \rho^{1\prime} = \rho^{2\prime}; \text{ and thus } \lambda_2 = 0.$$

20. The problem of the firm is identical to that described above, except now we write the self-selection constraints as

$$\theta_1 h_1 - y_1 - I > \theta_1 h_2 - y_2 + I$$
$$\theta_2 h_2 - y_2 + I > \theta_2 h_1 - y_1 - I$$

where I is the payment from the insurance company to the firm in the bad state (from the firm to the insurance company in the good state).

21. In the general theory of self-selection, it is shown that with only two states of nature a self-selection equilibrium dominates a pooling equilibrium, in the absence of transactions costs (see Stiglitz 1974b).

22. See the section on layoffs and contract complexity. Note, however, that with enforcement problems all the calculations concerning the relative merits of self-selection equilibria versus rigid-wage employment equilibria need to be redone.

23. There are, of course, other versions of asymmetric information models, yielding somewhat different results. Cooper, for instance, has explored a model in which firms are informed concerning workers' marginal rates of substitution. This model may easily give rise to underemployment equilibria. But the underlying assumption behind the analysis is unconvincing. While firms may plausibly be assumed to be imperfectly informed concerning an individual's opportunity costs, it is not plausible to assume, given that workers remain on a job, that there are significant variations in their marginal rates of substitution between leisure and income. (An exception would be provided by individuals who hold second jobs, such as taxi driving.)

24. We have drawn the line between implicit and explicit contracts somewhat more finely than we should have. Even when there is an explicit contract, reliance may be placed on reputation as an enforcement mechanism, because of the costs of resorting to the legal mechanism and because of the inevitable ambiguities associated with the terms of any contract. In addition, there is a long legal tradition stipulating that not all the terms of the contract can be enforced through the legal process.

25. Obviously, if the shocks at date t and $t=1$ are perfectly correlated, there is, in effect, only one shock; but then the assumption that the worker remains uninformed about the state of nature becomes implausible. Eventually, workers should learn that the firm faces bad prospects. So long as the state of nature eventually becomes known, the asymmetric information restrictions are irrelevant.

26. From the general theory of self-selection, contracts may entail randomness (see Stiglitz 1982a); how such random contracts are to be enforced appears even more problematic than how the nonstochastic contracts discussed so far are to be enforced.

For a discussion of optimal multiperiod contracts, see Stiglitz and Weiss (1983). Note that, since some of the shocks to the economy are common environmental shocks, the optimal contract should employ information from other firms, as in Nalebuff and Stiglitz (1983a, 1983b).

27. We have focused here on one side of the enforcement problem: ensuring that the firm does not cheat the workers. There is another side that has received attention: workers who have been subsidized in the bad state leaving the firm in the good state. If workers always left the firm whenever their wage was less than the value of their marginal product, the firm would never be able to pay workers more than their marginal product in the good states. There is an obvious solution: make individuals pay their insurance premium before they start to work; equivalently, since workers are normally hired in good states, pay the workers less than their marginal product for the first period of employment (see Holmstrom 1983).

28. Even if search were costly in time, but not in goods, and even if it were always successful, individuals who had a separable utility function but worked in a low

productivity firm would not be compensated by any severance pay if they were laid off. Indeed, if leisure and goods are complements, the optimal contract would entail negative severance pay, if that were feasible.

29. Several other papers have also focused on the issue of interfirm mobility. Holmstrom (1983) has considered its implication for the enforceability of contracts (with workers leaving in good states.) The paper closest in spirit to the Arnott-Hosios-Stiglitz paper (1983) is that by Imai, Geanakoplos, and Ito (1981), but they do not focus on the moral hazard issues that are central to Arnott, Hosios, and Stiglitz. For a partial survey see Ito (1982).

30. Obviously if U_{yh} is positive enough, the retained workers will be better off than laid-off workers. In the terminology of Arnott and Stiglitz, being laid off is a marginal utility increasing or decreasing accident depending on whether $U_{yh} \geq 0$; with full insurance, marginal utility increasing accidents always lead the individual experiencing the accident to be better off.

The result is even stronger if leisure and consumption are complements, in the sense that $U_{yh} < 0$. Those who are laid off have more time to enjoy their goods and thus receive more goods than those who are left to work. In Appendix A we show that, if leisure is normal, laid-off workers will be better off.

31. Though there are a few instances of "inverse seniority"—where unemployment benefits plus layoff pay are sufficiently generous that workers with greater seniority prefer to be laid off—this is more the exception than the rule. See, for instance, Bloom and Northrup (1977). In models with work sharing, the corresponding paradox is that workers' utility is higher in the bad state than in the good.

32. There are other ways of resolving this seeming paradox. For instance, as we noted earlier, if search is time intensive (but does not use goods), but always successful, then laid-off workers will not be compensated for the loss of time associated with search. They will be worse off than retained workers.

33. It seems to be merely a semantic quibble to claim that so long as there is some industry in which rationing does not exist there cannot be involuntary unemployment. The models we construct have the property that individuals who are identical (or nearly identical) are treated differently and have markedly different levels of expected utility.

34. So long as workers are risk averse, more risk averse than firms, firms will bear some of these costs. See Arnott and Stiglitz (1982) and also Hashimoto (1981).

35. Note that this problem could be resolved if individuals could be forced to pay all of their training costs, but this would give rise to a moral hazard problem on the part of the firm: it would have an incentive to charge individuals for allegedly training them and then fail to provide any training. This problem may be partly resolved by use of contests (Bhattacharya 1983) or promotion ladders (Carmichael 1983). Moreover, individuals may not have the capital to pay for all of their training costs. In any case, as we have noted, if individuals are risk averse, it is not optimal to force workers to bear the entire brunt of the risk that they may be ill-suited to the firm. As a factual matter, firms do bear some of the turnover costs.

36. To obtain an efficiency wage, one must show more than a dependence of quality on wages, but that quality increases sufficiently fast with wages that it does not pay firms to lower their wages in the face of unemployment. Conditions under which this occurs have been derived from Stiglitz (1976b, 1982a).

Some have objected to this theory on the grounds that firms eventually learn an individual's abilities; hence workers could be required to post a bond, which they would forfeit if it turned out later that they were not as good as they claimed. The objections to this are similar to those discussed earlier concerning the requirement to make individuals pay all of their training costs. Individuals may not have the capital to post the bond, and there is a moral hazard problem on the part of the firm. Some effective bond posting does occur, when individuals initially accept a lower wage, until they have proven themselves, but this imposes a further cost on individuals, in an inefficient intertemporal pattern of consumption.

Even when individuals are not well informed about their abilities, it may be beneficial for a firm to offer an above-market wage, to elicit a larger applicant pool, among which it can select those who are best matched with the firm.

What is at issue here is in part an empirical question: Do firms believe that by lowering wages they will lower the quality of their labor force, with a loss in productivity exceeding the savings in wages?

37. This version of the theory is developed by Shapiro and Stiglitz (1984). In their more general model, monitoring costs (and hence monitoring intensity) is endogenous. See also Calvo (1979).

38. The remarks in this and the next section are based on research in progress and therefore are of a more speculative nature than results reported earlier in this chapter.

39. See, for instance, John Taylor (1980), for a discussion of staggered contracts. The theory, as presented, does not explain why contracts should be staggered. Hosios has developed a theory, based on information costs, to explain why contracts in equilibrium would not be signed simultaneously by all firms.

40. For a more formal development of these ideas, see Stiglitz (1974b).

41. This result is an application of a more general result on market-mediated externalities in economies with incomplete markets and imperfect information (Greenwald and Stiglitz 1983).

42. There is the suggestion in the implicit contract approach that, since the terms of the contract, which lead upon occasion to unemployment, are signed voluntarily, the unemployment generated is not really involuntary unemployment; and that since the contract maximized expected profits, given the level of expected utility of the worker, since the contract is, in this sense efficient, the market equilibrium is efficient. While the first question, whether the unemployment is voluntary or involuntary, is mainly a matter of semantics, the second conclusion, that the market equilibrium is pareto efficient, is as we have noted incorrect. There exist, in general, governmental interventions in the market that can both increase profits and increase the expected utility of workers. (See Newbery and Stiglitz 1984; Arnott, Hosios, and Stiglitz 1983) (The result that—even when contractual arrangements between parties are "locally efficient"—the general equilibrium is not pareto efficient is more general and holds whenever there are problems of moral hazard or adverse selection. See Greenwald and Stiglitz 1983.)

REFERENCES

Akerlof, George A. 1984. "Gift Exchange and Efficiency Wage Theory: Four Views." *American Economic Review Proceedings* 74 (May):79–83.

———. 1970. "The Market for 'Lemons': Qualitative Uncertainty and the Market Mechanism." *Quarterly Journal of Economics* 84:488–500.

Akerlof, G. A., and H. Miyazaki. 1980. "The Implicit Contract Theory of Unemployment Meets the Wage Bill Argument." *Review of Economic Studies* 47 (January): 321–38.

Akerlof, George A., and Yellen, Janet. 1983. "The Macroeconomic Consequences of Near Rational Rule of Thumb Behavior." Berkeley: University of California at Berkeley. Mimeographed.

Akerlof, G. A., and J. E. Stiglitz. 1969. "Capital, Wages and Structural Unemployment." *Economic Journal* 79 (June): 269-81.
Arnott, R., A. Hosios, and J. Stiglitz. 1983. "Implicit Contracts, Labor Mobility and Unemployment." Princeton: Princeton University. Mimeographed. (Revised version of a paper presented at NBER-NSF conference, December 1980.)
Arnott, R. and J. Stiglitz. 1982. "Equilibrium in Competitive Insurance Markets: The Welfare Effects of Moral Hazard" (mimeo).
―――. 1981. "Labor Turnover, Wage Structures and Moral Hazard." Princeton: Princeton University. Mimeographed.
Arrow, K. J. 1964. "The Role of Securities in the Optimal Allocation of Riskbearing." *Review of Economic Studies* 31: 91.
Azariadis, C. 1983. "Employment with Asymmetric Information." *Quarterly Journal of Economics* 98:157-72.
―――. 1979. "Implicit Contracts and Related Topics: A Survey." In *The Economics of the Labour Market*, edited by Z. Hornstein et al. London: Her Majesty's Stationery Office.
―――. 1975. "Implicit Contracts and Underemployment Equilibria." *Journal of Political Economy* 83: 1183-202.
Azariadis, C., and J. E. Stiglitz. 1983. "Implicit Contracts and Fixed Price Equilibria." *Quarterly Journal of Economics* 98: 1-22.
Baily, M. N. 1974. "Wages and Employment Under Certain Demands." *Review of Economic Studies* 41: 37-50.
Barro, Robert J. and Grossman, Herschel I. 1971. "A General Equilibrium Model of Income and Employment." *American Economic Review* 61 (March):82-93.
Bhattacharya, S. 1983. "Tournaments and Incentives: Heterogeneity and Essentiality." Berkeley: University of California at Berkeley. Mimeographed.
Bloom, Gordon F., and Northrup, Herbert R. 1977. *Economics of Labor Relations.* Homewood, Ill.: Richard D. Irwin.
Borch, K. 1968. *The Economics of Uncertainty*. Princeton: Princeton University Press.
Burdett, Kenneth, and Dale T. Mortensen. 1980. "Search, Layoffs, and Labor Market Equilibrium" *Journal of Political Economy* 88: 652-72.
Calvo, Guillermo. 1979. "Quasi-Walrasian Theories of Unemployment." *American Economic Review* 69 (May): 102-7.
Calvo, Guillermo, and E. S. Phelps. 1977. "Appendix: Employment Contingent Wage Contracts." In *Stabilization of the Domestic and International Economy*, vol. 5, edited by Karl Brunner and Allan H. Meltzer. Carnegie-Rochester Conference Series on Public Policy, pp. 160-68.
Calvo, Guillermo, and Stanislaw Wellisz. 1979. "Hierarchy, Ability and Income Distribution." *Journal of Political Economy* 87: 991-1010.
Carmichael, Lorne. 1983. "Firm-Specific Human Capital and Promotion Ladders." *Bell Journal* 14 (Spring): 251-58.
Chari, V. V. 1983. "Involuntary Unemployment and Implicit Contracts." *Quarterly Journal of Economics* 98: 107-22.

Cooper, R. 1984. "Worker Asymmetric Information and Involuntary Unemployment." Cowles Foundation Discussion Paper 672R, April.

———. 1983. "A Note on Overemployment/Underemployment in Labor Contracts Under Asymmetric Information." *Economic Letters* 12: 81–87.

Cooper, R. 1981. "Risk-Sharing and Productive Efficiency in Labor Contracts Under Bilateral Asymmetric Information." University of Pennsylvania. Mimeographed.

Debreu, G. 1959. *Theory of Value.* New York: Wiley.

Eaton, B. Curtis, and William White. 1982. "Agent Compensation and the Limits of Bonding." *Economic Inquiry* 20: 330–43.

Gordon, D. F. 1974. "A Neoclassical Theory of Keynesian Unemployment." *Economic Inquiry* 12: 431–59.

Grandmont, J. M. 1982. *Money and Value.* Cambridge: Cambridge University Press.

Green, J., and C. Kahn. 1983. "Wage-Employment Contracts." *Quarterly Journal of Economics* 98: 173–87.

Greenwald, B., and J. E. Stiglitz. 1983. "Market Mediated Externalities: The Inefficiency of Competitive Economies with Imperfect Information and Incomplete Markets." Princeton: Princeton University. Mimeographed.

Grossman, S., and O. Hart. 1983. "Implicit Contracts Under Asymmetric Information." *Quarterly Journal of Economics* 98: 1223–56.

———. 1981. "Implicit Contracts, Moral Hazard, and Unemployment." *American Economic Review* (papers and proceedings) 71: 301–7.

Grossman, S., O. Hart, and E. Maskin. 1983. "Unemployment with Observable Aggregate Shocks." *American Economic Review* 91 (December):907–28.

Hall, Robert. 1980. "Employment Fluctuations and Wage Rigidity." *Brookings Papers on Economic Activity* 1:91–124.

———. 1975. "The Rigidity of Wages and the Persistence of Unemployment." *Brookings Papers on Economic Activity* 2: 301–35.

Hall, R., and E. Lazear. 1982. "The Excess Sensibility of Layoffs and Quits to Demand." *NBER Working Paper*, no. 864.

Hall, R., and D. Lilien. 1979. "Efficient Wage Bargains Under Uncertain Supply and Demand." *American Economic Review* 69:868–79.

Harris, J. E., and M. Todaro. 1970. "Migration, Unemployment and Development: A Two-Sector Analysis." *American Economic Review* 60: 126–42.

Harris, M., and B. Holmstrom. 1982. "A Theory of Wage Dynamics." *Review of Economic Studies* 49: 315–33.

Hart, O. 1983. "Optimal Labor Contracts Under Asymmetric Information: An Introduction." *Review of Economic Studies* 50: 3–36.

———. 1975. "On the Optimality of Equilibrium When the Market Structure Is Incomplete." *Journal of Economic Theory* 11: 416–43.

Hashimoto, M. 1981. "Firm-Specific Human Capital as a Shared Investment." *American Economic Review* 71 (June): 475–82.

Holmstrom, B. 1983. "Equilibrium Long-Term Labor Contracts." *Quarterly Journal of Economics* 98: 23–54.

Hosios, A. 1981. "Externalities, Efficiency and the Implicit Contract Theory of Employment." Princeton: Princeton University. Mimeographed.
Imai, H., J. Geanakoplos, and T. Ito. 1981. "Incomplete Insurance and Absolute Risk Aversion." *Economic Letters* 8: 107–12.
Ito, T. 1982. "Implicit Contract Theory: A Critical Survey." Center for Economic Research, University of Minnesota.
Leibenstein, J. 1957. *Economic Backwardness and Economic Growth*. New York: Wiley.
Malcolmson, James. 1981. "Unemployment and the Efficiency Wage Hypothesis." *Economic Journal* 91: 848–66.
Malinvaud, E. 1980. *Profitability and Unemployment*. Cambridge: Cambridge University Press.
―――. 1977. *The Theory of Unemployment Reconsidered*. Oxford: Blackwell.
Mirrlees, J. 1975. "A Pure Theory of Underdeveloped Economies." In *Agriculture in Development Theory*, edited by L. A. Reynolds pp. 84–106. New Haven: Yale University Press.
Moore, J. 1982. "Optimal Labour Contracts When Workers Have a Variety of Privately Observed Reservation Wages." London Birkbeck College. Mimeographed.
Mortenson, D. 1978. "On the Theory of Layoffs." Evanston, Ill.: Northwestern University. Mimeographed.
Nalebuff, B. J., and J. E. Stiglitz. Forthcoming. "Quality and Prices." *Quarterly Journal of Economics*.
―――. 1983a. "Prizes and Incentives: Towards a General Theory of Compensation and Competition." *Bell Journal* 14: 21–43.
―――. 1983b. "Information, Competition and Markets." *American Economic Review* 73 (May): 278–83.
Nalebuff, B. J., and R. Zeckhauser. 1981. "Involuntary Unemployment Reconsidered: Second-Best Contracting with Heterogeneous Firms and Workers." University of Wisconsin-Madison, Institute for Research on Poverty, Discussion Paper No. 675-81.
Neary, J. P., and J. Stiglitz. 1983. "Toward a Reconstruction of Keynesian Economics: Expectations and Constrained Equilibria." *Quarterly Journal of Economics* 98: 199–28.
Negishi, T. 1979. "Microeconomic Foundations of Keynesian Macroeconomics." Amsterdam: North-Holland.
Newbery, David M. and Joseph E. Stiglitz. 1984. "Pareto Inferior Trade." *Review of Economic Studies* 51 (January):1–12.
―――. 1982. "Wage Rigidity, Implicit Contracts and Economic Efficiency: Are Market Wages Too Flexible?" Princeton: Princeton University. Mimeographed.
―――. 1981. *The Theory of Commodity Price Stabilization*. Oxford: Oxford University Press.
Phelps, E. S. 1970. *Micro-Economic Foundations of Employment and Inflation Theory*. New York: Norton.
Polemarchakis, H. M. 1979. "Implicit Contracts and Employment Theory." *Review of Economic Studies* 46 (January): 97–108.

Polemarchakis, H. M., and L. Weiss. 1978. "Fixed Wages, Layoffs, Unemployment Compensation, and Welfare." *American Economic Review* 68: 909-17.

Rothschild, Michael A., and Joseph E. Stiglitz. 1976. "Equilibrium in Competitive Insurance Markets: An Essay in the Economics of Imperfect Information." *Quarterly Journal of Economics* 90: 629-49.

Salop, Steven. C. 1979. "A Model of the Natural Rate of Unemployment." *American Economic Review* 69: 117-25.

──────. 1973. "Wage Differentials in a Dynamic Theory of the Firm." *Journal of Economic Theory* 6 (August): 321-44.

Sargent, R. J. 1979. *Macroeconomic Theory.* New York: Academic Press.

Schlicht, Ekkehart. 1978. "Labour Turnover, Wage Structure and Natural Unemployment." *Zeitschrift fur die Gasamte Staatswissenschaft* 134: 337-46.

Shapiro, Carl, and Joseph Stiglitz. 1984. "Equilibrium Unemployment as a Worker Discipline Device." *American Economic Review* 74 (June): 433-44.

Solow, Robert. 1981. "On Theories of Unemployment." *American Economic Review* 91: 848-66.

──────. 1979. "Another Possible Source of Wage Stickiness." *Journal of Macroeconomics* 1 (Winter): 79-82.

Solow, R., and J. Stiglitz. 1968. "Output, Employment and Wages in the Short Run." *Quarterly Journal of Economics* 82:537-60.

Stiglitz, J. E. 1984. "Price Rigidities and Market Structure." *American Economic Review* 74 (May): 350-55.

──────. 1982a. "The Wage-Productivity Hypothesis: Its Economic Consequences and Policy Implications." Paper presented at the New York Meetings of the American Economic Association.

──────. 1982b. "The Inefficiency of the Stock Market Equilibrium." *Review of Economic Studies* 49 (April): 241-6.

──────. 1982c. "Alternative Theories of Wage Determination and Unemployment in L.D.C's: The Efficiency Wage Model." M. Gersovitz et al., editor. *The Theory and Experience of Economic Development: Essays in Honor of Sir W. Arthur Lewis.* London: Allen and Unwin, 1982.

──────. 1978. "Lectures in Macro-economics." Oxford: Oxford University. Mimeographed.

──────. 1976a. "Prices and Queues as Screening Devices in Competitive Markets." IMMSS Technical Report No. 212. Stanford University.

──────. 1976b. "The Efficiency Wage Hypothesis, Surplus Labor and the Distribution of Income in L.D.C.'s." *Oxford Economic Papers* 28: 185-207.

──────. 1974a. "Theories of Discrimination and Economic Policy." In *Patterns of Racial Discrimination,* edited by George von Furstenberg, pp. 5-26. Lexington, Mass.: Lexington Books.

──────. 1974b. "Equilibrium Wage Distributions." IMMSS Technical Report No. 154. Stanford University. Forthcoming in *Economic Journal.*

──────. 1973. "Approaches to the Economies of Discrimination." *American Economic Review* 62: 287-95.

Stiglitz, J. E., and A. Weiss. 1983. "Incentive Effects of Terminations: Applications to the Credit and Labor Markets." *American Economic Review* 73: 912-27.

Stoft, Steven. 1982. "Cheat Threat Theory: An Explanation of Involuntary

Unemployment." Boston: Boston University. Mimeographed.
Strand, J. 1983a. "The Structure of Implicit Contracts with Word of Mouth Reputational Enforcement." Oslo: University of Oslo. Mimeographed.
_____. 1983b. "The Structure and Efficiency of Reputational Labor Contracts." Stanford: Stanford University. Mimeographed.
Taylor, John B. 1980. "Aggregate Dynamics and Staggered Contracts." *Journal of Political Economy* 88 (February): 1–23.
Weiss, Andrew. 1980. "Job Queues and Layoffs in Labor Markets with Flexible Wages." *Journal of Political Economy* 88: 526–38.
Wilson, Charles. 1977. "A Model of Insurance Markets with Incomplete Information." *Journal of Economic Theory* 16: 167–207.
Yellen, J. 1984. "Efficiency Wage Models of Unemployment." *American Economic Review* 24 (May): 200–205.

* * *

COMMENT BY CHRISTOPHER PISSARIDES

I found Joseph Stiglitz's paper extremely interesting. In fact, when I started reading it, it soon became obvious to me that I was going to have one very serious problem when discussing it, in that I was agreeing with everything it said. I thought with a paper of this length there must be something that I could say, but the only comments I could make were more by way of summary rather than substantial criticism. But since it was a long paper followed by a long presentation, I will try and give you a very short presentation here, of what I consider to be the main points of the paper.

The first explanation of wage rigidity discussed by Stiglitz is the implicit contract explanation. This explanation is theoretically satisfactory because a profit-maximizing firm will have no incentive to reduce its wage when the demand for output falls. If it did so it would create too much income fluctuation for workers, and risk-averse workers would not like it. So a firm that wanted to offer as good a job contract as possible to its workers would have an incentive not to reduce its wages. However, layoffs also cause fluctuations in workers' incomes; so a firm would also have an incentive not to lay off workers, unless it was able to compensate workers so that their incomes did not fluctuate when they were laid off.

As a theory of unemployment, however, the implicit contract theory is not satisfactory. There are two elements in it that we may single out for criticism. The first one is not so important, although the second one is.

The first is that the theory implies that unemployment is either equal to or less than the unemployment we would get in spot markets. This is not a very serious criticism because we do not know how much spot unemployment there is. For example, say that in a Walrasian world unemployment was as high as 20 percent. If now we get 10 percent unemployment with contracts and this unemployment has different characteristics from Walrasian unemployment, then the contract explanation of unemployment is still worthwhile, because we learn something about the features of that unemployment.

However, what I consider to be a more serious criticism of this theory is that the unemployed workers in implicit contract models are not necessarily worse off than the employed workers, and that goes against our understanding of unemployment. We think of unemployment as being costly so that workers do not like to be unemployed, yet in those models there is a condition that makes workers equally well off at the margin, regardless of whether they are employed or not. Associated with that marginal condition, there is an average condition that usually works the wrong way, in that the unemployed worker has higher average utility than the employed worker under very weak conditions on utility functions. So, on average, workers with contracts should prefer to be unemployed than employed.

There are several extensions of the model, some of which are more promising than others. Asymmetric information, or what Stiglitz calls the observability problem, does not seem to improve things. In fact, it makes overemployment more likely because now the firm will have an incentive to lie in bad states and report that the state is good, in order to get more work out of its workers. Risk aversion on the part of firms might give some underemployment, but it is not an assumption on which we would want to base a theory of unemployment. Apart from the limited appeal of the assumption, it is not clear that this approach to unemployment can give us anything more than a trivial amount of underemployment.

Theories of unemployment that rely on the complexity of contracts are appealing, because casual empiricism tells us that it would be very difficult to write contracts with a full set of contingencies. But such theories are unsatisfactory to the extent that results depend on what we assume can be written in contracts, and what can be written in contracts is not part of the theory. For example, suppose that, for the sake of simplicity, contracts are restricted to making money wages contingent on a single price. Which price we choose to name will normally make a difference to the market outcome, for example, whether it is output price, the consumer price index, or, as in the Newbery-Stiglitz model, the export price. There is as yet no theory, or even convincing empirical evidence, that can tell us what is feasible and what is "too complex" for real-world contracts.

The next extension of moral hazard and labor turnover is more appealing, because firms may have preferences about the behavior of their workers, without sufficient tools to control it. For example, a firm may want to control the search behavior of its workers, and one outcome of this may be layoff unemployment.

In the case discussed by Stiglitz, the firm would like some workers to leave; so it lays them off without sufficient compensation. If the workers are worse off on layoff than employed, they will search more intensely for an alternative job when they are laid off. However, firms may have incentives to keep their workers if they have accumulated firm-specific skills, especially if the depressions are expected to be short. In such a case they might compensate their workers on layoff generously, at least for a short period after layoff.

However, there is another way in which firms may control the behavior of their laid-off workers, and this works in favor of more layoffs. Firms may discourage job search by increasing the recall probability, that is, by reducing the expected duration of the layoff. The existence of this tool is likely to change the firm's policy toward more unemployment and less wage reduction, since the tool becomes effective only when the worker is made unemployed. Thus, in the case where the firm does not want the worker to leave because of firm-specific skills, it may still lay off to save the wage costs. It could then discourage workers from searching for another job by recalling frequently and laying off other workers if necessary.

Efficiency wage models break away from the framework of contract models and concentrate instead on the quality of labor. The basic idea is that wage reductions reduce the quality of labor; so the firm may avoid them. I find this an exciting idea, though we do not yet know how well it can stand up to the kind of scrutiny that the models of job search and implicit contracts have been subjected to. Nevertheless, the idea does look promising, and since this conference is devoted to Keynes, I might add that this idea is not quite in any of Keynes' writings, but it is in Hicks' *Theory of Wages*. Although not quite a perfect substitute, it is close enough, and it conforms to the law that if it is not in Keynes, it must be in Hicks.

For industrial economies the efficiency wage hypothesis takes two forms. First, a higher wage may improve the quality mix of labor; that is, it may induce more able workers to take the firm's wage offer. Second, the higher wage may make existing workers work harder. The firm may, for example, offer a wage for a particular job and recruit by applying a hiring standard if it can observe the quality of applicants. If it cannot observe the quality of applicants, it may still be able to recruit better people because the high wage will attract higher quality applicants. Then, if there is a decrease in the demand for output, the firm may be better off if it laid off the lowest quality workers, or the median worker by random choice of layoffs, than if it reduced wages. Wage reductions are more likely to induce the more skilled workers to quit.

Workers may work harder when the wage is high and when it does not fluctuate in response to small changes in demand either for reasons of morale, as discussed by Akerlof, or simply because workers know that they will be rewarded with employment at a good wage when times are bad, if they work hard when times are good. In multiperiod models similar incentives may be offered by rising wage profiles. But a rising wage profile requires a perfect capital market, otherwise workers' consumption will fluctuate too much. If workers cannot borrow cheaply, the firm may instead achieve the same incentives as a rising wage profile by paying well from the beginning, but maintaining the threat of unemployment for later periods, if the worker's work effort is not sufficiently good.

Finally, a firm may avoid wage reductions in a recession to reduce the chances of quits of trained workers. Unless workers can be made to pay for their entire training costs, labor turnover is costly to the firm. A high wage reduces the turnover rate; so firms may prefer it to a lower one.

In all these models labor is of different quality, and what it does depends on the wage rate. It seems that an important step toward a formalization of this theory is to relate workers' quality to their response to wage fluctuations. For example, are more able workers more likely to quit in response to a given wage reduction than less able ones? Do wage comparability arguments matter? These are questions that are largely unanswered.

* * *

COMMENT BY KARL BRUNNER

The author presented a massive paper, and when I received it two days ago I wondered about my capacity of absorbing all that material within such a short time limit. I may suffer some divine retribution for what I did to my discussants on occasions in the past years, but this time I had an occasion to read it quickly. I do regret that I could not ponder it in the way it deserves to be pondered. I find it interesting and stimulating.

It is also neatly and cleanly presented as you would expect from Joe. It is certainly a paper worth a detailed examination.

The problems of wage rigidity, employment patterns, and unemployment belong to the core of macroeconomic concerns. A serious reexamination of the contract theory and the efficiency wage theory seems most appropriate at this stage. We experienced evolutions on the labor markets of various countries over the recent years that were generally held to be highly improbable. We found that some money wages declined, and so did some real wages. We also found that general and full indexations agreements of long standing—apparently untouchable—broke down under the reality of the market forces. There also emerged changes in employment and unemployment patterns. Substantial shifts occurred between layoffs, permanent separations, and particularly shifts between layoffs on one side, or what we call in Europe partial unemployment, and what you call work sharing in the United States. Typically labor hoarding in Switzerland occurred over recession. There were, in general, few layoffs, and this contributed to holding the unemployment rate at a comparatively low level. This pattern was clearly visible in industries employing few foreign workers. The old pattern has now been replaced by a massive appearance of work sharing and partial unemployment. This evolved essentially as a consequence of the change in unemployment compensation. Since 1975 unemployment compensation is now applicable to the working days that a firm cuts out of the week. A worker obtains unemployment compensation for each weekday lost. So labor hoarding was replaced by partial unemployment. All these new experiences naturally challenge us to reexamine our state of analysis.

Employment, unemployment, and wage rigidity are important features of Keynes' legacy. Wage rigidity formed, however, neither a sufficient nor a necessary condition for his basic conclusions. Wage rigidity is introduced quite ad hoc as a device to stabilize the *nominal* system. Before we proceed with a discussion of wage rigidity, it is important to clarify what we really mean by it. It is not something that one can see out there. I cannot see wages being rigid like I can see Joe Stiglitz sitting there. Wage rigidity, basically, only has meaning in the context of a completely specified theory when it is defined by the context of the theory. Wage rigidity is thus a highly theoretical term ultimately assessed by the empirical relevance of the containing theory. We need to explore somewhat further and characterize the context of the term. We recognize, in general, that an economy is subject to the operation of a wide array of transitory or permanent shocks. These shocks continuously modify market conditions. Rigidity of wages means now that wages do not fully reflect all ongoing shocks at all times. Within the context of the standard rational expectations market clearing model, all prices and wages are fully flexible; that is, they reflect fully all ongoing shocks. In this sense, there is no price rigidity at all. If you look, on the other hand, at the rational expectations models that I worked on with Alex Cukierman and Allan Meltzer in the *Journal of Monetary Economics*, price rigidity occurs in the sense that prices do not reflect all ongoing shocks. They only reflect a component of these shocks, namely those that agents perceive as comparatively permanent shocks. The perceived transitory shocks are not reflected in the price-setting behavior of agents. This procedure shows, incidentally, that the notion of wage rigidity does not involve a rejection of equilibrium analysis. An equilibrium always exists relative to the relevant information expressed by perceived permanent shocks. Deviations of actual shocks from those perceptions impose adjustments on real magnitudes.

I emphasized that wage rigidity plays a very limited accessory function in Keynes' analysis. Actually he offers us a real theory of employment and output with a real business cycle. Within this basic core of the real theory of employment and output, underemployment equilibrium is set by the real conditions of the economy, essentially independent of nominal shocks and nominal affairs. They may enter, however, via the long-term uncertainty of the system, and to this extent a feedback on the real conditions may emerge. But wage flexibility in the context of an underemployment system produces a permanent deflationary process. the nature of expectations induced by this deflation would affect the outcome. Keynes seems to emphasize a prevalence of extrapolative expectations, in contrast to the regressive expectations assured for the bonds markets, and "anything goes" on the stock markets. We find thus in his analysis a strange combination of expectational patterns.

Turning back to the labor market, however, we find that the social fact of wage rigidity imposed on individual behavior as an extraneous entity serves to anchor nominal values. It serves in Keynes' analysis as the role of the money stock in classical theory.

This analysis is really quite unsatisfactory. Wage rigidity appears removed from economic analysis and separated from the interaction between motivated individuals. Wage rigidity, moreover, seems to have no real significance. Economic analysis would suggest that "wage rigidity" measured unemployment and that observed employment patterns are closely linked. An exploration of this linkage is really the concern of this paper.

The contract theory is subjected to a very careful and detailed examination. Stiglitz emphasizes that the contracts structured in the theory involve essentially insurance arrangements. He elaborates on the various aspects involved, the observability conditions, enforceability, and other issues that need to be considered in this context. However, the crucial question remains: Does this explain the interrelation between wage rigidity and unemployment, or does it explain anything about unemployment? The author concludes correctly that this approach does not bear on our issue. The world described by these models maintains full employment in a specified technical sense or produces in some cases even "overemployment." Whatever the contractual relation in the interrelation between wage rigidity and unemployment may be, it will require an entirely different approach to cope with this problem.

The efficiency wage theory is the second theme in the paper. Consider the production function expressing output as a function of the input of labor in physical units multiplied by an intensity or effort measure λ (see equation [15]). This intensity index appears as a function of the wage paid by the particular firm, the array of wages obtainable at other firms, and the unemployment level U. The wage offered by the firm itself has a positive effect on the effort index, and so does the unemployment rate, whereas the wages paid by other firms affect λ negatively.

This formulation seems a good summary expression to subsume the class of efficiency wage theories. Stiglitz properly discards the nutrition theory as irrelevant for our purpose. But there remain four more theories that are possibly of some significance. The turnover theory, the theory that emphasizes imperfect information about the quality of workers, and the theory that emphasizes imperfect information about the action of workers, basically involving the problem of monitoring and shirking, seem to offer, in my judgment, the most promising avenues for exploration. Akerlof's fairness theory, on the other hand, appears to me somewhat dubious, at least until further evaluation.

The alternative theories can be usefully characterized and differentiated in terms of the λ function. This function not only differs in its general form according to the theory expressed, but also in terms of the arguments included. Different theories may require inclusion of different events or different types of real shocks and possibly nominal shocks. These differences suggest that the alternative theories within the general class probably produce a substantial array of diverse propositions. A rather extensive research program would be required to explore and assess these ramifications.

The issues raised by Stiglitz invite me to probe most tentatively a bit further. The failure of the "contract theory" with respect to our problem does not produce an alternative contractual approach. I have been much influenced in this respect by ages of discussions with Armen Alchian, William Meckling, and Allan Meltzer. These discussions wrestled with possible price-theoretic (i.e., nonsociological) explanations to the phenomenon of "inflexible" prices and wages. The failure of existing "contract theory" results, in my view, from its intellectual background and starting point. It seems crucially conditioned by the Arrow-Debreu paradigm. With this background, phenomena sensitively associated with transaction costs, monitoring, and information problems will be emasculated or neglected. The important labor market institutions and relevant contractual relations are barely integrated into approaches with this starting point.

Consider a different procedure. We encounter in reality a diffuse uncertainty beyond risk, particularly with respect to the kinds of shocks occurring. Shocks continuously modify market conditions, and agents are similarly confronted with inferences problems, whether these shocks are comparatively transitory or comparatively permanent. All managers of the bank's money desk have to make this decision every day. They do not put it that way, but they have to decide whether huge reserve inflows are transitory or more permanent. Are the inflows at the tail of a distribution, or are they reflecting a change in the distribution? Managers will make radically different portfolio decisions depending on what their assessment is. In one case they will just make a federal funds operation, not even a Treasury bill operation, and in the other case portfolio adjustments reach rapidly beyond securities to loans.

Direct your attention to setting up a firm. No firm will be set up in view of transitory market conditions. You will require much more permanent conditions for this purpose. A less extreme but similar condition frequently holds for price setting. If one changes prices very rapidly, you impose serious costs of information and inconvenience on your potential customers. Whenever such costs and inconveniences occur with some weight, competition between suppliers induces firms to set their prices over some time. The relevant time period varies with the conditions characterizing a firm's position. The resulting price may be higher on the average, but potential customers are compensated by lower information costs and lessened inconvenience. This potential explanation of price and wage rigidity does not appear, on prima facie grounds, inconsistent with an "efficiency theory" of wages.

Some questions need be addressed to this theory. The argument in the production is the product of λ with the physical volume of labor. It follows that a lower-intensity level raises the marginal product of labor. It appears to me that the multiplicative occurrence of λ poses a problem. A better procedure seems to involve a separate occurrence of λ with a positive cross derivative with respect to the physical volume of labor input.

Another aspect refers to an important omission in the λ function. The intensity level is in my judgment to a large extent conditioned by the organization of the firm. This organization influences the incentive structure characterizing the firm. It reflects, moreover, the control and monitoring mechanisms that assign responsibilities and modify shirking. Organizational choices may reinforce or obstruct the effect of the wage on or offset the negative effect of other firms' wage offers. Organizational choices are frequently associated with the total package of an employment offer, and they influence the latter's effect on λ. Most likely, the nature of the function thus depends quite sensitively on organizational choices.

Prices seem another important omission from the λ function. Their absence implies that real conditions do not matter and "money illusion" rules supreme. Money wages are not set or formed irrespective of prices. Indexation and other arrangements suggest this connection. Without an explicit integration of prices, the efficiency wage formulation cannot properly be linked up with a full macroeconomic scheme of unemployment and the wage structure.

Lastly, the dynamic interaction of the whole system seems particularly interesting. Global shocks operating on the unemployment level impose adjustments on the whole wage structure and wage levels. This change in the whole wage structure unleashes further adjustment in the unemployment rate and output, until the system ultimately would come to a rest again.

It may be worthwhile to develop such an analysis in order to explore the determinants of the normal level of unemployment. In this context the nature of the λ function could assume a crucial role. The resulting analysis may ultimately not offer a relevant explanation. An exploration along these lines of normal unemployment, which emerges from the equilibrium solution of an interaction between the system of wage structures in response to all kind of shocks, could still offer some useful material. Alternatively, normal unemployment could be defined as the average rate of unemployment, given the shocks that continuously impose adjustments on the wage structure with productivity and unemployment effects occurring as a result.

The efficient wage formulation seems also to offer a justification for the Austrian thesis. This thesis holds that, with a single labor union for the whole country, the complex interaction between various competing unions is removed. The adjustment of wage structures can be simultaneous and immediate under the circumstances. The social adjustment costs are consequently smaller. However, this argument neglects the monopoly problem and the internal conflict of a single union.

The expectational problem has been rather cavalierly disregarded so far. The workers' *perception* of other firms' wage structures affects the intensity level. But this perception, and the corresponding perception about prices, involves an inference problem based on the information confronting the worker. Those expectational elements enter the process conditioned by institutional arrangements as, for example, the choice of organizational structure within firms. Such structure affects packages of wages and work conditions that could influence the speed of adjustments. We touch here on issues of social policy bearing on the choice of institutional constraints on organizational structures. Different constraints may modify the range and social cost of adjustment and thus influence the achievable welfare.

* * *

COMMENT BY RICHARD LAYARD

I agree very much with the spirit of most of this paper. I thought it was very satisfactory, but I have three comments. The first is on the very last bit where Joe is rather cavalier about the question of nominal wage rigidity, which I found somewhat surprising, particularly at this conference. I always thought that the sort of thing we teach as Keynesianism had to do with the rigidity of the nominal wage, and the inconsistency between the nominal wage and the money stock or some other nominal magnitude. Certainly in public debate these days, most of us think in terms of the bottom left-hand corner in Axel's diagram. When we think about why unemployment has gone up with all these governments deflating around the world, we surely basically think of it in terms of some nominal inertia in wages and with the growth in the money demand variables coming down faster then the rate of inflation of money wages. This seems to be a very important area to study, and some of the things that were said in the paper do throw light on it. But a possibly important way of looking at it, which is not referred to very particularly here, is the difficulty, when you have staggered timings of wage settlements, of workers preserving their real incomes in the face of a nominal deflation when they are going through staggered drops. If nominal demand falls, and all the workers resettle at the same time, they can all have the same real incomes but at lower nominal wages and that will be fine. But if nominal demand falls and we are the next ones to settle, then we drop down by the amount of the fall in nominal demand, and the price level continues on the basis of the wages that other people who have not yet settled are being paid. So we will be the ones to suffer. That seems to be an important explanation of this major difficulty of transition, which most people would think of as a sort of central Keynesian proposition that we teach.

Coming to the question of real shocks as opposed to nominal shocks, some of what is said here is very relevant. There is another model that one could perhaps explore, in which peoples' feelings or morale depend on their real wage relative to the real wage that they think is fair, which is based on their past experience. Then if you have a productivity drop, it is not in the interests of the employers to drop real wages by the same amount as the productivity drop because of the morale effect. They will drop it by less, and that is a source of the unemployment resulting from the oil shock and the like. This is an important rival way of looking at these effects to the interesting explanations that Karl Brunner and his colleagues have been putting forth.

Finally, I would like to comment on these models as they relate to the natural rate. I still feel that they are most powerful in thinking about the properties of the natural rate. Obviously the basic difficulty with all models relating to the natural rate, including the ones that I was talking about yesterday, is whether they are the least bit plausible in terms of magnitude. Unemployment cannot be 50 percent. It is somewhere between 1 and 20 percent. It is not obvious from any of these models other than the supply and demand one, which we are rejecting in adopting these wage-setting models, why the natural rate of unemployment should be under a fifth. It is particularly not obvious in any of the models such as George Akerlof has been advocating, where the whole thing is very much a bootstrap theory and the wage has basically got to be what it is because people are going to be in trouble if they change it. If one wants to choose between theories, one of the important criteria in choosing is whether the theory gives you any feeling at all for why the magnitude of the natural rate is what we see.

* * *

COMMENT BY COSTAS AZARIADIS

We have to give the speaker some time to respond to the discussants' comments and also open the floor to general discussion. Before we do that, I shall appeal to the "fairness doctrine" of broadcasting under which certain individuals are entitled to equal time when their ideas are imperfectly rendered by others. The first thing that struck me as I read this paper was a passage in Scott Fitzgerald to the effect that it is the mark of great intelligence to be able to hold in one's mind two opposing ideas and still be able to function. Joe passes this particular test with flying colors: on the topic of today's paper, he holds at the same time in his mind several opposing ideas and has coauthored (with David Newberg and others) several opposing, and interesting, papers that articulate these views.

The first substantive point that I want to stress is that turnover costs to a firm depend not only on the wage the firm itself pays, but also on the wages of all other firms. Since, in a general equilibrium model, the wage policies of firms are endogenous, it has to be the case that equilibrium turnover depends on the search costs of all individuals and also on the process by which meetings between jobs and workers take place. So this particular theory of turnover costs shares some common ground with search theory, in particular, the problems that search theory has in explaining cyclical unemployment. The most important of these is that quits are highest at the peak of business cycles, not at the trough as search theory predicts.

The paper reiterates the provocative idea that Joe and Carl Shapiro have had about unemployment as a disciplinary device for workers. This is an explanation of unemployment, but it is a bit one-sided because it looks at unemployment queues as a way to dissuade workers from breaching their implicit contract with their employer. The particular problem Shapiro and Stiglitz address is shirking, that is, the failure of workers to exert themselves sufficiently at work.

Firms have valid incentives of their own to breach implicit promises that are hard to monitor, such as overtime employment or even job security. Vacancies may be thought of as a disciplinary device for firms. If vacancies exist, then workers are very valuable at the margin, and firms would think twice before they breach a contract. If one looks at the possibility of breach not only from the workers' side but also from the firms' side, it is not clear whether the outcome is unemployment or vacancies. The reason for this indeterminancy is that the model of Stiglitz and Shapiro is one of asymmetric or private information. Private information causes an inefficiency in the labor market that may take the form of too little or too much employment. The direction of the inefficiency depends on preferences, on who the informed party is, and on other factors. But from first principles alone, we cannot be sure about the outcome, unless we are willing to think further as to how implicit contracts are enforced in the first place.

Many economists view implicit contracts as mechanisms that mimic the allocations of an Arrow-Debreu world. My own view of this literature is that it exploits elements that are special to the relationship between workers and their employer. Employers know things about their workers and workers know things about their employer that outsiders, third parties, are not privy to. That is what makes the insurance exchange so much easier in the workplace than outside it. It is like a husband and wife team. Each one possesses information about the other that the outside world simply does not have. This is completely different from the Arrow-Debreu model in which all information is public, where everybody knows everything about everybody else that is of any economic relevance.

My last remarks are addressed to the problem of enforcement, by far the most important one in Stiglitz's criticism of implicit contracts. Contracts are usually thought of as schedules of wages and employment expressed as functions of some state of nature. What mechanisms bind contractants to these schedules?

One mechanism, studied extensively by Radner, Townsend, Carmichael, and others, is reputation: if somebody deviates from the terms of the contract, the deviation becomes widely known, and the deviant finds it difficult to locate trading partners in the future. That works very well if the contractual relationship is repeated and if, furthermore, the future is important in comparison with the present, in other words, if the discount rate is very low. If the discount rate is very high, reputation does not work all that well.

The other method of enforcement is by a third party, a monitor, arbitrator, or court of law. That is where interesting problems arise, and Joe has brought up some of them. In order for a court to enforce a contract, it has to be able to observe all the prices and all the quantities specified in it—the employment status, hours worked, and wage rate of every worker. That is an unreasonably large informational burden to place on someone who is outside of the special relationship called a contract. Outsiders can be expected to observe at low cost only certain aggregates or averages, but not very much in the way of idiosyncratic detail. We may think, for instance, that courts readily observe wage rates but find it more difficult to observe quantities.

How does one design and enforce contracts when the rate of discount is high and outsiders are poorly informed about the trades among contractants? One potentially useful idea, due to Clive Bull and Yves Younès, is that whatever part of the contract cannot be enforced by courts should be enforced by the self-interest of the contractants. If, for instance, hours of work cannot be observed by courts, then the terms of employment implicitly specified must be in the short-term interests of each party. Thus, if 40 hours of work per week are specified implicitly for some state of demand, then it must be in the interest of both the worker and the firm to trade that amount. Workers cannot be compelled to work

40 hours if they do not want to, that is, if 40 hours exceed their labor supply at the going (and observable) wage rate. And the firm cannot be forced to use 40 hours of work if this is more than it desires at the going wage rate.

Contracts that are partially self-enforcing are a topic I find particularly interesting, and one I hope to see develop further in the years to come.

* * *

REPLY BY JOSEPH STIGLITZ

I will not answer all the questions that are raised. Let me try to organize my comments into a couple of major areas.

First, in the context of the problem with the efficiency wage models, I agree very strongly that the specification that I gave in this paper was obviously deliberately made simple in order to illustrate the basic principles of how this can generate unemployment. And I think that, if one wants to get an interesting business cycle theory out of this, one is probably going to have to generalize it in some important ways. Some of the suggestions that Karl Brunner put forward, I think, were particularly apropos, such as introducing prices and trying to clarify how the organizational and incentive structures affect λ. These are all important aspects of those extensions. A question was raised concerning the particular specification of the production relationship (output is a function of λ and workers employed), in which output is a function of productivity of a worker times the number of laborers. I have worked on extensions where one does not have to have that particular specification; it complicates the analysis, but the results come out consistent with what I have reported here.

The second point I want to emphasize (and basicaly again I agree with what has been said) is that one of the consequences of these models is that they make the optimal wage paid by one firm dependent on the wages paid by other firms. These interactions, I think, are very important in describing the behavior of the economy and lead to the interesting questions that Karl raised concerning how certain changes in the negotiating process will lead to changes in the nature of those dynamics. I think that is an interesting question to pursue.

One aspect that I talked about a little in the paper is that, if there are staggered contracts, these models give rise to slow dynamics in adjustment. I conjecture, but I have not proved that, if one went from one equilibrium where there is a given low level of unemployment to another equilibrium with an equilibrium level of unemployment, the dynamics of the transition could well entail a higher period of unemployment as part of the transition process. I think an investigation of that is an interesting question for future research. At this point, I just have two comments. First of all, although staggered contracts have been used a lot in recent literature, I think one really needs to have a theory that explains why they are staggered. Some recent work by one of my students, Arthur Hosios of Toronto, has tried to give an explanation based on imperfect information of why the equilibrium of a competitive economy would entail staggered contracts. Secondly, the question is raised about whether staggered contracts can lead to rigidities in nominal as opposed to real wages. I tried to give an example in the context of the paper where the theory can lead to rigidities in nominal wages, but let me say that I feel a little bit uneasy about these theories. In environments in which the countries have experienced inflation over an extended period of time, one would have thought that the contracts themselves would become extensively indexed. Contracts, even though they are staggered, would not be based on nominal variables.

This brings me to the general question that Richard Layard raised concerning nominal versus real wage rigidity. I am ambivalent about this. I am most at ease in the real-real story, where there are real shocks to the economy and there are real rigidities. I can be persuaded that in the short run I can get some nominal-nominal rigidities of the kind that can occur in the economy in which inflation had not been part of life, and then inflation became part of life and there is a transition. But I find it a little bit difficult to believe that most of those rigidities would persist if the economy were experiencing, as a regular part of its life, inflation and particularly variability in the rate of inflation. It is not that one cannot construct models that have nominal rigidities or show nominal rigidities, but as a permanent part of a world that has always been experiencing inflation it is just hard to believe that there would not be an extensive degree of indexation.

Let me turn to some of Costas Azariadis' remarks. Let me first say that I was teasing Costas a little bit. I think that the implicit contracts theories have made a very important contribution to our understanding of macroeconomics. There is something about the relationship between the worker and the employer that one wants to try to capture that is essential in understanding employment fluctuations. The literature can be viewed as an attempt to try to capture exactly what that is. The problem is that usually our models do not completely capture our ideas; they capture only part of our ideas. But then people look at those models and they say that model cannot be explaining what it purports to explain. But the idea is obviously broader than the particular model. I think the line of discussion that Costas expanded upon concerning the importance of the enforceability problem is central: it is important to understand what kinds of contracts are or are not enforceable, how they are enforced, and what restrictions enforceability imposes. I also agree that all these enforcement problems are two-sided problems; there are problems of the workers honoring their side of the contract and the firm honoring its side of the contract. What needs to be done, really, is to bring both of these sides together; as a research strategy we always tend to look at only one part of the problem at a time because it is difficult to do more than that. The criticism that Costas put of the turnover models, or the search costs model, is a criticism of the earlier search theories, most of which simply postulated an exogenous quit rate function and did not derive it endogenously to the structure of the model, but there has been work trying to derive equilibrium wage distributions. There is at least the hope that the structure of the equilibrium wage distributions is such that it changes as the cycle changes; so some of the peculiarities that have been noted in the earlier search literature would not apply to these more general versions of turnover models.

Let me reiterate, in conclusion, that this paper is meant to outline the state of where we are and to suggest directions of what I think are fruitful lines for future research. If it manages to stimulate discussion and reaction, it will have achieved its purpose.

Index

aggregate supply, Lucas type, 141
Akerlof, George, 186
anticipated inflation model (AIM), 2
Arrow-Debreu, 60, 217-18
asymmetric information, 207; bilateral, 175
auction market, 52
axiom of reals, 98

Barro, Robert, 2
Barro and Grossman, 57
Bretton Woods, 5, 46
Brunner and Friedman, 34
business cycle, 190; credit cycle, 37; disequilibrium model, 38-40; equilibrium model, 38-41; Hicks, 96; monetary, 36-37; real, 36-37

Clower-Leijonhufvud model, 138
competitive model, 186, 191
consumption-based asset pricing theory, 66
consumption beta model, 81, 90
consumption deflator, 68
contract: contingent, 175; staggered, 220; theory, 210, 211
convertibility, 36-40
coordination failure, 135
Cowles, Alfred, 67

disaster model, 76
disequilibrium, 3, 56
disinflation, 143
dividends, 68-69, 102

Edgeworth substitutes, 166
efficiency wage model, 119, 182-93, 208, 210, 212, 219
efficient markets, 65-77, 89-90, 105-6, 108
elastic expectations, 57
elasticity of labor supply, 126, 168
enforceability, 176
entrepreneural economy, 59
ergodicity, 95-96
expectations, 32, 33
explicit contracts, 176

factor-price-frontier, 128
Fisher, Irving, 59, 63
flex-wage market, 126
Friedman, Milton, 34
Friedman and Brunner, 34
Friedman and Schwartz, 2

Gibson's paradox, 2
gold convertibility, 37
gross substitution, 96

Hahn, Frank, 142
Hicks, Sir John, 9

imperfect information model, 55
implicit contract, 176-78, 217; explanation of wage rigidity, 206; theories, 155-82, 220-21; with unobservability, 163
implicit insurance, 154; contracts, 158-59
incomes policy, 113-26
inflation, 4; premium, 3; expectations, 2
informational assumptions, 4, 99
intertemporal substitution, 54, 96-97
involuntary unemployment, 53, 57, 140
irrationality hypothesis, 93
iso-profit curve, 162, 170

Keynesian: economics, 1; model of auction markets, 52

labor-market distortions, 134
labor-turnover, 184; model, 190
liquidity trap, 53, 78
long-term interest rates, 78-80
Lucas, Robert, 2, 56, 62

MAP, 152
marginal efficiency of capital (MEC), 33
marginal rate: of substitution, 161-64; of transformation, 161-64
marginal utility of leisure, 154
market clearing, 1, 60
Marsh and Merton, 75
Marshallian: demand curve, 136; equilibrium method, 33; supply curve, 136
micro-foundations, 60
monetarism, 1-2
monetary regime, 4
monetary theory of production, 59
money demand: stable, 2
moral hazard, 179-81

natural rate: hypothesis, 2, 3; of unemployment (NAIRU), 2, 111, 136-42, 145, 149-51, 216
new classical economics (NCE), 1, 52
nominal disturbance, 37
nominal expectations, 5
nominal rigidities, 191-92
nominal scalar, 62
nominal shocks, 6, 216
non-accelerating inflation rate of unemployment (NAIRU) 145-46

observability problem, 207

Pareto efficient, 145, 157, 191
partially unionized economy, 123-25
pecuniary externalities, 191
perfect equilibrium, 177
Phillips curve, 2, 46, 56, 150
Poincavé, 43, 44
profits, 175

quality-efficiency wage model, 187-88
quit rate, 116, 133, 184
quits, 115, 140, 149

Radcliffe Report, 2
random walk theory, 65-72, 75
rational expectations theory, 1, 52, 56, 78-80, 89-90
real disturbance, 32
real rigidities, 191-92
reservation wage, 62
risk aversion, 167-68
Robertson, Sir Dennis, 34-35

Sargent, Thomas, 2
Sargent and Wallace, 2
savings-investment inequality, 53
Say's Law, 43, 137-41
search model, 55-56
self-selection constraints, 162-63
Shackle, G.L.S., 96
shocks, real, 32, 216
short-side rationing, 138
sociological theories, 186

stabilization policy, 61; fiscal, 2
stability, 60
Standard and Poor Composite Stock Price; Stock Index, 67
Stiglitz, Joseph, 52
substitution effect, 126

tax, wage-inflation, 112
TIP, 113, 146
term structure of interest rates, 78–80
Tobin, James, 2
Tract on Monetary Reform, 44
transmission mechanism, 60
turnover costs, 217
turnover theory, 212

unemployment, 58
unions, 121–23, 134; mark-up, 123–24
utility functions, 160–61, 167–73
utility of income, 181

vacancies, 119–20
variance bounds test, 92

wage subsidy, 144
wage rigidity, 52, 59–60, 126, 153–54, 191–92, 210–11; nominal, 53–54, 215, 220; real, 220
Walrasian wage, 156
Walrasian unemployment, 207
wealth effect, 67

About the Authors and Contributors

James L. Butkiewicz: Ph.D., University of Virginia, 1977. Dr. Butkiewicz is Associate Professor of Economics and Associate Dean of the College of Business and Economics at the University of Delaware. He has published in the areas of monetary and fiscal policy effectiveness and the origins of the Great Depression.

Jeffrey B. Miller: Ph.D., University of Pennsylvania, 1976. Dr. Miller is Associate Professor of Economics at the University of Delaware. He has also been a Visiting Professor at Northwestern University. Dr. Miller has published in the areas of economic planning, incentive systems in economies and organizations, and anti-inflation policies.

Kenneth J. Koford: Ph.D., University of California, Los Angeles, 1977. Dr. Koford is Associate Professor of Economics at the University of Delaware. He has held teaching appointments at Washington University, St. Louis; Vassar College; Connecticut College; and Occidential College. He has published in the areas of the microeconomic foundations of macroeconomics, public choice, and industrial organization.

Costas Azariadis: Ph.D., Carnegie-Mellon University, 1972. Dr. Azariadis is currently a member of the economics faculty at the University of Pennsylvania. He has also held teaching positions at Carnegie-Mellon University and Brown University. He has published widely in the areas of implicit contracts in labor markets and economic theory.

Barry Bosworth: Ph.D., University of Michigan, 1969. Dr. Bosworth is a Senior Fellow in the Economic Studies Program at the Brookings Institution. He has served as Director of the Council on Wage and Price Stability and on the staff of the Council of Economic Advisors. Dr. Bosworth has held academic appointments at Harvard University and the University of California at Berkeley. He is the author of numerous articles and papers on various aspects of economic activity.

Karl Brunner: Doctor of Economics, University of Zurich, 1943. Dr. Brunner was Professor of Economics at UCLA for many years and then the Everett D. Reese Professor of Economics at Ohio State. He is now the Fred H. Gowan Professor of Economics at the University of Rochester. He has served as President of the Western Economic Association.

Professor Brunner is the founding editor of the *Journal of Money, Credit and Banking* and the *Journal of Monetary Economics*. He is also co-organizer, along with Allan Meltzer, of the Shadow Open Market Committee. Dr. Brunner has written many articles as well as edited and written several books in the areas of monetary theory, macroeconomics, and international economics.

David Colander: Ph.D., Columbia University, 1976. Dr. Colander is Christian S. Johnson Professor of Economics at Middlebury College. He has held teaching positions at the University of Miami, Nuffield College, Oxford University, and Vassar College and was a Brookings Fellow in 1977–78. He has published in the areas of anti-inflation policies and microeconomics foundations of macroeconomics.

Paul Davidson: Ph.D., University of Pennsylvania, 1959. Dr. Davidson is Professor of Economics and Associate Director of the Bureau of Economic Research at Rutgers University. He has taught at the University of Pennsylvania and has been a Senior Visitor at Cambridge University. His professional activities include participation on the Brookings Economic Panel, and he has been a member of the Board of Editors of the *Energy Journal* and is presently the editor of the *Journal of Post Keynesian Economics*. Dr. Davidson is the author and coauthor of several books and numerous articles. He has testified before Congress on such topics as antitrust, energy, and monetary policy.

Richard A. Jackman.: B. A. Cambridge. Professor Jackman teaches at the London School of Economics and Political Science. His primary research interests are in the area of labor economics.

Richard Layard: M.S., London School of Economics, 1967. Since 1974 he has headed the Center for Labour Economics at the London School of Economics. In 1980 he was named Professor of Labour Economics at the London School. He has published extensively in the areas of income distribution, labor supply and demand, and unemployment.

Axel Leijonhufvud: Ph.D., Northwestern University, 1967. Dr. Leijonhufvud is Professor of Economics at the University of California at Los Angeles and has served as department chair. He was recently a Visiting Fellow at the Institute for Advanced Studies at Princeton University. He has published numerous papers on macroeconomic theory and interpretations of Keynes and has authored several books, including *On Keynesian Economics and the Economics of Keynes: A Study in Monetary Theory*.

ABOUT THE AUTHORS AND CONTRIBUTORS

Christopher Pissarides: Ph.D., London School of Economics, 1974. Dr. Pissarides is a coeditor of *Economica* and a Lecturer in Economics at the London School of Economics. He was a Visiting Professor at Princeton University. He has published numerous articles in the areas of employment, wages, and macroeconomics.

Laurence Seidman: Ph.D., University of California at Berkeley, 1974. Dr. Seidman is Associate Professor at the University of Delaware. He has held teaching positions at the University of Pennsylvania and Swarthmore College. He has published extensively in the areas of tax-based incomes policies, public finance, and macroeconomics.

Robert J. Shiller: Ph.D., Massachusetts Institute of Technology, 1972. Dr. Shiller is Professor of Economics at Yale University. Previously he was a research economist at the National Bureau of Economic Research and has held faculty positions at the University of Pennsylvania and the Massachusetts Institute of Technology. He is noted for his work in the area of macroeconomics fluctuations and financial markets. Several of his most recent papers have examined the relationships between expectations, interest rates, and asset prices.

Joseph E. Stiglitz: Ph.D., Massachusetts Institute of Technology, 1966. Dr. Stiglitz has taught at the Massachusetts Institute of Technology, Yale University, and Stanford University. In 1976 he was appointed Drummond Professor of Political Economy at Oxford University. Professor Stiglitz has written many articles and several books and has been coeditor of the *Journal of Public Economics*. He has also served on the editorial board of the *Journal of Economic Theory, American Economic Review*, and *Energy Economics*. In 1972 he was a Fellow of the Econometric Society, and in 1979 he received the John Bates Clark Medal, awarded every two years by the American Economic Association to the most distinguished economist under age 40.